A New Sociology of Work?

A selection of previous *Sociological Review* Monographs

Theorizing Museums*
ed. Sharon Macdonald and Gordon Fyfe
Consumption Matters*
eds Stephen Edgell, Kevin Hetherington and Alan Warde
Ideas of Difference*
eds Kevin Hetherington and Rolland Munro
The Laws of the Markets*
ed. Michael Callon
Actor Network Theory and After*
eds John Law and John Hassard
Whose Europe? The turn towards democracy*
eds Dennis Smith and Sue Wright
Renewing Class Analysis*
eds Rosemary Cromptom, Fiona Devine, Mike Savage and John Scott
Reading Bourdieu on Society and Culture*
ed. Bridget Fowler
The Consumption of Mass*
ed. Nick Lee and Rolland Munro
The Age of Anxiety: Conspiracy Theory and the Human Sciences*
eds Jane Parish and Martin Parker
Utopia and Organization*
ed. Martin Parker
Emotions and Sociology*
ed. Jack Barbalet
Masculinity and Men's Lifestyle Magazines*
ed. Bethan Benwell
Nature Performed: Environment, Culture and Perfermance*
eds Bronislaw Szerszynski, Wallace Heim and Claire Waterton
After Habermas: New Perspectives on the Public Sphere*
eds Nick Crossley and John Michael Roberts
Feminism After Bourdieu*
eds Lisa Adkins and Beverley Skeggs
Contemporary Organization Theory*
eds Campbell Jones aid Rolland Munro

*Available from Marston Book Services, PO Box 270, Abingdon, Oxon OX14 4YW.

The Sociological Review Monographs

Since 1958 *The Sociological Review* has established a tradition of publishing Monographs on issues of general sociological interest. The Monograph is an edited book length collection of research papers which is published and distributed in association with Blackwell Publishing. We are keen to receive innovative collections of work in sociology and related disciplines with a particular emphasis on exploring empirical materials and theoretical frameworks which are currently under-developed. If you wish to discuss ideas for a Monograph then please contact the Monographs Editor, Rolland Munro, at *The Sociological Review*, Keele University, Newcastle-under-Lyme, North Staffordshire, ST5 5BG.

A New Sociology of Work?

Edited by Lynne Pettinger, Jane Parry, Rebecca Taylor and Miriam Glucksmann

Blackwell Publishing/The Sociological Review

BLACKWELL BUBLISHING
350 Main Street, Malden, MA 02148-5020, USA
9600 Garsington Road, Oxford OX4 2DQ, UK
550 Swanston Street, Carlton, Victoria 3053, Australia

First published 2005 by Blackwell Publishing Ltd

Library of Congress Cataloging-in-Publication Data applied for

ISBN 140513903X
ISBN 13: 9781405139038

A catalogue record for this title is available from the British Library.

Set by SNP Best-set Typesetter Ltd, Hong Kong.

Printed and bound in the United Kingdom by Page Brothers, Norwich.

The publisher's policy is to use permanent paper from mills that operate a sustainable forestry policy, and which has been manufactured from pulp processed using acid-free and elementary chlorine-free practices. Furthermore, the publisher ensures that the text paper and cover board used have met acceptable environmental accreditation standards.

For further information on Blackwell Publishing, visit our website:
http://www.blackwellpublishing.com

Contents

Acknowledgements

The ESRC funded much of the original empirical work reported in this book, (the chapters by Esther Dermott, Jane Parry and Lynne Pettinger develop their PhD research, Clare Ungerson's chapter derives from research undertaken under the auspices of the ESRC Future of Work Programme, and Miriam's Glucksmann's from her ESRC Professorial Fellowship). We wish to acknowledge this assistance. We are also grateful for their support in funding the seminar in September 2003 where the papers in this volume were first presented.

Rebecca Taylor and Jane Parry would like to thank the Policy Studies Institute, in particular the encouragement and advice of Steve Lissenburgh, Alex Bryson and Jim Skea. We are also indebted to the University of Westminster's Regent Street Polytechnic Fund for financing some of the time spent on this book.

Lynne Pettinger would like to thank the Sociology department of City University, London, where she held a post-doctoral fellowship from October 2002–2004. In particular, the guidance and stimulation provided by Rosemary Crompton was much appreciated.

Part 1
Conceptualizing work

Confronting the challenges of work today: New horizons and perspectives

Jane Parry, Rebecca Taylor, Lynne Pettinger and Miriam Glucksmann

Introduction

The question mark in the title of *A New Sociology of Work?* is deliberate. Without it we might appear to be making grandiose claims. Our intention, however, is not to replace an existing field with a new one but to generate broad-ranging discussion about the nature of work and ways of theorizing and researching it. All four editors of this book have wrestled with debates within the sociology of work in relation to our own research projects. What brought us together was our search for conceptual tools that would enable us to understand particular sets of experiences and activities that were outside a narrowly employment-focused definition of the field. Where we found innovative conceptual development being conducted, however, it was either in relative isolation or in fields other than work and employment. There was a clear need to consolidate these advances, and reinvigorate debate in a way that would provide a more inclusive and sophisticated basis for research on work in the 21st century.

With this intention we organized a workshop at the Policy Studies Institute in London in autumn 2003. This was funded by the Economic and Social Research Council and brought together a group of researchers who were actively engaged in looking at issues that, in some cases, appeared only loosely connected to the study of work. Participants' research interests covered substantive areas as diverse as prostitution, voluntary work, fathering and community work. In different ways, these challenged conceptual frameworks by unpicking taken-for-granted assumptions about work's boundaries, definitions and spheres (Taylor, R. F. *et al.*, 2003). The workshop stimulated considerable discussion and debate amongst the contributors, and the idea of bringing the issues raised by the papers together in an edited collection, to expose them to a wider audience, gained momentum. This book, and the questions it poses, is the result. Its central concerns are with widening debate, extending conceptual boundaries and forging new paths in social science research.

The workshop helped us identify five themes that link the papers and provide a focus for the present volume. These act as refrains throughout the book, linking chapters and highlighting innovative elements. They are:

- *The nature and definition of work* – this involves a fundamental questioning of what we mean by work. Examining work's conceptual boundaries stimulates the development of conceptual structures and tools that can accommodate work's diverse forms.
- *socioeconomic, spatial and temporal dimensions of work* – here we explore the permeable, often blurred boundaries between the domains within which work occurs (public and private, formal and informal, legal and illegal, market and non-market) and the temporal structures which define work activities (for example, work time versus leisure time).
- *the embeddedness of work in other social relations* – this theme engages with the difficulties in separating work from other social relations, such as familial ties and friendships.
- *the interconnections between work in different spheres* – here we consider how forms of work are organized at a social structural level, so that changes in one type or function of labour affects work in other areas.
- *the commodification and remuneration of work* – the link between pay or wages and work can not be taken for granted. Whilst some forms of labour may become increasingly commodified others may be economically devalued or re-valued in terms of other perceived rewards.

The central aim of this publication, then, is to initiate and develop an empirically grounded understanding of the nature, dimensions, and relations of different forms of work. Work is not assumed to be a discrete activity carried out in exchange for remuneration in institutions (although it can be) but, rather, is conceptualized as being embedded in other domains and entangled in other sorts of social relations. To be clear, it is not suggested that employment is no longer a relevant category. Indeed paid work and employment remain critical to debates within the sociology of work. However, we argue that these may be better illuminated when conceptualized in the context of a broader understanding of what constitutes work. A perception of the variety of ways that people engage in work in contemporary society could offer a more accurate depiction of the complex, messy, dynamic trajectories that encapsulate people's working lives. From this perspective for example, life-stages not normally associated with work, such as time spent in education, retirement or unemployment, take on new interest for the sociologist of work.

Most crucially, the project has far-reaching implications for how we understand social inequalities. A movement away from the fixed boundaries of occupation, for example, raises new questions about the relationship between work and social class, and between work and gender relations, and ethnic and age-based differences. Occupation may indicate class position but class position also defines orientation to work in its broadest forms – from domestic labour to voluntary work. *A New Sociology of Work?* foregrounds the way in which inequalities manifested in one domain have a re-iterative relationship with behaviours and values in another domain.

The implications of the project for social policy are extensive. In exploring work at the boundaries, *A New Sociology of Work?* provides a counter to the preoccupation of policy makers with employment as the only work of value. 'Third way' politics, including New Labour in the UK, has, through work-focused employment programmes amongst other things, increasingly tied citizenship and benefits to having a paid job (Hirsch and Millar, 2004). Those outside or excluded from employment are not recognized as 'working'. At the same time, it has more frequently turned to informal work to compensate for failures in its or the market's provision (for example, in the case of care work) creating a fundamental contradiction between a limited understanding of work in the former case, combined with a practical reliance on substitutes for paid workers. By drawing attention to the ways individuals operate within family, community and societal contexts, the approach we are proposing challenges the individualization of work/benefit systems and suggests that employment is not always or the only solution to social inequality.

Before we outline the contributions made by the 12 chapters it is important to situate these themes and debates in relation to both dramatic changes within the world of work and key developments in the sociology of work in recent decades. These allied contexts have informed our thinking and provide the context for the theoretical questions that define the 'New Sociology of Work?' project. The first section of this introductory chapter, *Working lives in the 21st Century*, maps out key changes in the world of work: the issues that are pressing today and the implications these have for the questions we ask and the ways we understand work. The subsequent section, *Landscape of the sociology of work*, briefly outlines some important conceptual and theoretical developments that have taken place over recent years. This provides an epistemological context to the book's central debates, acknowledging influences and anchoring our critique. Both these sections are highly selective and neither is a literature review in the traditional sense; rather they draw on key texts to locate the 'New Sociology of Work?' project in relation to current academic debates, and research agendas in the field.

Having sketched the backdrop, the penultimate section of this chapter, *Towards a new sociology of work*, maps out the contribution to the debate provided by each of our chapters and the five cross-cutting themes linking them. These themes loosely map onto a five-fold organizational structure that provides a framework for setting out some critical commonalities and differences across the various chapters. The five section to the book are entitled: conceptualizing work, re-examining paid employment, privatized work, work on the boundaries, and international comparisons

For the editors and contributors, this book provides an important point of consolidation, a marker documenting our emerging conceptual ideas and research questions. We hope it will also offer a useful resource for academics and students who are thinking about traditional and contemporary forms of work in new ways. This book is about raising rather than answering questions. Our aim has been to generate debate and more empirical research that will continue to seek out the margins and to refine definitions and conceptual understandings. In the final section of this chapter, *Further questions, future research: where next for the New Sociology of Work?*, we explore the empirical and conceptual potential of the ideas that we have outlined. We anticipate that it will form an important stage in a series of evolutions within the sociology of work to bring about more inclusive and sophisticated concepts and methods for understanding work.

Working lives in the 21st Century

Changes to the organization of work and labour around the 21st century have raised new questions and issues for the sociology of work. The proliferation of electronic modes of work and the increasingly global scale of economic operations and competition have consequences not only for occupations and skills, but also for organizational forms. Other transformations arise from processes of commodification and decommodification and blurring of the boundary between public and private sectors of the formal economy. These bring some forms of work that were previously undertaken on a non-market basis into the market for the first time while shifting others out of it. New work practices promoting flexibility, especially in relation to time and space, lie behind the reorganization and relocation of many forms of employment. All these impact on people's working lives in profound ways which alter not only their conditions and experience of work but also the meanings and significance it has for them, as mapped out by various projects in the ESRC's 'Future of Work' Research Programme[1]. When unpaid work is also brought into view, the depth of change is even more striking. A massive growth of care work and the heightened importance of voluntary and community work to the public domain add new dimensions to the current reconfiguration of work.

Paid work itself is increasingly likely to cover categories other than full-time permanent work, and the full-time permanent (male) worker of old is less likely to be able to rely on a full-time unpaid worker/wife in the home (Walby, 1997; Yeandle, 1999). In an era of transnational corporations, footloose organizations, short-term economic choices and flexible working, for many the idea of standard employment or a job for life has fallen by the wayside (Felstead and Jewson, 1999). Some commentators have argued that paid working lives are now dominated by flexibility and insecurity (Beck, 2000), though others suggest this is something of a myth (see for example Robert Taylor, 2002). Sennett (1998) suggests that new capitalism is destructive of the individuals caught up in it, who become isolated, untrusting, rootless. The flexible firm demands a flexible workforce, one which might work long hours in addition to their contracted working time, and which is available to service customers early in the morning or late at night (Jenkins, 2004). As jobs in certain areas have become more 'flexible', career paths less defined, and hours of work more variable and non-standardized, individuals' means of getting through their working lives must also change.

The ability of corporations to transfer production from one region to another further contributes to the uncertainty of employment in the 21st century. Whilst manufacturing industries were previously the most vulnerable to this trend, the service sector has now also moved in this direction, as call centres are shifted from Europe and North America to South Asia (Huws *et al.*, 2001; Mirchandani, 2004). It is not only the production of goods and services that can shift from place to place, the movement of people is also important. Increasing interest in migrants as a source for domestic, care and service work in metropolitan countries (Glenn, 1992; Lutz, 2002; Momsen, 1999) have opened up the debates around public and private work and drawn attention to the global reshaping of domestic work.

Whilst the workplace in industrial societies is usually assumed to be in a physically distinct location from the home, research has highlighted situations where this is not the case. Two forms of homework have been identified, one a traditional type of women's work, generally low paid and marginal, the other, a new form facilitated by technological developments and predominantly the realm of middle-class professionals, both male and female (Felstead *et al.*, 2005; Huws *et al.*, 1999; Osnowitz, 2005). Homeworking highlights the increasingly troublesome nature of traditional temporal and spatial dimensions of work. For homeworkers, paid work is (re)located in the nominally 'private' sphere and hence the social meaning of space alters. Furthermore, the social meaning of time is transformed: home workers have no fixed end to their working day and no firm delimitation between paid work, unpaid work and non-work.

The sorts of work that occur in the home vary between times and place, suggesting that fixed understandings of 'work' are incommensurate with the realities of diverse working practices. Where it is concentrated amongst poorer sectors of the community/globe, homeworking means workers (usually women) combine paid employment with domestic duties in the same place and at the same time. The conceptual implications of home-based work have been hinted at by, amongst others, Prügl and Boris, who draw attention to the way in which it 'illuminates the permeable quality of such conceptual boundaries' and suggest the difficulties in thinking about workers without reference to their social location (Prügl and Boris, 1996:7). Even in the traditional workplace, the routines and disciplines of office space are being relocated and transformed, whether at hot desks or in touchdown areas, in home offices, airport lounges or on trains (Felstead *et al.*, 2005; Halford, 2004).

With more women engaged in paid work (Crompton, 1999), the ways in which individuals and families experience and balance different forms of work are ever-changing. Obtaining a 'work-life balance' is predominantly conceptualized as involving the juggling of paid work and care work (Crompton, 2002; Houston, 2005). Information communications technology (ICT) industries, work intensification and cultures of working that encourage long hours often make a 'work-life balance' purely notional (Perrons, 2003). Although the term implies a problematically sharp distinction between 'work' (by implication, paid work) and 'life' it highlights the interconnectedness of different forms of work. Long working hours in one area of the economy has implications for other people's work in other sectors of the economy: services such as childcare or retail must be available for longer. By calling attention to interrelationships of work time, location and economic sector, and the lack of fixity in work-time, this analysis has implications for time beyond paid work, and thus for an understanding of temporality as implicated in generating at least one of the blurred boundaries of work.

The question of who cares – for children and the elderly – has an ever-increasing resonance given the return of women to the workplace, changing patterns of family formation and geographical location (kinship networks are less likely to be available than in previous generations) and an ageing population. The shortage of people to undertake care work becomes critical and highlights an increasingly complex array of care options: paid and unpaid, public and private, formal and informal, regulated, and unregulated. With the state reluctant to step in, the burden frequently devolves to families, many of whom respond by turning to the marketplace and buying in care. These changes not only impact on individuals or households but also have global ramifications, as the world's poor fill in the care deficit (Anderson, 2000; Ehrenreich and Hochschild, 2003). The implications on the provision of care for our understanding of work are many, as practices cross boundaries between different domains. Unpaid private care work may be commodified, whilst care previously supplied by the state may shift to the family. This movement of work practices demands a more sophisticated model of the organization of labour than one that polarizes work activities as either public or private.

Landscape of the sociology of work

A great deal of research has been conducted into these, and other, changes to the world of work, which is beyond the scope of this chapter to review. What is increasingly noticeable is how these developments create problems for commonsense understanding of what workers do, and for traditional sociological conceptions of work. In this section we suggest that, despite the attention paid to new forms of work, their implications have not been fully addressed at a conceptual level. We look at the recent evolution of the notion of work and contend that the time is now right for further theoretical developments to manage the empirical sophistication and real-world complexity of 'work'. In doing so we also set out a mandate for the 'New Sociology of Work?' project.

Traditional sociological explorations of work tended to equate it with full-time waged employment. This somewhat reductive legacy derives from their foundation in economics and industrial sociology (Pahl, 1988; Tancred, 1995).

Glucksmann (1995) argued that the creation of disciplinary boundaries within academia mirrored the industrial differentiation of institutions, whereby work became the domain of classical economics with questions of the monetarization and quantification of labour central. As a result, work was conceptualized around dichotomies of paid and unpaid labour, and public and private spheres. These produced a narrow definition of work as either paid employment in the public sphere or unpaid domestic labour in the private sphere (Taylor, R. F., 2004). Such an understanding of work has continued to influence the discipline almost up to the present. Forms of labour that are outside these distinct spheres, such as voluntary work or work for the community, work that is sporadic, informal or even illegal, have either been pushed to the margins or excluded from the field entirely.

However these conceptual boundaries have been subject to serious challenge since the 1970s and through the 1980s and 1990s. Second-wave feminism of the 1970s made a crucial contribution when it questioned the taken-for-granted assumption that work undertaken in the private sphere of the home was not 'work'. The achievement of the domestic labour debate was to counter the marginalization of women's domestic labour by mainstream theory 'through the recognition that housework, the "labour of love" performed by women, was a form of work' (Beechey, 1987:126). Feminist research went on to play a crucial role in illuminating the realities of women's employment. The gendered nature of employment processes signalled by the entrenched nature of inequalities continue to motivate research in the field (indicatively, Bradley, 1989; Cavendish, 1982, Crompton, 1997; Fitzsimons, 2002; Jenson *et al.*, 2000; McDowell and Pringle, 1992).

A crucial addition to the debate was Hochschild's *The Managed Heart* (1983), which introduced the concept of 'emotional labour' in relation to service sector workers, such as flight attendants. This theme has subsequently been explored in many other occupations, including nursing (James, 1989), beauty therapy (Sharma and Black, 2001), call-centres (Callaghan and Thompson, 2002), waitressing (Paules, 1996; Wharton, 1996), and service sector work more generally (Abiala, 1999; Macdonald and Sirianni, 1996). A focus on emotional work, later also including issues of sexuality and embodiment, offered a more holistic perspective and an important advance on a narrowly defined labour process paradigm, offering deeper understanding of the activities and social relations involved in the conduct of work. With the spread of interest in emotional labour across disciplines, a new-style personhood/identity approach to the analysis of work (Adkins and Lury, 1999; du Gay, 1996; Knights and Wilmott, 1999) has diverged from more traditional approaches to emotional and personal skills. These offer important new angles to the sociology of work, by drawing out companies' growing awareness of the resources that are brought into the workplace by their employees' nominally private lives.

Changes were also occurring more centrally within the field of sociology, Pahl's mold-breaking collection *On Work* (1988) mounting a serious challenge to employment-centred approaches to the sociology of work. Calling for recognition and exploration of all aspects of work, across spheres, he insisted on the necessity of taking into account the social relations within which labour activities were embedded, themes he had previously set out in *Divisions of Labour* (1984). Since then, insistence that the sociological vision should include as work a broader range of activities has slowly but definitively reshaped the sociology of work. Researchers are looking beyond employment to household provisioning (Gershuny, 2000), informal economic activity (Williams and Windebank, 2003), other forms of exchange such as LETs schemes (Aldridge *et al.*, 2001), the wide variety of 'caringscapes' (McKie *et al.*, 1999) and the labour embedded in other activities such as acting (Dean and Jones, 2003). The revival of economic sociology and the emergence of the new field of cultural economy (developments drawn on by a number of our contributors) have given further impetus to these shifts. In these and many other ways, new approaches to work, often in response to the huge changes in the forms and organization of labour mentioned above, have begun to open up and remap the sociology of work.

Towards a new sociology of work

The 'New Sociology of Work?' project advocated here does not rest on a single theoretical perspective or a narrow substantive focus on particular forms of work. Rather, it is concerned to question the myriad forms of 'work' and explore their socio-economic basis and diverse social relations. It argues for a re-examination of the nature and definition of work so as to avoid squeezing new work practices into old models and categories, and in order to generate more nuanced conceptual frameworks and tools of enquiry that are inclusive of labour undertaken at or outside the margins of what has conventionally been understood as work.

Re-conceptualizing work involves bringing to the forefront of our analytical prism an appreciation of the complexity of the dynamic and interconnected character of work relations. The same activity may be paid and treated as formal employment, or be undertaken informally or on an unpaid basis; such differences have implications for how it is understood and socially evaluated. In such circumstances what counts as 'work' may be contested both by those performing it and social researchers. Similarly, rather than isolating work from non-work activities the project becomes one to explore the points at which they become entangled and embedded as well as differentiated. The 'work' aspect of some relationships may be inseparable or indistinguishable from other dimensions – for example, emotional, sexual or religious. Care can be work, but it can also be about affective ties. Work can also be creative or social; it may be embedded in consumption and leisure. Work is not necessarily conducted within profit motivated, market-like exchange relations (Williams, 2004). The locations within which work takes place are not always discrete; the workplace may be the home or someone else's home, and time spent working may also be time spent engaged in a creative activity (McRobbie, 1998; Richards and Milestone, 2000). The product of that activity, a painting or a book or piece of music, may be sold but it may also be given away or exchanged. The existence of unemployment benefits or familial assets may make that particular piece of creative work possible. All these factors can be brought to bear on the way we understand the activity as work.

When viewed comparatively, there is nothing fixed, determined, unchanging or uniform about the division of labour. Consequently we confront enormous variability historically and across the globe, not only in the construction of jobs and work tasks, but also in who they are allocated to and on what basis. Reflecting such principles, national occupational structures are often strongly gendered and ethnicised, in such a way that work relations are at the same time also gender and ethnic relations. The lines of division, however, and their relative strength, rigidity and fixity vary between cultures and over time, so that divisions of labour are always specific to particular times and places. How deeply rooted the division of labour and its allocation is in traditional beliefs or ideological discourses of various kinds will have a bearing on how open it is to challenge and change.

Several of these themes utilize or build on the 'total social organization of labour' approach developed by Glucksmann (1995, 2000a) and summarized in her chapter below. This relational framework refused the distinction between work and employment in favour of a more inclusive understanding of work as taking place in differing socio-economic forms and as interconnected with many other, often non-work, relationships. Instead of attempting to draw a boundary around something that could incontrovertibly be seen as 'work', this approach, on the contrary, entails drawing attention to the blurry line between work and not-work, and to the connections between work activities undertaken in different socio-economic spaces. In sex work, labour is sexual and sexuality is work, and so it would be pointless to try to disentangle these as distinct components. Or, to take another obvious example, if men's ability to take part in waged employment is predicated on women carrying out unpaid or informal labour to their benefit, then both of these would need to be taken into account to promote any proper understanding of either. Bringing such blurriness into the field of vision rather than excluding it by artificially narrowing the focus, will inevitably introduce new theoretical challenges and analytical uncertainties. But these should render social analysis more adequate to what it is trying to comprehend and also make it more stimulating for researchers.

Structure of the book

Contributions to this volume are organized into five sections: conceptualizing work, re-examining paid employment, privatized forms of work, work that challenges the boundaries of the public and private spheres, and international comparisons.

Conceptualizing work

This introduction and Miriam Glucksmann's chapter comprise Part 1 and are concerned with establishing the remit of the new sociology of work. Glucksmann's chapter significantly develops her earlier conceptual framework of the 'total social organization of labour'. Demonstrating the interconnections between work undertaken in different socio-economic relations and spaces has been central to this approach. Here she focuses specifically on the issue of interconnection, and attempts to disentangle analytically different kinds of linkages between various work activities. She distinguishes between four dimensions of such interconnection: across the processes of production, distribution, exchange and consumption; across the boundaries between paid and unpaid work, market and non-market, formal and informal sectors; the articulation of work with non-work activities and relations; temporality and its significance across the other three dimensions. Outlining these with reference to a range of developments in the contemporary world of work, she proposes new tools for coming to grips with some of the big questions raised by the 'New Sociology of Work?'

Re-examining paid employment

Part 2 concerns the sphere of employment traditionally associated with the sociology of work, but each of the three chapters presented here offers an analysis of the complex ways in which paid employment is embedded in a wider set of social relations.

Lynne Pettinger's contribution draws upon ethnographic research in the retail sector to examine the social relations of work, and the interface between work, consumption and 'private' lives in this public sphere, through a study of friendships on the shopfloor. She draws attention to how the social relationships associated with particular occupations are important in understanding occupational participation and expectations, and in organizational regulation of the workforce. Pettinger argues that working in consumption spaces involves both work and play and highlights the blurring of boundaries between work and non-work relations through exploring the importance of the social relations of friendship in understanding retail workers' labour processes and practices.

This is followed by Wendy Bottero's critique of traditional stratification theories based upon occupational measures. Bottero endeavours to develop a class analysis that takes into account the broader social spaces of relationships and, like Pettinger, argues for a consideration of the work embedded in social relationships that do not have their origin in the workplace, in this case to understand social mobility and the meaning of occupations. Bottero's chapter works towards an enhanced understanding of inequalities, by suggesting ways

© The Editorial Board of the Sociological Review 2005

of measuring social class that look beyond occupation to social and cultural factors.

Finally in this section, Angela Coyle analyses how a 'family-friendly' flexible workforce has been pursued in specific feminized labour markets (in this case the UK's NHS) via key temporal and spatial transformations in the organization of work. Coyle draws attention to the impact of this strategy for individuals' working experiences. She suggests that the sorts of working patterns demanded by the NHS are not necessarily those which might best enhance 'family-friendly flexibility', and draws attention to the new inequalities of time that may be promoted by policies entailing 'family-friendly flexibility'. The implications for this are worker discontent and, increasingly, exit from health-care professions.

Privatized work

Part 3 switches the focus to privatized forms of work, arguing for their comparability with traditional labour activities and drawing attention to enduring gendered patterns. One key theme in this section is the interconnections between forms of work in different domains, in this case how work in the private domestic sphere is closely tied to work outside that sphere.

Looking at one aspect of the work performed in the home, Esther Dermott examines fathers' interpretation of their involvement in childcare, and in particular their disassociation of these activities from their paid work, drawing out crucial differences in terms of the meaning and organisation of labour performed in different spheres. Dermott explores how the work of fathering is understood in relation to the social relations of paid employment, with stark differences apparent in the responsibilities inherent in the concepts of 'good parents' and 'good workers' for men and women. Dermott explicitly relates this to a theme central to the 'New Sociology of Work?' – time – arguing that time has different meanings for fathers, depending on whether they are talking about their home or work lives.

A fascinating contrast to this is provided by Diane Reay's research with mothers, which is utilized to consider the substantial shift of educative work from the public into the private sphere, and the gendered and classed interpretations that parents utilize to incorporate educational expectations into their repertoires of work. Reay picks up on a key theme of the 'New Sociology of Work?' project in discussing how work in one sphere (such as paid employment) impacts upon work in other spheres. She highlights how the work of education is being privatized, with *mothers* increasingly expected to take responsibility for some of their child's learning within the home.

Both Dermott's and Reay's chapters suggest that, whilst recent concern with women's movement into paid employment has sidelined the importance of domestic labour, nonetheless changes in employment practices have a great bearing upon its organization. For example, Reay points out that one of the reasons why middle-class mothers are able to dedicate so much time to their children's education is because they are paying working class women to perform practical domestic tasks within their homes.

Work on the boundaries

The book's fourth substantive section looks at some of the work that has typically been overlooked by the sociology of work – labour that does not sit comfortably within definitions of work as either paid employment in the public sphere or domestic labour in the private sphere.

Rebecca Taylor's chapter opens up this debate by discussing a traditional form of work rarely acknowledged in the sociology of work: voluntary work. Voluntary work as unpaid work in the public sphere falls outside existing definitions of work, effectively providing a test case for building a more inclusive theoretical framework. Referring to research on workers in two voluntary sector organizations, Taylor argues that understanding volunteering as work provides a new dimension to people's work histories. Taylor's qualitative research is used to uncover the diversity of unpaid work performed both within and outside two public sector voluntary organisations, and to explore how participation is related to individuals' capital and orientations to work. As with Bottero and Reay, Taylor's chapter has implications for the understanding of class based inequalities, as it demonstrates how voluntary work as unpaid public work can be as crucial in understanding class position as occupation in the traditional sense.

Prostitution has also been sidelined by conventional approaches to work. Jackie West and Terry Austrin's chapter highlights how sex work can be understood more clearly when it is conceptualized as work and its relationship to the market is fully considered. Their cross-cultural analysis of prostitution examines this informal, and often semi- or illegal, form of work, revealing its social relations and the multiple ways in which such 'invisible' labour may be organized and regulated. West and Austrin's insights bring new dimensions to the question of the embeddedness of work in other social relations, including the legal and market context.

Jane Parry's chapter picks up on work performed across these formal and informal, public and private divides, by looking at the gendered and classed patterning of community work. She focuses on post-mining populations, a group whose entire landscape of work has been transformed by industrial restructuring. Parry's paper draws attention to the blurred boundaries between work located in different spheres, prompting definitional concerns: community work at various times encapsulates informal and voluntary work, paid employment and domestic labour, as well as leisure time, and draws upon a range of statutory, voluntary and informal sectors. The interconnections between work in these different spheres are highlighted by the restructuring of coal mining in the Welsh Valleys, with the resulting unemployment and re-employment leading to changes in men's and women's involvement in both paid and unpaid work.

International comparisons

In the final part of the book, three authors employ cross-national comparisons to engage with issues raised by 'New Sociology of Work?' These focus particularly on care work and the implications for the social organization of the labour of commodified care. The restructuring of welfare and changing patterns of care, the decline in state-provided care and the concomitant increase in care provided by family members, raise a number of issues for how labour is organized in different spheres and the nature of these different types of work relations and conditions. These cross national comparisons provide another reminder that there is little that is fixed about the social organization of labour.

Pat and Hugh Armstrong focus on changes to work in the Canadian healthcare sector, and their implications for distinctions between the care that goes on in the private and public spheres. The Armstrongs' analysis of Canadian healthcare highlights the increasingly blurred boundaries between care performed in a multiplicity of public and private spheres and sectors, linking these to recent managerial strategies. Their historical review of changes in the organization of Canadian healthcare brings into relief the redistribution of commodifable care and its effects upon women working in care-related roles. They demonstrate clearly the interconnections between work in different spheres, and the social inequalities resulting from, or enhanced by, the marginalization of particular forms of care work.

Meanwhile, drawing on cross-European comparative research on different ways that domiciliary care work has been commodified, Clare Ungerson highlights some, perhaps unexpected, consequences arising from the recent introduction of personal budget schemes which enable care recipients to purchase their own care labour. She focuses on the varying arrangements, regulatory regimes, and methods of payment directed at relatives, care workers or other types of helper, and explores the implications of these configurations for the meanings and emotional resonance of care relationships for the parties concerned. Her evidence suggests fascinating associations between the nature of particular employment relationships and labour contracts and the different qualities and dimensions of emotional relationship that emerge between care employer and giver. In so doing Ungerson introduces a quite new dimension to the study of emotional labour and opens up fundamental questions relating to the generation and place of emotion in work relationships.

Finally, Margarita de León draws out the connections between welfare state structures, family forms and patterns of childcare. León's chapter provides a comparative analysis of how various European welfare state regimes impact upon the balance between different forms of paid and unpaid work, using childcare as an example of the social organization of labour. She traces the implications of women's paid employment participation for the labour invested in social care and child care, and relates these to the broader organization of work in contrasting European welfare state regimes.

Further questions, future research: Where next for the 'New Sociology of Work?'

The debates that we have instigated here raise questions which we hope will provide a catalyst for future research, conceptual development and exchange among the research community. The many discussions that have arisen during the life of this project have given rise to four particular areas where research might profitably focus.

Further analysis of the boundaries of work

The questions 'what is work?' and 'what is not work?' are fundamental to the 'New Sociology of Work?' project. Conceptual recognition of the multiplicities and complexities of the notion of 'work' and the possible ambiguities regarding what counts as work, open up a number of important avenues. The plethora of activities that currently sit on the margins of what is considered work, such as illegal and criminal activities, different types of community work, unpaid work for unions and political activism, and creative work such as painting, writing or acting, would all benefit from attempts to understand how they are constituted as work and relate to other work activities. Other activities may not initially appear to be work, but would provide a fascinating addition to understandings of the nature of work in contemporary society if analysed in the light of these conceptual debates. Personal maintenance work, for example, is considered a vital part of the labour involved in particular occupations (Witz *et al.*, 2003), and may be privatized or consumed. Can consumption be considered a form of labour? One of the challenges here is, rather than trying to label everything 'work', identifying the extent to which it is useful to apply the tools offered by analyses of work to a wider range of activities.

The social organizations of labour at the macro and micro level

An important avenue for further research is the combination of paid and unpaid, public and private, formal and informal labour that constitutes a country's labour profile at a given historical moment. This means exploring the reasons behind the variations in the organization of labour between different countries and welfare regimes and raising questions about which types of work are privatised, who engages in voluntary work, and what are the drivers of change, where the type of work or function carried out in one sphere shifts to another. These comparisons have implications for understanding the organization of labour at the global level. They raise questions about the increasing power and reach of global corporations, the impact of corporate employers on local working practices and ways of life, changing global divisions of labour, the impact of migration on the way labour is organized and the forms of labour that proliferate.

At the micro level, exploring the way individuals and families organize their labour involves a recognition that people may have more than one job or area of work. This is more than simply a description of 'portfolio working' or the juggling of several freelance positions (Gold and Fraser, 2002). Exploring people's multiple engagement in work also entails a holistic examination of how (and why) they organize and manage activities that might include employment, voluntary work, community work, informal economic activity and domestic labour. It also means taking into account that labour is organized across a family unit not just by the individuals within it. This raises questions about how issues of managing work for individuals at the micro level map onto the macro organization of labour. Future research in the sociology of work needs to be attuned to the multiple layers and complexity that define people's working lives.

New social inequalities

A third set of questions relates to how rethinking work impacts on our understanding of social inequalities. The transfer of work between spheres, and the intensification of particular forms of work, may alter existing inequalities of gender, class, ethnicity, age, disability and/or ill-health. At a conceptual level, several chapters in this volume emphasize the need to revisit the traditional relationship between class and work, and to establish connections between the two in cultural as well as economic terms. As paid employment within occupations represents only part of people's working lives, understanding the relationship between different forms of labour and class positions can only accentuate the reinvigoration of class analysis.

Policy implications

This move towards creating a more inclusive definition of work has significant implications for official uses of the term 'work'. At the policy level, welfare to work programmes, with their assertion of the primary importance of paid work, are ill equipped to understand what it is people do when they are not in employment and there is little available research to counter this deficit. Clearly the more inclusive conceptualization of work needs to filter down into policy and practice, and research that strives to give work a broader definition has the potential to impact upon how the state supports and relates to those not in paid employment: the 'workless', the unemployed and the economically inactive. A more holistic approach to researching people's working lives would provide a much more complete picture of economically productive (if unpaid) activities.

Conclusion

A New Sociology of Work? sets out to broaden existing perspectives on work and create a number of ideas for the future direction of research into work. The five main themes of the project – the questioning of the definition of work; the interest in social, spatial and temporal elements of work; work's embeddedness in other social relations; the interconnections between spheres of work; and the involvement of the market in this – can potentially encompass a broad range of research questions. The chapters that follow engage with the themes in very different ways. We hope that they stimulate discussion and further research into the complexity of work and working lives in the 21st century.

Notes

1 Which ran from 1998–2004; for further details see: http://www.leeds.ac.uk/esrcfutureofwork/index.html

Shifting boundaries and interconnections: Extending the 'total social organisation of labour'

Miriam Glucksmann

Introduction

This chapter attempts to refine and enhance my 'total social organisation of labour' (TSOL) approach and so contribute to a new sociology of work. It does so by developing and exploring a broad analytical theme – the differing modes of interconnection between work activities – for its investigative potential and explanatory relevance across a variety of fields of work and employment.

A brief review of recent empirical and conceptual developments in relation to work is followed by discussion of the TSOL perspective and its uses. Although a focus on the connections linking work conducted in different socio-economic spaces is central to this perspective, the notion of interconnection itself and the character and range of possible interconnection has not been addressed in detail. The main part of the chapter takes on this task and is devoted to analytically thinking through and separating out different sorts of interconnection between work activities. Four dimensions are schematically distinguished:

1. across the processes of production, distribution, exchange and consumption;
2. across the boundaries between paid and unpaid work, market and non-market, formal and informal sectors;
3. the articulation of work activities and relations with non-work activities and relations;
4. differing temporalities of work and the significance of temporality across the other three interconnections.

These propose a (by no means exhaustive) variety of prisms or lenses that slice reality in different ways, so directing analytical attention to diverse kinds of linkage that in practice will be overlapping and inseparable. If the broad objective of the new sociology of work is to open up new domains and issues for investigation, then it also requires the equipment to do so. The main purpose of this chapter in distinguishing between different interconnections of work is to contribute to such a project by developing some conceptual tools that may help pinpoint and think through some major contemporary changes in work.

Transformations of work

Technological innovation, the implementation of information and communication technologies in all fields of economic life, the increasing complexity and density of global interconnection, restructuring between market and non market sectors, and reconfiguration of temporal arrangements all have profound effects for the organisation and experience of work. The emergence of new occupations, skills and divisions of labour, far-reaching alterations in employment relations, patterns of participation and the reorganisation of working time are just some of the changes currently occurring in paid employment. To these must be added equally significant developments in non-market and unpaid work, including proliferation of the modes and extent of care work, the growth of voluntary or community work in the public domain, and shifts in both directions across the commodity/non commodity divide. As such changes impact on individuals and households, the questions of work/life balance, time pressure, and tensions between competing responsibilities and timescales assume salience in public policy as pressing problems of working life today.

Recent empirical studies reveal both the depth and breath of contemporary change, but as most focus on one development alone (such as flexibility, subcontracting and remote outsourcing, insecurity, work/life balance, portfolio careers, new modes of managerial control or labour process), usually from a specialist disciplinary perspective, they cannot be expected to offer comprehensive analysis of the broader changes. New paradigms and theoretical approaches are emerging to account for changing realities and their implications, amongst the most suggestive emanating from a renascent economic sociology (e.g. Granovetter, 1992, 1985; Granovetter and Swedberg, 1992; Swedberg, 2003; Smelser and Swedberg, 1994; Slater and Tonkiss, 2001; Callon, 1998; Metcalfe and Warde, 2002), the new field of cultural economy (Ray and Sayer, 1999; Du Gay and Pryke, 2002) and spatially inflected work in economic geography (Wrigley and Lowe, 1996; Dicken, 2003; McDowell, 1997; Perrons, 2003). The concern to research the linked stages of an integral process (Cockburn and Ormrod, 1993; Du Gay, 1997) or to outline contrasting configurations of economic processes (Harvey *et al.*, 2002) evident in economic sociology and cultural economy, together with attempts to analyse the social and cultural in the economic and vice versa (Lash and Urry, 1994; Ray and Sayer, 1999; Du Gay and Pryke, 2002) all offer novel ideas for thinking about recent empirical developments. Common to many of these is the project to overcome conceptual boundaries, especially between the study of consumption and production, for example, by thinking in terms of 'systems of provision' (Keat *et al.*, 1994; Fine *et al.*, 1996; Warde and Martens, 2000) or of 'instituted economic process' (Harvey, 2002; Harvey *et al.*, 2001; Harvey and Randles, 2002).

From the 'total social organisation labour' . . .

The discussion here reflects and benefits from all of these initiatives. For many years I have been working with the concept of the 'total social organisation of labour' (Glucksmann 1990, 1995, 2000a). Originally the central thrust was to draw attention to the interconnections between labour undertaken under different socio-economic relations or in differing socio-economic spaces. As outlined in Chapter 1, the TSOL refuses a distinction between work and employment, arguing for an inclusive concept that acknowledges as work many forms of labour that are not remunerated or that may not be differentiated out or recognised as activities separate from the relationships (social, cultural, kin, etc.) within which they are conducted. It is concerned with connections between work across boundaries, the shifting and permeable character of such boundaries, and with the formation and dissolution of boundaries as an object of study. Given that work activities may shift historically between the commodity and non-commodity sphere, or between production and distribution, a TSOL perspective is concerned not with establishing a classification but rather with the overall articulation of interconnected work activities. Taking the manner of articulation as the central object of investigation means recognising the variability and multiplicity of linkages and connections.

The TSOL is thus a relational conception focusing on modes of linkage and connection, articulations, intersections, configurations, patterns, networks and so on. Transformations over time between different organisations of labour are a central concern. By analytically unpicking and rejointing connections and relations it becomes evident that explanation of the distribution of labour across spheres and boundaries cannot be internal to any one sphere, but must refer to the higher level of how labour is organised across and between them.

In substantive research I have developed the TSOL at macro, meso, household and individual level to explore historically changing social divisions of labour within and between the commodity and non-commodity sectors of the economy. *Women Assemble* (Glucksmann, 1990) focused on the linked series of changes affecting women's work in both paid employment and the household that accompanied the transition to mass production in Britain during the inter-war period. The 'new industries' produced a range of goods that were specifically aimed at household consumption, recruiting hundreds of thousands of women to factory employment, who in an earlier generation might have worked as unpaid homemakers or paid domestic servants, simultaneously transforming household labour with the availability of consumer durables, ready-made food and clothing and other new commodities.

In *Cottons and Casuals* (Glucksmann, 2000a), I analysed the connections between gendered divisions of labour in paid employment and domestic labour for two groups of married women workers in Lancashire in the second third of the twentieth century. Here spatial and temporal dimensions were introduced to the TSOL approach, complementing the central concern with informal local economic transactions, differences within gender and divisions of labour inter-linked across home and work.

My subsequent research concerns have shifted towards exchange, distribution and consumption, and to the links between the work undertaken in different parts and stages of a process considered in its entirety. The TSOL perspective was deployed in relation to retail (2000b), and to call centres, the latter being one of the most rapidly expanding forms of business organisation (2004a). Here the focus is the connections to and place of call centres and their labour forces in the wider overall economic process or business activity of which they are a part, developing a relational conception of the call centre as one phase in an integral process of provision or production through to consumption. From this perspective, call operating work is seen as heterogeneous, part of a larger and variable occupational structure. Looking in greater detail at one type of call centre work, telephone retail (Glucksmann, 2004b), and at the encounter between front line service workers and consumers, a TSOL approach explores how the telephone alters the nature of both consumption and sales work, and the respective competencies required of both parties to the interaction.

Throughout this research, using a 'total social organisation of labour' frame-work facilitated analysis across and between work performed under differing socio-economic relations and of work with similar content but undertaken under disparate conditions. A TSOL approach has also been productive for other scholars, for example in research on the connections between paid work and domestic responsibilities in women's changing employment profile (Crompton, 1997), on insecure forms of employment (Charles *et al.*, 2002; Charles and James, 2003), on the last century of health care work in Canada (Armstrong and Armstrong, 2004), and on strategies of former South Wales mining communities in responding to a transformed set of economic circum-stances (Parry, 2003). In research on voluntary work, Rebecca Taylor (2002, 2004) significantly develops the TSOL by extending it to the field of unpaid work in the public sphere and also *across* spheres.

... to interconnections between work activities

While these various studies demonstrate the value of taking the articulation between different forms of labour as the object of investigation, there are a number of weaknesses in the TSOL formulation thus far and ways in which it may be strengthened. It is not intended as a 'finished' conceptual framework, but one that is constantly developing in relation to the substantive material it confronts.

First, the TSOL has definite limitations in that it cannot itself explain the distribution of work. In other words, the organisation and distribution of work cannot be explained solely from within work. While we can understand how some kinds of work are predicated on others also being undertaken, or how some forms of work interact with others, or how the contours of particular occupations take shape in relation to each other, the organisation and distribution of work between economic spaces is not self-explanatory. In order to enhance the explanatory capacity of the TSOL, particularly with respect to change, reference is required to a higher level of analysis than work itself, focusing on the relationships connecting the sectors in which labour is undertaken. *Women Assemble* did attempt this by locating the changes in women's paid and unpaid labour in an analysis of the transformation between the household and market economies that accompanied mass production and consumption. In the work on call centres this higher-level explanatory framework is also evident in the emphasis on the relation between variations in the intermediary function of call centres and the type of economic activity in which they are engaged. However, the higher-level explanatory frame requires further explication. This is especially so in relation to the first two dimensions of interconnectedness of work activities to be discussed (across overall processes of provision/production to consumption, and across socio-economic mode).

A Polanyian-derived 'instituted economic process' approach is particularly helpful in this connection on account of its concern with how economic processes are historically and socially instituted in particular configurations. Contrasting the place of the economy in pre-literate, archaic, pre-modern and 19th century British societies, Polanyi had argued for the historical specificity of the economic given 'the shifting place of the economic in society . . . in which the economic process is instituted at different times and places' (Polanyi 1957: 202). What is differentiated out as 'economic' or understood as 'work' may vary significantly between different societies and over time, depending on how economic processes are embedded and instituted in particular cases. Adopting this approach, the different parts or stages of an economic process may be seen as a relational complex of interdependent parts. An 'instituted economic process' perspective makes it possible to view provision or production, distribution, exchange and consumption as a configuration along these lines, and for present purposes this particular relational complex may provide the higher level analytical frame for explaining the distribution and organisation of labour across and between sectors.

Second, some issues require further specification or refining. Others would benefit from being made more explicit. A case in point is the basic notion of 'interconnection' between different forms of work, given that this may be of quite different kinds. Bearing this in mind, the following sections separate out and conceptualise in turn the four analytically distinct kinds of interconnectivity of work activities distinguished at the outset. The prime focus here will be the manner and modes of interconnection, rather than the domains and boundaries crossed.

Interconnections between different work activities undertaken in different parts of an overall process are analytically distinct from interconnections between work activities conducted within diverse socio-economic relations or economic spaces. Similarly, the interpenetration with and relative extent of

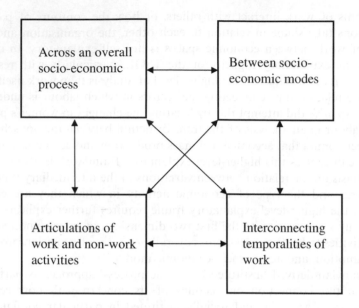

Figure 1: Interconnections of Work Activities

differentiation of work activity from other social and cultural relations is also of a distinctive nature, as is the manner by which work activities mesh in temporal interconnection.

These four dimensions are interdependent and so in addition to being considered separately on their own account, they are also to be analysed in combination in relation to each other. Figure 1 attempts a simplified representation.

It is important to remember that any particular process will 'possess' or be characterised by all four dimensions, each of which will have their own characteristics, intersecting or combining with each other in a specific manner. Separating out the dimensions involves slicing the same subject matter a different way, and approaching it with a different set of questions and concerns. Thus any overall process will have different phases or stages, broadly of provision or production, distribution, exchange and consumption. These may be undertaken through a variety of modes, including the possibility of different phases being delivered through different modes (e.g. production through the market, and distribution through the public sector as in the case of public transport). Similarly the work undertaken in both the phases and the modes may be more or less undifferentiated from other relationships (e.g. in marketised care of the elderly, the work of paid carers is still likely to involve an emotional aspect). And each of these also has a temporal dimension. A complex picture thus emerges which is not readily amenable to diagrammatic representation, especially as each dimension takes a variety of forms that are not dualistic oppositions or to be conceived as positions on a linear continuum.

The remainder of the chapter elaborates a schematic conceptualisation of the differing kinds of interconnectivity of work activities, by pulling together, refining and drawing out these themes. An exercise in analytical precision such as this represents a preliminary step in enhancing the potential of the TSOL to confront contemporary transformations of work.

Dimension 1: Interconnection of work activities across economic processes

The first dimension singles out the interconnectedness of work activities across the processes of provision or production, distribution, exchange and consumption, with a special focus on the transformation or emergence of processes and the new occupations, skills, divisions of labour and organisations of work associated with them. Particular processes or fields of economic activity are characterised by their own distinctive overall division, integration, and succession of the stages involved in work activity. Work undertaken at different points in a process may vary historically and/or shift between different stages, often as a consequence of new technologies or organisational innovation. The interdependencies of labour connecting all those involved in 'an overall process of provision/production and consumption', are likely to be relatively less geographically restricted than previously to particular locations, and more nationally or globally dispersed.

Denoting a process in its entirety raises a terminological problem. 'Circuit' of 'production to consumption' is not right since it suggests a pre-given, single and continuous sequence. It also implies linearity in which production precedes consumption when changes in consumption also impact on the rest of the process. In the absence of an adequate alternate, I shall refer to 'overall processes' of provision and/or production and consumption. 'Provision' is an inclusive term, encompassing production and other means of 'providing' the services and goods with which call centres are associated. 'Overall' implies that the shape and complexity of the process are not pre-given, but the object of analysis.

As suggested above, changes in the distribution of work cannot readily be explained from within work but may be better appreciated by reference to their wider context, that is, the changing pattern of interconnectedness that results from re/structuring of the overall process and of the different stages of work activities. It is in relation to this dimension that the 'instituted economic process' perspective is especially relevant. Within this paradigm, production, distribution, exchange and consumption (PDEC for short) may be viewed as distinct but mutually dependent and interrelated processes forming a relational complex. Each undergoes distinctive processes of institution along with the relations between them 'which are inherently a source of variation' (Harvey *et al.*, 2001: 59). The focus will be how the four processes are instituted, how relations between them become stabilised in distinctive configurations enduring over a

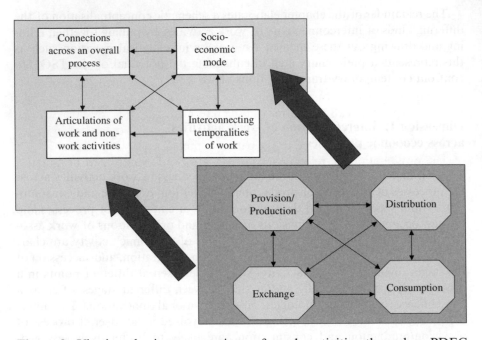

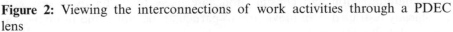

Figure 2: Viewing the interconnections of work activities through a PDEC lens

given space and time, and the patterns of mutual dependency and asymmetries of power across such a relational complex of processes.

Incorporating into the TSOL approach consideration of this higher level configuration across an overall economic process would undoubtedly strengthen its analytical range and capacity. TSOL and PDEC represent different analytical cuts that may be applied to the same process, separately or conjointly. Of course, configurations, and transformations of configurations, of production, distribution, exchange and consumption may be analysed in their own right. It is also possible to view them through the lens of the TSOL, focusing primarily on their labour component. Conversely it is also possible to view TSOL through a PDEC lens, which is what I am beginning to do here (See Figure 2).

Several benefits are gained by deploying a processual approach towards the overall configuration of work. First, it elucidates evolving patterns of work activity that could not be gained from concentrating on individual occupations or workplaces; second, it helps explain how work is distributed across vertical and horizontal occupational structures; and third, it raises to the surface basic questions about the drivers and dynamics of transformation involved in the changing interconnectedness of labour activities.

Clearly, technological innovation, industrial restructuring and economic change are crucial considerations in analysing shifts in mode of interconnection across a PDEC process. The spread of internet and call centre technologies, for example, provides a ready instance of this dimension of interconnected work activities. As information and communication technologies are developed to establish new businesses and forms of transaction, new kinds of work emerge (for example, web designers, script and prompt writers, and magnetic resonance imagers) with their own skill requirements and occupational structures. The work performed by call operators and the intermediating role they play can be properly understood only in the context of the broader division of labour of the business activity, as suggested in the earlier comments on call centres.

The proliferation of ready-made food – a second example, to be pursued at greater length – has been accompanied by a progressive reconfiguration of labour between the market and household, a new range of occupations and an alteration of the relation between production, distribution, retail and consumption, and in the nature of work that is done at each stage in this overall process. Instead of buying food raw materials in shops and preparing the finished meal at home primarily through unpaid domestic labour, meals for a long time now have been produced under market conditions as commodities available for purchase either partially or fully prepared, with correlative shifts of labour out of the home and into food preparation factories and retail outlets selling the new goods. Packaging, distribution, advertising and sales also expand and alter in line with the extension of the food commodity sector, workers being recruited to perform many different kinds of work, some of which were not previously undertaken as paid employment. Vegetable chopping, dough making, and sauce mixing are tasks that increasingly are undertaken in food factories, a highly feminised, and frequently ethnicised, form of paid work that would previously have been done by women unpaid and on an individual scale for immediate consumption in their own homes.

In the present day UK, the leading supermarkets are responsible for the majority of ready-made food sales. They are also amongst the largest employers in the country. Many check-out staff, responsible for effecting the sale of food goods, are women who in earlier generations, like the food production workers, might not have engaged in the paid employment which now encourages them to purchase the same goods that they are selling, but rather devoted more unpaid labour time to food preparation at home. Thus a reconfiguration of women's work occurs between household, factory and retail outlet.

Turning to another part of the overall process, the supermarkets have established large regional distribution centres for the rapid transfer of their perishable food products from factory to the network of retail outlets spread throughout the country. Here a new range of workers is employed, including stock controllers, fork lift truck operators, logistics experts, computer software programmers, not to mention the fleet of lorry drivers. This part of the process is more likely to be male dominated.

A different part of the overall process will be dedicated to advertising and marketing. In the era when branded ready-made food was dominant, advertising was designed to create or enhance the demand for ready-made in general (labour saving; more global and varied than you could make at home; high quality; low cost; and so on) and for particular brand meals. Today competition between supermarkets tends to revolve around the particular companies with their own-brand products.

Each of these phases of the overall 'provisioning' of ready-made food involves in turn commensurate changes up and down the line: research and development into new plastics for packaging materials; the production of specialist refrigerator units for lorries; focus groups, market research, and shopper profiling to provide information to assist the design of advertising campaigns.

The point to take from an ever-extendable example such as this is that the various stages and parts of the process, and the different work activities under-taken in them, are connected with each other in a particular configuration of production, distribution, exchange and consumption. None can be properly appreciated on its own outside of the wider system of which it is an integral part, and understanding of the division of labour and occupational structure rests on the broader frame of reference.

Dimension 2: Socio-economic mode: interconnectedness across boundaries between paid and unpaid work, market and non-market, formal and informal sectors

It is vital to adopt an inclusive approach to work as comprising all labour activ-ity since it is undertaken within a wide variety of socio-economic relations. While paid employment is the dominant mode in modern industrial societies, work is also conducted in a multiplicity of ways, many of which are on an unpaid basis in the household, community and the public formal sphere. Bound-aries between socio-economic modes have always been permeable, the same work activity crossing between domains. Perhaps rapid change and global inte-gration make this more evident today.

Given ever-increasing multiplicity and proliferation of both market and non-market forms of work, which may be connected to each other, it is more realis-tic to conceive of the economy as a 'multiplex' combination of modes, rather than as a dualism between market and non-market forms. Employment in the public or state sector is characterised, if not driven, by many of the same con-siderations as the private sector (rate for the job, productivity deals, recruitment and retention, labour market profiles), even if conditions of employment differ and the employer is bound by more regulated standards of accountability. More-over, while many contemporary welfare states financially resource welfare, they do not always provide the services themselves. Subcontracting by the state and public sector to private firms produces a blurry distinction between state and private employment, graphically described in Polly Toynbee's account of hospi-tal portering in the UK (2003: 55–84). The National Health Service (NHS) con-tracts out a large proportion of its cleaning, portering and other ancillary work, largely to Carillion, a French owned company, who in turn subcontract to employment agencies. When Toynbee worked as a porter in this context, it was often unclear exactly who she was responsible to: the agency who took her on, their client Carillion, or the hospital she worked at. Emulating the 'hollowing out' of private sector firms, subcontracting in the public sector is integral to a policy of reducing the directly employed workforce, creating complex new links with and dependencies on the market.

It is similarly unhelpful to counterpose as dualisms paid employment and unpaid household labour, as is common in many commentaries on women's work, since unpaid labour may be performed in a wide variety of environments other than the household and paid work can be undertaken as formal employment or on the basis of informal exchange, and in the commodity or non commodity sector.

The second dimension of interconnectedness of socio-economic mode problematises the relation between work and employment through a focus on interactions across boundaries and shifts of work activities between modes. In the following four examples the prime concern is the nature of such interactions, and their implications, rather than enumeration or classification of modes.

The first comes from *Cottons and Casuals* (2000a). To understand how domestic labour was effected by the two groups of women, weavers and casual workers, required reference not only to the unpaid labour they undertook at home and to their paid employment, but also to the network of local informal exchange and to their husbands' occupations. Weavers' wages were relatively high, enabling them to purchase the services of other women, for example, to do their washing or childcare. Moreover, their husbands' earnings were on a par with their own, predisposing a more equal domestic division of labour than might have been the case had there been a large difference in their respective contribution to household income. For the casual workers the situation was reversed: not only did they take total responsibility for work in their own households but they also worked formally and/or informally for pay, selling domestic labour to formal organisations and to other women. Their husbands usually worked in insecure and (male) gender-segregated occupations that were associated with a tradition of secrecy over wages and construction of housework as 'women's work'. While weavers were able to buy time with money and so reduce the amount of unpaid labour they undertook, the casual women workers gained money only through additional expenditure of labour time. In the overall picture then, four interconnections across socio-economic mode came into play: the woman's paid work and her domestic labour, her husband's employment, and their relation to informal exchange.

The second example is care work, which is connected across and shifts between formal and informal provision, paid and unpaid, in historically changing ways in different countries (see Clare Ungerson, this volume). In the UK, for example, the reduction in state support especially for mental health care in the late 1980s, under the policy of 'care in the community' divested the government of major employment costs in the affected fields and transferred care work onto families, usually women, who assumed responsibility but were not paid. As a concerted Labour government policy since 1997, state and voluntary sector involvement in care work are becoming increasingly intertwined, both financially, through increased state support to voluntary organisations, and in provision, as the voluntary sector assumes ever more responsibilities for supplying front-line services. Another way of putting this is that the government now resources others to perform a range of care work which in the past it had directly undertaken[1]. Simultaneously the private sector is rapidly expanding into childcare, recognising day nurseries as having significant business potential, while also withdrawing from care homes for the elderly often on the grounds that government regulation makes profit margins unviable[2]. In these various ways, the public sector, profit-making businesses, non-profit voluntary organisations and charities inter-connect in an intricate network to provide care. The same service may be supplied within differing socio-economic relations, which also affect the mode of 'employment' of care workers.

Very different issues are to the fore in different countries. In Taiwan, for example, the absence of developed welfare provision may provoke serious strain as increasing proportions of women join the paid labour force. Traditionally in Taiwan (and this example could be multiplied around the globe) care was undertaken by the extended family. The generation of women who are now middle-aged were able to combine motherhood and work through reliance on their own mothers to care for children. But the social and economic changes of which their own employment is one instance also imply that they will not do the same for their own daughters. Nor will those daughters be readily able to undertake elder care. So the paid-unpaid work interconnection between two generations which facilitated women's entry to paid employment in the late 20th century is no longer viable in the 21st. This poses a keenly felt 'personal' problem for many younger Taiwanese concerned at the lack of public recognition of the need for a new care regime, an absence currently filled by private individuals employing migrant domestic workers (Lin, 1999; Lan, 2003).

Voluntary work – unpaid public work – provides a third example. Inter-connections between 'voluntary' and other socio-economic modes of work exist both at the personal individual level (many individuals undertaking both paid and unpaid work in different combinations over the life course (viz. Taylor, 2002; 2004)) but also at the national societal level, with wide international differences in the amount, organisation and endorsement of voluntary work and in how it is financially resourced. It is not high on the agenda for the Nordic countries. Their policy of bringing as much work as possible into paid formal employment results in lack of encouragement, if not disdain, for unpaid public work as exploitative. In the Netherlands, by contrast, many young elderly engage on a voluntary but relatively formal basis in care work, especially relief of family carers, 'subsisting' on the pension from their previous employment (Burger and Dekker, 2001). In this scenario, voluntary work is in effect supported through employers' and state contributions to pensions, producing an indirect but nevertheless definite connection between paid and unpaid work, past and present, and between state, private and individual finance routed via retirement pensions. Age and stage in the life course are integral to this kind of interconnection, as were intergenerational considerations in the Taiwanese case.

Non-market forms of consumption 'work' presupposed by products and services produced through market employment provide a final and very different example of interconnection of work activities across socio-economic mode. Whilst vacuum cleaners, electric drills and hair washing products are all made in factories on the basis of market employment, their use or 'consumption' presuppose that unpaid 'work' will be undertaken by the consumer, either as housework, or DIY, or grooming. The middle years of the 20th century saw the decline of laundries as commercial enterprises, superseded by people doing it themselves in laundrettes and later in their own homes. The production of washing machines for domestic rather than industrial use was predicated on a new form of work being undertaken in the home, requiring new skills on the part of the 'consumer'.

The aim of these four examples is to bring into sharp relief the shifting place of labour activity in different modes of provision, the formation of new boundaries and interactions across them, and how their interrelations are directly or indirectly mediated. Questions about how major social change and economic restructuring affect interactions across boundaries between market and non-market, formal and informal, work activities define a wide-ranging and important area for investigation.

Dimension 3: Articulations of work and non-work activities: the multidimensionality of labour activity

The third dimension addresses the interpenetration, boundaries and articulations between work and non-work processes. It raises the basic question 'what is work' and how it is instituted as an economic activity, to be understood as a theoretical, empirical and historical question rather than one of definition. Three distinct research areas where issues relating to work/non-work are central and theoretically contested may be brought together here: 'embeddedness versus differentiation', 'emotion' work and 'aesthetic labour', and consumption 'work'.

The first, 'embeddedness versus differentiation', concerns forms of labour (primarily unpaid) that are more or less undifferentiated from non-work activities or relationships (especially characteristic of care, the household, and pre-industrial societies). In such circumstances work rarely exists in a 'pure' form, as is clearly evidenced in pre-industrial or agricultural societies where the 'economy' is not separated out as a separate domain (Glucksmann, 1995). But a significant proportion of labour in advanced industrial societies may also remain undifferentiated from informal, household, familial or community relationships which contain other components in addition to work. Domestic labour and care of children and the elderly are the obvious examples, where work may be fused with a wide range of different emotions and relationships.

While the embeddedness of work is 'normal' and analytically unproblematic for the disciplines of anthropology and history, it presents more of a challenge to approaches in sociology or economics which have conventionally rested on a view of their subject matter as differentiatedly 'social' or 'economic'. Coming to terms with the challenge involves recognising that differentiation is likely to be a relative, rather than an 'either-or' matter. Embeddedness too will be a matter of degree, and also a question of what is embedded in what and the manner of embeddedness. So, work may be differentiated to a certain extent, totally or not at all from other relations, and in studying particular cases and instances, the degree of differentiation will be an important area for specification.

Embeddedness is also likely to affect the experience of work. When labour is unpaid, those undertaking it may subjectively understand it as an expression of 'love' or 'neighbourliness' and not acknowledge it as work. And this will further problematise the question of work/non-work by bringing into view possible discrepancies between the interpretations of actors and researchers.

The second area for which 'emotion' work is very much a shorthand, focuses on jobs where in addition to emotions, aesthetics, interpersonal skills, and/or sexuality comprise an essential component and are combined with technical and professional competencies. This has been an increasingly significant theme in research on women's work from Pringle's study of secretaries in the late 1980s, and Adkins' (1995) of tourism employees, through to Witz and colleagues' work on the style economy (Warhurst and Nickson, 2001; Witz *et al.*, 2003), Entwistle's on fashion models (2002), and Pettinger's study of high street fashion store sales assistants (2003, 2004). Expansion of service industries has been accompanied by the proliferation of occupations where interpersonal skills, appearance and comportment represent both a requirement of the job and a means by which firms compete for market share.

Although especially characteristic of interactive service work and the 'new economy' where extensive research has focused on call centres, flight attendants, tourism and the leisure industry, we should not forget that emotional engagement, personal attributes and people skills have always been presupposed by far more traditional (usually female dominated) occupations such as nursing, hairdressing and beauty therapy (Sharma and Black, 2001), not to mention paid care work (Qureishi, 1990; Ungerson, 1999).

Conflicting views exist about the extent to which 'sociality' is a recognised or formalised part of such jobs (see Lynne Pettinger's chapter in this volume). Unpicking the different dimensions of work and non-work that are intertwined in the performance of particular forms of labour and establishing exactly how they articulate represents a major extension to the understanding of work, and a stimulating frame for further research.

The third, new, area, 'consumption work', would explore the 'work' involved in practices of consumption and whether such 'work' is extending into new domains. Routine practices such as shopping, driving, grooming, and appreciating cultural goods, for example, may variously be interpreted as work, consumption, leisure, or an undifferentiated combination of these (see Chapter 1 of this volume). Buying and using goods and services commonly demands labour to be undertaken in addition to whatever gratification, pleasure, fantasy or desire are also involved. While routine household shopping has long been viewed by feminists as work, cooking, operating a dishwasher, washing machine or video recorder, playing computer games, or assembling an outfit to wear, can be understood both by actors and/or by those studying such activities in a variety of ways.

Moreover, the ability to engage in consumption practices often relies on the 'work' of knowledge acquisition and learning specific practical skills, so raising the question of whether, or in what sense, the acquisition of skills necessary to undertake consumption constitutes work. Cooking and preparing meals could be a fruitful example to investigate for a complex fusion of work, non-work and skill acquisition.

Also relevant here is previously paid work that is transmuted into unpaid and apparently non-work activity. For example, when domestic servants disappeared in the early 20th century in the US and UK they were replaced by the ideal housewife running her ideal home, and a construction of domestic labour which emphasized its positive, emotional and rewarding features far removed from the hard drudgery and heavy work associated with earlier images of maids (Cowan 1983).

This third dimension of interconnection of work activities draws together distinct and often disparate areas where the nature of work is contestable (since it is always combined with other non-work activities, relationships or emotions), and so foregrounds analysis of the changing historical character of work.

Dimension 4: Interconnecting temporalities of work

As well as having its own significance as a mode of interconnection of work activities, temporality is also conceived as a 'golden thread' running through and connecting the first three dimensions. The term temporalities denotes the social organisation of time in durations, cycles, synchronies, sequences and rhythms, and their articulation.

Recent years have seen an explosion of research and policy attention to work-time, both in itself and in relation to non-work time, often in the context of a perceived increase in time pressure and 'shortage'. Concerns have centred on consolidation of '24/7' society and its global implications, erosion of 'standard' working time and disappearance of the normal working day, the EU working time directive and its implementation, the work/life balance or, more accurately, 'imbalance', the value of time-use study, and of time measures for estimating value and output, including initiatives for satellite accounting of non-paid work such as those undertaken by the UK Office for National Statistics (UK 2000 Time Use Survey, Household Satellite Account).

Strictly speaking these concerns primarily address employment and clock time. Yet the temporal dimensions of work are multifaceted and extensive, calling for an approach which is not restricted to standard linear time. Because time can be ordered and regulated, and enter social processes including work and employment in innumerable different ways, the possible structurings of time, or temporalities, are almost infinite. Successfully managing different temporalities, and integrating working with non-working time has probably always posed a challenge for individuals and households, but one that may now be accentuated as older modes of integration are eroded. The time shortage debate (Schor, 1992; Robinson and Godby, 1997; Gershuny, 2000; Southerton *et al.*, 2001) may be better interpreted in relation to the disruption or alteration of pre-existing temporalities (including subjective experience) than in terms of measurable time poverty (Southerton and Tomlinson, 2003; Harvey, 1999).

The temporal dimension is also evident in the rhythms, cycles, sequences, continuities and discontinuities of work, all of which may be transformed in relation to alterations in the overall process of production, distribution, exchange and consumption. For instance, to return to an earlier example, the production of ready-made meals shifts working time from unpaid household labour to paid employment in factories, warehousing, transport, and retail outlets. The need for ready-made sandwiches to be fresh imposes a temporal imperative of speed and co-ordination throughout the process of production, distribution and exchange right through to final consumption, where eating sandwiches may replace previous modes of (definite) timed lunch breaks with grazing. Call centres adopt a plethora of new information technologies to alter the temporal organisation of work for businesses (including rerouting calls to remote locations) but also for call operators and clients/customers, in addition to extending 24/7 operations and speeding up global communication (Glucksmann, 2004b).

As the previous three dimensions all have a time aspect, this fourth theme focuses on the significance of temporality as integral to their inter-relation with each other. Alterations in the processes of production, distribution, exchange and consumption (dimension one) also shift the articulated temporalities for all those engaged in the work activities of factories, logistics, retail outlets and households. Shifting work between different modes of provision (dimension two) often requires new articulations of temporalities between them. The embeddedness or differentiation of work from non-work activities (third dimension) likewise involves a fairly obvious structuring or restructuring of temporalities. Moreover, changes in the temporalities of some people's non-work consumption activities may interconnect or clash with changing temporalities in the work activities of others who provide consumption products or services. A recent report on the provision, or rather lack of provision, of childcare for people working what used to be called 'unsocial hours', highlights the knock-on and contradictory effects of temporal shift. More and more people work in the evening or at night or weekends, yet few childminders are prepared to take children outside of 7am to 7pm, Monday to Friday, concerned about the impact on their own families of working longer hours (Mooney and Statham, 2003).

Analysing the changing temporalities both within and between each dimension of interconnectedness (the overall socio-economic process, market/non-market, work/non-work), and the drivers of such change, comprise the principal foci of this fourth dimension. Perhaps there is greater potential today than in previous historical epochs for changes of temporality within one dimension to generate tensions or contradictions with others. And in such circumstances there is unlikely to be any overall integrative temporal regime.

Conclusion

The objective of this chapter has been to suggest a relational conceptual framework by bringing together four dimensions of interconnectedness of work activities: across economic processes, modes of provision, the interfaces of work and non-work, and the temporalities of each of these three. Not only do these dimensions co-exist and combine, but changes within each are likely to bring about changes within and between other dimensions.

An analytical approach highlighting the multiple interconnections of work will have many other implications than those explored in this chapter. From this perspective, for example, workers may be understood as being constituted, both collectively and individually, as a particular point of intersection of interconnectedness in four dimensions. So too may consumers. And given that workers are also consumers and vice versa, it is perhaps more appropriate to think in terms of worker-consumers. Multiple and variable interconnectedness of the four dimensions is manifest in differently constituted workers, consumers and worker-consumers. Moreover, interconnectedness makes them a locus of constraint and conflict which are part of the dynamics of points of intersection.

The research agenda implied here involves work of different kinds: new empirical research addressing each dimension; synthetic work building on the variety of perspectives and knowledge of different disciplines whose subject matter is work and employment; and theoretical work to refine, clarify and develop the conceptual framework.

My hope is that recognition of the distinctiveness and interdependence of these dimensions of interconnectedness of work activities provides a basis for addressing fundamental questions relating to the nature and dynamics of transformations of work within a broader and deeper analytical framework. The principal objective of such a research vision which seeks out the multiple ways in which work is conducted and the shifting boundaries between employment, work and non-work is to contribute to the re-invigoration of the sociology of work.

Notes

1 An estimated increase of 40 per cent in income received by charities from government between 1991–2001 (Glennerster, 2003: 14, citing Kendall *et al.*, 2003) provides convincing evidence of their increasing use by the state as a means of delivering social welfare services.
2 The childcare market was worth £2.15bn in 2002, more than five times as much as in the early 1990s (*Guardian*, 6 May 2003) and market provision of childcare is set to expand considerably in coming years.

Part 2
Re-examining paid employment

Friends, relations and colleagues:
The blurred boundaries of the workplace

Lynne Pettinger

Introduction

This chapter illustrates the blurred boundaries between work and non-work relations and their interface in the nominally 'public' sphere of paid employment by examining the role of friendship in the workplace in getting and keeping a retail sales job. Patterns of sociability are constructed around pre-existing ties and social networks, and along lines of age, occupational position and gender. Social relations between work colleagues are a relatively neglected dimension of workplace studies, although friendship and sociability are important for both workers and employers as indicated, for example, by Korczcynski (2003). For workers, family and friendship relations are instrumental in gaining and keeping employment in the retail chain stores that are the focus here, with socializing at work important in shaping who stays in work and who progresses from marginal to central roles (for example, from temporary to permanent work). Socializing with work colleagues is an important part of the working lives of shop assistants, and compensates in some way for the less favoured aspects of retail work, such as low pay, low status and emotional demands placed by customers.

Social similarity and social connections between colleagues benefit employers in regulating staff turnover. Social relations between colleagues contribute to the selling environment by enforcing and enhancing particular forms of sociability on the shopfloor. This creates 'atmosphere' for customers and 'team identity' for employees. Being sociable with colleagues demonstrates workers' ability to be sociable with customers and may produce a socially homogeneous shopfloor, as friendships are based around an affinity between like-minded people. This can aid stores in performing their branding strategy (Pettinger, 2004) as it means the workforce can be configured as part of how the brand is performed on the shopfloor. The existence and strength of a workplace community, however, may at times militate against the formation of effective service relationships, as socializing with colleagues when on the shopfloor may preclude interacting with customers.

Glucksmann's Total Social Organization of Labour (TSOL) involves a relational view of work, whereby work is allocated to different structures or institutions in a society, with there being an interdependent relationship between different sectors or ways of organizing work (Glucksmann, 2000a:19–20). This is explicitly a relational analysis, intended 'to elucidate the configurations and patterning of social relations and to throw light on the interlocking or intersectionality connecting together different social processes' (Glucksmann, 2000a:156). The TSOL approach has previously been used to explore how work in one sphere is connected to work elsewhere. Here, I will draw on the approach to study one occupation. In the case of service sector work there are a number of possible applications of a TSOL perspective, including unpacking the relationship between work and consumption and grounding the skills and attributes commonly associated with doing service work – most famously, emotional labour (Hochschild, 1983) – within a wider context that recognizes the importance of the non-work lives of the employees under question. Friendship networks, explicitly relational in themselves, are an under-acknowledged part of this. Notably, however, and unlike the formulation of the TSOL put forward by Glucksmann (1995; 2000a), my analysis foregrounds the way in which non-work relations are brought into the workplace and underpin formal employment relations. The central question concerns what sorts of social relations are involved in 'work'.

Studying the retail sector is revealing of how getting and doing a job incorporates elements that go beyond the paid employment contract and relationship, and impinges on wider social relations. This chapter draws on an ethnographic study of women's clothing chain stores conducted in south-east Britain 1999–2001. Three main strands of data collection are reported here. Firstly, 'worker observation', a period spent by the author employed as a sales assistant in a store called 'Distinction'[1], when participant observation was conducted. Secondly, 'shopper observation', a period of participant observation that entailed visiting seven different high street chain stores on around 20 distinct occasions in the role of a shopper to observe the workforce[2]. Thirdly, a series of qualitative interviews with shopfloor sales assistants are incorporated into the discussion (see Pettinger, 2003; 2005 for more methodological detail). One strand of this research involved studying the interactions between colleagues, which I characterize here as friendship and sociability. I begin with discussing the nature of friendship and sociability, asking whether these apply to the arena of paid work. I then go on to explore the important manifestations of friendship and sociability I identified in sales work, looking at how people get jobs, the friendship networks in workplaces, those excluded from these networks, and how the organization of work structures friendship. I conclude with some comments on the importance of recognizing how workers enter paid work as fully social beings, bringing social relationships from the 'private' sphere into their working lives.

Friendship

Friendship is '. . . a relationship built upon the whole person' that 'aims at a psychological intimacy' (Pahl, 2000:163) and tends to be associated with the private sphere (Pahl, 2000:13). Pahl contends that a new form of 'friendly' society has emerged, with friendship relations increasingly important: 'we are increasingly socially and culturally determined by our friends' (2000:172). Friendship is based around social similarity, with 'affinity' (Rezende, 1999:80) arising where friends tend to be of similar age, gender and class. Affinity means friendship may supersede organizationally imposed social hierarchies in work situations, making workplace friendships more significant than organizational roles. This may tend towards producing a socially cohesive and homogeneous shopfloor.

Somewhat optimistically, Pahl suggests that the evolution in the nature of friendship he suggests happened in the 1990s may lead to a more egalitarian society, and one which 'is subversive of market-based social relations' (2000:164), as the reciprocity involved in friendship is not calculated one. He implies that the market does not impinge on friendship in any way. On the contrary, however, and as this chapter shows, friendship relations are in many ways fundamental to market relations, as one of the forms of affinity between colleagues is their shared consumption behaviour – from shopping trips to shared ideas about a 'good night out' – as well as their work promoting consumption. Pahl's is a somewhat idealized account of friendship, one that neglects the importance of social contexts in defining friendship and providing the opportunity for friendship. Pahl makes a series of problematic assumptions and statements. His argument for the near-irrelevance of the workplace rests on an understanding of work as universally negative, rather than as a potential location for the creation and maintenance of meaningful friendships. It assumes that individuals are increasingly deinstitutionalized, liberated from the constraints of occupational identities, people 'who work to live, not live to work' (2000:164). Yet my research suggests that the workplace is crucial to the formation of some friendships, and that friendship is important in defining work. Work is not universally negative, but is potentially a source of meaningful social support and as social identity.

Work friends for Pahl are demoted to being 'friends of convenience', or acquaintances, and labelled as instrumental. He suggests friendships at work are relationships that 'do not depend on specific confidences or intimacies and are relatively superficial' (2000:118), and likely to end when one or the other leaves the job. This is in part true: the sociability present on the shopfloor need not signify deeper emotional ties, but it is not the whole story. Pahl assumes a separation of spheres: that public and private are consistently distinct, and that work is separate from family, friendship and consumption. This problematically negates the possibility for a more complex interaction between 'public' and 'private' (as Taylor and Armstrong and Armstrong note elsewhere in this volume). Despite the common separation between public and private, and general assumption that friendship is located in the private sector, the workplace is an important focus for friendship (Bell and Coleman, 1999). To some extent, Pahl acknowledges the possibility of this when he says: '[f]riendship exists largely through an involvement in certain activities, which generate sentiments which, in turn, encourage further activities' (Pahl, 2000:14), although he is not explicitly referring to the world of work. Working together in often high-pressure service environments is, for my respondents, one part of this, as will be seen. Indeed, friendship at work may be increasingly significant as a result of long working hours and family breakdown (Hochschild, 2001). With work repositioned as central to individuals' social support networks, Hochschild (1997) argues that workplaces are providing an escape from the pressures of family life, a source of support, identity and meaning, as family life is not the 'haven' it is supposed be. Friendship in the workplace offers an important line of analysis in developing a full understanding of many current themes in the sociology of work, such as the role of work in the formation of identities, and the relationship between work and home. Of course it is not the only significant form of interaction between colleagues. Less emotional relations of sociability are also present.

Sociability

Sociability is involved in the performance of friendship, but has a wider significance in service work, where interactions are central. Simmel's idea of sociability gives some insight into how the interactions are influenced not by 'skills' and 'attributes' long acknowledged to be marketized, but by everyday ways of being and interacting. Sociability, according to Simmel, is 'the pure essence of association' (1949:255), that which is left when more 'serious' elements of interactions between individuals are removed. It arises quite naturally, as 'an impulse' (Simmel, 1949:254), visible in how workers 'pass the time of day' with each other and with customers. Sociability, for Simmel, is disconnected from serious aspects of life, and is instead a 'social game' in itself, whereby interactions with others are devoid of serious intent, being a 'play-form of association' (Simmel, 1949:255). Here, 'talking is an end in itself' (Simmel, 1949:259) and the content of the conversation is irrelevant for as long as it is not too serious. Chatting and playing on the shopfloor is not, contra Simmel, free from connections from serious aspects of life, rather it acts as a counterbalance to these, making up for the stress of service work. For example, the response to a demanding customer may be to mimic the customer for the amusement of colleagues.

In my own research, whilst in many instances deeply held affective ties of friendship between colleagues could be observed, for example between workers who had been friends before joining the store, the dominant pattern of interaction was a sociability similar to the Simmelian definition. Simmel, however, overplays the suggestion that sociability is abstracted from social context; quite the reverse is true. Sociability occurs in the workplace, a workplace that is also a consumption space and hence is constrained by the demands of the organization and the market. Simmel argues that when sociability is directed towards an objective purpose, it loses its particular meaning and becomes false (Simmel, 1949:256). In my research, sociability had an instrumental aim in contributing to organizational success in two ways. Firstly, it contributed to the creation of a relatively socially homogenous workforce that suited the brand strategy and targeted customers by including and excluding workers from the dominant social groupings. Secondly, the sociable impulse that workers demonstrated in their interactions with each other could be harnessed to enhance customer service provision. By creating affective sociable ties with customers, largely through chatting to them, workers contributed to the store ambience and to customer service.

This last point, that the behaviour of workers is fundamental to the service interaction, is what lies behind the majority of research into interactive service work, which focuses largely on relations between workers and customers (as in emotion work studies), or between workers and managers (du Gay, 1996). As attested by Benson (1988), however, interactive service workers, particularly retail workers, face a third direction: to each other. Sociability is of particular importance in the service sector, where 'the *emotional style of offering the service is part of the service itself*' (Hochschild, 1983:5, italics in original) and employees are enjoined to be sociable with customers. This sociability is implicit in the studies of emotional labour that have dominated service sector research in recent years (Paules, 1996; Sharma and Black, 2001). It is rarely explicitly defined, however, as sociability, as a set of personal characteristics, such as being outgoing, bubbly or bright; rather it is presented as a requirement to manage one's own emotional reaction and to create a particular emotional reaction in others. The focus tends to be on workers interacting with customers, with insufficient attention paid to the context of these interactions in the wider domain of the service environment – for example, in the emotional support colleagues provide for each other. This is not to suggest that emotion work is not a crucial part of service work, far from it, and much interesting research has been done in this area (Macdonald and Sirianni, 1996; Bolton and Boyd, 2003). The discussion is well-rehearsed, however, and will be set aside here. This chapter foregrounds sociability itself as an important element of retail service work.

Getting a job: informal recruitment mechanisms

I turn now to exploring the manifestations of friendship relations and the performance of sociability in the retail shops I studied. 'Personal communities' (Pahl, 2000:145), or friendship networks, were important in gaining employment. This, I argue, has two main elements: new recruits in the stores I studied often knew current employees in some way, and promotion or other contractual changes were related to 'fitting in' to the workplace social group. For most of my interviewees, some form of nepotism was at play and they were assisted in getting their jobs by friends who already worked in the store, relatives, or by

knowing the managers. This usually explicitly involved being passed information about vacancies. McGauran (2000) found that managers in Dublin shops,
wanting people to fit in, preferred to employ one gender of staff. She found
recruitment was often by word of mouth, which she suggests 'is most likely to
be distributed among persons of the same gender' (2000:628), perhaps because
employees recognize the existing gender structure at work and so act to support
that. I found, however, that word of mouth recruitment in stores that employed
both men and women was not confined to one gender.

Granovetter (1973; 1974) famously emphasized the 'strength of weak ties' in
helping individuals to get a job. He argued that social networks are instrumental in getting work, with those who are relatively removed from an individual's
immediate circle able to inform the individual of job opportunities they were
unaware of. Hannan (cited in Pahl, 2000), on the other hand, suggests that close
friends are more significant in helping unemployed people find employment than
distant friends. In my research, both 'strong' and 'weak' ties were relevant.
Alison's[3] job came about because her brother was already employed in Canyon;
Phil's at Fashion Junction was acquired through a casual acquaintance. His
experience illustrates the general pattern:

> 'I'd been to Ipswich for an interview for another job and the owner of this franchise
> . . . they had another little private shop, and a friend of mine . . . worked Saturdays
> and I got to know her through him . . . I walked past one day . . . and she just came
> out . . . and asked me.' (Phil*)*

He began working part time, becoming full time after 6 months. Phil did not
have any previous experience of customer service work, and so the informal
recruitment process was essential. Both Laura and Tara did not know anyone
in the shops where they now worked, but submitted application forms 'cold'.
Only Laura, however, turned her temporary employment into a permanent job,
using the social connections she had established to help her stay on after her
initial contract expired:

> 'Initially it was a Christmas job at a concession . . . I became friendly with the 'Real
> Men[4]' bosses and said I was looking for work after Christmas and they said they . . .
> would find some work for me' (Laura).

This internal and word-of-mouth recruitment is perhaps a feature of how the
labour market for service occupations that do not require formal qualifications
is largely a local labour market, and so community connections come into play.

Once in a job, getting on with people at work was recognized by my interviewees as important for instrumental reasons, especially to progress in the store.
Tara suggests:

> 'If they like you, and a position arises, I think you might quite easily be put in to like
> an assistant manager or supervisor's positions' (Tara*)*.

This did indeed seem to be the case at Distinction, where I conducted worker
observation. Moving from part time to full time work was common here, with

part time work used as an extended selection process for full time workers. The same was true of switching from temporary to permanent work, and there was ongoing murmuring on the shopfloor about who of the Christmas temps would be kept on and who wanted to stay (a number could not wait to leave). Whilst there was no single cohesive social group and many disagreements between workers, social connections were important. This is seen most clearly at Distinction in the case of Luke, who moved from being a part time temporary worker to a full time and permanent one, a big leap to make.

Luke was initially employed on a long-term temporary contract (16 hours per week). He had a number of pre-existing ties to the store: his girlfriend (Claire) and her best friend (Vicky), key members of his social circle, both worked in the children's department, Vicky being the manager. This gave him an entry point not only to the job, but also to the social network of the shop, and facilitated his progress in the store. He had a degree from a local further education college, and was able and hardworking. When a permanent post was advertised, several people from the branch and outside applied but the main competition was between Luke and Jo, a part-time permanent worker. Luke was given the job, in part because of his social connections, as well as his abilities and willingness to lead other workers and to take on extra shifts at short notice. Luke's promotion caused some tension and heightened divisions between his and Jo's friends, based to some extent around the different departments; Jo's friends were mostly on ladieswear (the downstairs), Luke's in the upstairs departments[5]. Much of the tension bubbled beneath the surface and it was not easy to get a clear picture of who felt what[6]. What was clear to me was the way in which Luke had been able fully to enter the workplace culture because of his social ties, facilitating his transition into secure standard employment. These divisions between departments are examined more closely in the following section.

Social networks inside and outside work

Ethnographies of the workplace have found friendship to be a significant feature. Feminist ethnographies of work such as Westwood (1984), Pollert (1981) and Cavendish (1982) all point to how friendship and socializing at work made it easier for women workers to get through the day. Westwood, for example, found that friendship was an integral part of the shopfloor culture, marked through celebrations, the exchange of food and such like (1984:89–101). What was significantly different for the customer service workers I focused on was the presence of customers in the domain of social interaction.

Marshall (1986), in his ethnography of bar and restaurant work, makes some interesting points about social relations in service work. He stresses how the boundaries between workers and customers are permeable, in particular how workers become customers at certain times precisely because of the friendships and social interaction that are critical to doing bar work. A key point, also appropriate to retail, is that in restaurants, 'the usually discreet activities of work and play are here taking place side by side' (Marshall, 1986:34). He concluded that there were fuzzy boundaries between work and leisure: 'the convergence of work and non-work lives is focused on the particular workplace itself' (1986:44), and workers socialized at work. Socializing at work was endemic in the retail stores I studied, reflecting these fuzzy boundaries, although there were also a number of differences in the style of interaction. Opportunities for play or consumption at work were fewer for retail workers than for Marshall's bar staff, but were present, even actively created by workers. Interactions with customers also differed; the customers of shops were more likely to be strangers than 'regulars' at the bar Marshall (1986) studied. This may have contributed to a work culture in shops that was more closed to outsiders as affective ties between workers and customers were not formed, the workplace community being the enduring social relationship.

Friendship networks at Distinction were formed along lines loosely related to age, gender, position in the workplace hierarchy and membership of particular departments. This mix of personal and job specific factors interacted in complex ways and I trace some of the main divisions. Friendship was not the only form of connection: sexual and family relationships were also apparent – interviewees Alison and Zoë both worked with family members (brother and cousin, respectively), and Luke and Claire, and Sam and James at Distinction were in relationships. This is a finding similar to Adkins (1995), who showed how family relations were important to employment in the hotel sector. However, in this instance, women's employment was not conditional on the employment of their partners, as Adkins found.

The older workers, who were overwhelmingly female, did not socialize together outside work in the same way as many younger workers did, mainly because of their family commitments. They did, however, share confidences about their own and their partners' and children's lives and so knew each other quite intimately, especially those who had worked together for several years. A group of workers in their late 20s and early 30s, often with some form of supervisory role, and mostly full time, saw more of each other outside work: Kate, the manager, for example, would stay at Emma's[7] house. They did go out together but did not talk about it at work much, reflecting perhaps how social lives were less significant markers of identity for this group.

For younger workers, however, the social groups appeared very important, with the groups being larger and more socially active. Pahl (2000) notes how friendships are particularly important for adolescents and young adults, who are likely to have wider social circles. Sam was an extreme case of the emphasis on social interaction between colleagues, someone whose social life at work appeared to be her main priority, and an extension of her social life outside work. It was her main topic of conversation, and indeed her main occupation, as she would often find a reason to escape the busy women's department and go upstairs to menswear to chat to her friends. These relationships were enacted outside work, largely on nights out but also through shared shopping trips or exercising. On New Year's Eve, Vicky (a department manager) held a party to which many of her work friends (and a few from outside work) were invited, demonstrating the centrality of the workplace as a source of friends.

My interviewees generally took the friendships they had at work seriously, saying these were important to them. This was partly a means of making work easier: 'we all sort of work quite well as a team up here anyway' (Nicole), or making up for the problems of the work: 'the people were really nice, you know, but the actual work itself wasn't very nice at all' (Tara). Perhaps most important was the personal enjoyment derived from spending time with likeminded people: 'I enjoy the team a lot. The people are good, they are really good fun' (Helen). This was the case even when colleagues were not seen to be good at their work: 'We all get on really well, there's a really nice atmosphere . . . although some of them aren't brilliant at dealing with people' (Chris). This was real problem for Chris and Phil, working at the same Fashion Junction store, who criticised the franchise owners for poor management and certain of their colleagues for being rude to the customers, suggesting some contradictions between work and social relations. Chris and Phil themselves were very good friends, with a great deal in common, only part of which was their attitude to work. Others spoke in similar terms:

> 'I was really glad that I was broke, and I had to work because I've made a whole load of friends . . . I get on with my colleagues immensely. We see each other socially as well, so we do enjoy our work as we all like the people we work with.' (Laura)

Friendship at work was not a universal experience, however. Both Becky and Beth felt isolated from the social relations on the shopfloor, in Becky's case because she felt supervisors treated the family and close friends also working at the store preferentially. Zoë said at first that she was not that close to any of her colleagues, because they were younger than she was. During our conversation, she realized she did spend time out of work with some of them, going to gigs or for a drink, but maintained that they were not emotionally close, having different life ambitions and doing different activities outside work.

The workplace at Distinction did not only see friendship relations, it was also a site for conflict, gossip, backbiting and bitchiness, serving to exclude some individuals from the workplace community – one limit on the extent of work-place sociability. For example, other workers often mocked Diane, a temp who was unpopular because she found much of the work hard and never stopped talking (perhaps suffering from an excess of sociability!). There was even violence on the shopfloor: the boyfriend of a female staff member came into the store and hit a male employee. The police were called and the aggressor given a caution. Tensions between workers were transferred onto the shopfloor, and played out in front of customers. During shopper observation in Number 1, I witnessed a female Asian and a black male employee having a heated argument, and later the same woman was taking to task another worker over the same issue. Thus workforce relations are not always positive, and sometimes act to the detriment of shopfloor harmony when played out in front of customers.

Close social relations between colleagues and a particular style of shopfloor sociability, whilst bringing benefits to the organization, may also entail problems.

Divisions and hierarchies

Benson (1988), discussing the work cultures of sales assistants in American department stores in the early years of the 20th century, explored how colleagues from within departments marked events such as engagements and marriages with parties, how they shared dressmaking skills and home-cooked food, and how the shopfloor helped people meet potential marriage partners. Friends from departments would eat together and go on holiday together. All these are important ways by which social relations are enacted, and their modern equivalents were apparent in contemporary UK chain stores. Benson (1988) identified the prevalence of divisions between departments and homogeneity within departments and suggests this produced and complemented a strong work culture. Whilst Benson does not describe this as friendship, it seems an obvious conclusion to draw. She focuses instead on the solidarity between colleagues, directed against management, consumers, workers from other departments and those from within the department who did not play by the implicit rules:

> 'Solidarity grew out of the intense social interaction which co-workers shared; huddling, or gathering together and talking, was the most universally remarked feature of saleswomen's work culture' (1988:245).

Similar patterns were apparent at Distinction, within departments in particular. Distinction, operating in a localized labour market, saw affinity being produced between colleagues/friends who shared social and work environments. Affinity crossed work-imposed hierarchies to some extent, particularly for permanent workers. I will now consider some of the main divisions imposed by the structures of the workplace. This section deals with the divisions on the shopfloor resulting from the organization of work, beginning with the impact of management on friendships and sociability.

a) Management

Social networks at Distinction sometimes crossed hierarchies imposed by the job, as in the case of Vicky and James, both managers and both at the centre of a social network. This had the potential to produce conflicts between the friend role and the supervisor role. Managers could use their relative power to organize work to influence inclusion into the workplace culture and social groups. At Distinction, friendship patterns influenced who was assigned which task. Reprimands may be avoided because of the ties of friendship – Sam, for example, was 'allowed' to do less work than others because of her proximity to

James, her partner and the menswear manager. My interviewees spoke about a range of tensions in the stores where they worked. Becky (Cheap Chic) complained of favouritism in task allocation, with the supervisor's sister (who worked only on Saturdays) getting the more prestigious jobs. At both Amanda Jane and Fashion Junction, problems with the management were at the root of workplace tensions. Helen and Nicole both said their manager, Anita, had neglected Amanda Jane and its employees in favour of Jones (a 'sister' store operating on the same site). She was also felt to have favourites, giving time off to her cousin over Christmas, against regulations. Helen commented:

> '. . . we couldn't complain, they'd all been here so long they were really close, family close, so we couldn't really say anything . . . if you went to her [Anita] with a complaint, if she didn't like you then she wouldn't give you hours'.

The manager in this instance quite explicitly used her power to organize aspects of work to stifle dissent and privilege certain workers she was closer to. Elsewhere, power was not so blatantly wielded, but tensions between managers and workers were manifested in other ways.

Jenny, a manager at Distinction, was not generally popular in the store because of the social distance she appeared to maintain. Unlike other managers, Jenny made status distinctions clear through her interaction style. Not only was she unwilling to chat, she would describe the sales assistants as 'girls', a word used to refer to groups of relatively low status women, regardless of age. In contrast, others drew on sociable relations to minimize the distance between managers and staff: Mel, assistant manager of ladieswear, was very open with the stress she felt at work, and store manager Kate's staff presentations invariably concerned her activities outside work[8]. However, Jenny was less concerned with using work demarcations (rather than social ones) to maintain her status as manager; she would to help unpack deliveries of goods. Other divisions were apparent, some based on job titles and roles, others on departments. I will consider next one fundamental division that influenced sociability, that between permanent and temporary workers (temps).

b) Marginalized workers

In Japan, Kondo found that company outings were part of a discourse that presented and perpetuated the idea of the company as family, with part-time workers usually excluded (Kondo 1990:162). Part-time and temporary workers were also excluded from the work cultures of American department store saleswomen (Benson, 1988:250). Once again, in the different context I studied, similar results were apparent. Throughout my research, temporary workers were seen as 'other' by the core permanent workforce and denigrated for this. Beth, a temp at a different Distinction store, commented on the attitude to temps prevalent where she worked, reporting how she felt she had been spoken to harshly in front of customers because of her status. Other workers had justified making dismissive comments about temps to her with 'Yeah, well I don't mean you' (Beth). In the course of my worker observation[9], Luke (on the day his permanent job was made public) made a comment about 'Christmas temps' when talking about his next shift. He complained he was doing 'replen'[10] from 12 to 9pm with 'just a temp to help during the day'. I must have looked shocked or outraged as he apologised for saying it in a seemingly derogatory way. Hannah, one of the youngest permanent employees, was often friendly and helpful, yet she too could be dismissive of temporary employees, suggesting one of the more timid temps, Rachel, was cheeky to ask for a lift home from a colleague who lived in the same area, but who she did not know. This marked out what she saw as the domain of acceptable sociable relations.

Even the most sociable temps did not prosper in Distinction without pre-existing social ties: common history, shared friendships and other similarities making the difference. Hannah, a permanent employee aged 16 and Sarah, a temp, both shared an interest in men in the army[11], for example, and then found they knew some of the same people. The temporary workers at Distinction were not invited to the staff Christmas party, further evidence of how temps were set apart from the main body of employees and not integral to the social relations of the shopfloor. This was felt by many to be unfair and unfriendly. The permanent/temporary division occurred in other stores as well. Tara, for example, a temporary worker at a discount store, went to the Christmas meal with her colleagues, but not to other social events, explaining: 'I'm not really in with their sort of thing.'

These episodes reflect how permanent workers often operated with an assumption that temps were incompetent, and indicate their low status and exclusion from social networks. However, other permanent workers were far more open and friendly. The divisions were therefore not clear-cut. Luke, whose story I discussed above, shows that some temps did become part of the work culture by building relationships with permanent workers. Indeed, exclusion from social networks had an effect on temps' work, and thus had a negative impact on the organization. Missing out on the spread of information could lead to errors in customer service provision, for example, promising orders that could not be fulfilled. Many of the temps I spoke to agreed to not having enjoyed working at Distinction: Emily, Anna and Diane could not wait to leave. None had felt welcomed, talking about how people they had met didn't recognize them, saying there were too many temps to distinguish between them. Annabel told me with delight that she was leaving as she had got a full time permanent job, as a clerk for a large furniture store, and had 'had enough of how unfriendly it is here'. The dissatisfaction did not appear to be noticed by managers, who even participated in sidelining temps.

The stress on 'getting on' with colleagues is, especially for temps, a way of selecting those who will fit well in the store culture. Those temps who were taken on permanently also have a chance to join the social networks in the future, when they will be more of a good investment in getting to know than the transitory Christmas workers, implying that sociability itself may be a form of labour. The partial exclusion of temps perpetuates the store's work culture, as those who are successful at gaining long-term employment have often proved themselves on a temporary contract to be 'one of us'. The recruitment process is thus extended beyond the initial hiring. Ability and sociability cannot be entirely separated, especially given that being social is an element of the customer service work, and so getting on with colleagues is a good test of this. Contractual differences between workers were not the only source of tension. The spatial organization of the shop, particularly the division into departments also affected friendship relations.

Sociability on the shopfloor

Organizations are tapping into workers' 'social vitality' (Goldthorpe *et al.*, 1969), making use of it in the selling and service workers perform. For example, during the early hours of the first day of the January sale at Distinction, my job was to stand and chat to the customers queuing to pay (as well as to monitor the progression of the queue). Thus sales consultants at Distinction were constructed as sociable, friendly, helpful customer service providers and inculcated into company norms of service right from the start. This vitality has several dimensions, however, and is not only directed to the customers. Canyon used this strong peer group as a way of monitoring performance, by putting up posters comparing workers' customer service success.

The spatial arrangement of the shopfloor was an important means of structuring sociability at Distinction. Workers on the shopfloor were somewhat isolated from each other, whereas those on the till, and to a lesser extent on the fitting room, were able to communicate with each other more easily, and often with justification. Workers could talk unobserved by management on the fitting room. The staff room was the most directly sociable zone, where friendship relations were freely permitted. Work did invade this space as it was used, along with the men's toilets, to store stock prepared for the sale and so there was often scarcely enough room to move around. Only on one occasion during my observation period did work dominate the staffroom conversation: on the first day of the biannual sale, a chaotic and stressful time, rendered especially hard as the till had broken down, causing stress for customers and particularly for workers. The conversation was about how unreasonable customers were for complaining about having to queue, when they should have realized what it would be like. The same anecdotes were repeated through the day, especially a story of Luke being threatened by a customer queuing outside and James swearing at a customer. The feeling of a battle between 'us' and 'them', workers and customers, changed the dynamics of sociability in the staff room, making it more open and less cliquey than was the norm, with the divide between permanent and temporary workers more permeable. This points to how friendships with colleagues, and the social support they provided, were important in counteracting the often demanding and stressful nature of customer service provision, going beyond what Broadbridge *et al.* (2000) found about how companionship ('comradeship') at work was an important source of job satisfaction, although they did not explicitly consider how stress at work could be mediated by colleagues.

A sociable atmosphere could operate to the detriment of customer service. On several occasions when researching as a customer ('shopper observation'), especially at a Distinction store in central London, where the store layout meant that there were always people working at the entrance to the fitting room, and at Canyon, I felt that I was unwelcome for interrupting conversations between colleagues, or trying to get past them. A similar effect was produced when staff did not pause in their conversations when fulfilling their service obligations, or if they wandered away from their customer service positions to join in with friends elsewhere, to avoid feeling left out. Social relations were sometimes more important than customer relations, especially at Canyon, where the social relations between workers were well developed and important, perhaps as a result of the company's apparent preference for outgoing, friendly employees. This was far rarer at other (and busier) stores, with workers being more spread about and gathering in smaller groups (of two or three, rather than four or five, as at Canyon). Benson (1988) argues that ignoring customers and carrying on chatting with each other is a way of keeping customers in their place. I would suggest that the neglect of the customer is not always so self-conscious, arising more subtly from the sociable nature of the shop floor and need for management to grant some autonomy in service provision to their staff.

Social interactions at work were obviously conditioned by the work setting, with many conversations I overheard during shopper observation being about work. At Amanda Jane one day, two young assistants were talking about which jobs that they had been allocated to do that shift, complaining that the person who was on the till was lazy compared to them. At Number 1, I overheard two senior workers discussing one of the members of staff, a young man who had to be told not to hang around the ladies fitting room such a lot and had been told off for swearing. Work conversations could easily segue into more general chatting, sometimes inspired by the work or the products. Chatting to colleagues whenever possible, was a way of making time pass more quickly and was the main form of sociability. However, managers would tell workers off for chatting if they thought that customers were being neglected (although they too would chat if they had the opportunity). Some workers spent more time in conversation than others did, and this was a source of conflict on the shop floor. Both Sam (mentioned earlier) and Sarah, a temp, stirred up resentment amongst other workers for not being where they were supposed to be because they were chatting elsewhere, hence sociability is seen as having an appropriate time and place. The chatting reflects the importance of the shop environment as a place to socialize as well as to work. Workers coped with quiet periods by playing or discussing their lives outside work, usually social activities and relationships. Work itself was also a topic, especially between relative strangers.

At busy times, and in the busier stores, there were fewer opportunities to talk. Instead of socializing with each other, workers had to socialize with customers, a very different interaction to that which occurs between colleagues. Like the bar and restaurant staff studied by Marshall (1986), retail employees could adjust the pace of their work to suit customer demand, filling in quiet times by talking to each other. The two Fashion Junctions I observed indicated this clearly. In central London, workers were much busier, and it was a rarer to see them chatting for a long time with each other, unless they were doing something else at the same time, for example, three assistants were talking whilst tidying a table of jumpers[12]. At Lakeside, in contrast, the store was far quieter and there was more playing. I saw workers using one of the umbrellas on sale like a sword and then opening it suddenly, one singing along to the music, and one modelling a hat from the display with a scrunched up piece of paper hanging out of his mouth. In each case, it was a male assistant who was playing. Female assistants were seen talking but were not so disruptive, suggesting sociability has gendered dimensions. Play did not have to involve co-workers: I came out of the fitting room at Storm to find a girl balancing on a portable rail, making it move by throwing her body forwards, explaining she was really bored.

Nicole talked in her interview about the value of such play:

'We can have a laugh. You need to, definitely . . . it does make a big difference. If we're happy and friendly than obviously the customers are going to get better deal . . . We're not unprofessional in any way, but we do get on.'

This suggests that not only does play help the workers deal with the stress of customer interaction, but can also make the shopping environment more pleasant for the customers. Elsewhere, sociability took different forms, from flirtation, finding common cultural references, or exchanging details about their families[13], and this depended on who was working together at each moment. Social interactions, developing into friendships, remain significant elements of retail service work, as is likely to be the case in other work domains.

Conclusion

I have given many illustrations of how work life is affected by social relationships, sometimes where colleagues were also friends and family, with local community and labour market conditions coming together. The 'psychological intimacy' (Pahl, 2000) and emotional support that are characteristic of the sort of friendships that Pahl describes are visible on the shopfloor. These friendships sometimes pre-date working relationships, giving support to Pahl's suggestion that friendship is something apart from the public sphere. However, existing friendships are altered by being played out on the shopfloor, and new friendships are formed which are significant both in and out of work. It is noticeable how these friendships are not purely located and constructed at the emotional or psychological levels but have a tangible and practical element, as evinced in the ways in which friends and relations influence getting and keeping jobs. This need not make the emotional content any less.

Furthermore, the day-to-day interactions between colleagues that do not approach being described as friendship, are nonetheless often sociable (reflecting Simmel's idea of sociability, or a form of 'temperate friendship' (Hill and McCarthy, 2000:38)), and also influence the domain of paid employment. Performing sociability, in the Simmelian sense, is one part of the expression of friendship. It also has a wider significance, referring to the casual interactions that are common on the shopfloor, between friends, between colleagues who do not know each other well, and between workers and customers. The social interactions between workers are at times reflections of deeper emotional ties, at others simply ways of passing the time. Sociability is not always the free-floating, decontextualized interaction of Simmel, rather a version of sociability is apparent, grounded by the context of the workplace, the tasks being performed, and any growing acquaintanceship between colleagues (which may end up as friendship).

The incorporation of non-work-related social relations, such as friendship, adds another dimension to the attack on the reduction of work to paid employment highlighted in the introduction to this collection. Individuals actively draw on their 'private' lives in constructing their working lives, and in particular their social networks may be brought into the workplace. Furthermore, employers make use of skills, attributes and capital that are not explicitly included in the employment contract but which draw on non-work elements of employees' lives. For service work, this is commonly thought of in terms of the emotion management skills and emotional labour that service sector workers perform. Here, I show that it is not only workers' tacit skills but their social milieu that is used as a resource by organizations.

Glucksmann suggests the 'Total Social Organization of Labour' can be applied to an individual workplace (2000a:162). In this context, connections between colleagues that encompass friendship and family relations have a noticeable and significant effect on various aspects of the work and employment relationship. Sociability and friendship between colleagues are instrumental in getting and keeping jobs, in being promoted and in belonging to the workplace culture/community. Friendship influences work, and work can lead to the formation of friendships, extending work relations beyond the working day.

Friendship impinges on the work being done, for example, it affected how tasks were allocated and customer service provision. Social interaction is central to the production of the shopfloor as a place for work and for consumption. Not only are interactions between strangers – customers and workers – important, so are relations between colleagues. The recruitment of friends and acquaintances and the prevalence of friendships at work produces a workplace where employees are socially similar. The 'affinity' between colleagues enhances the work environment in several ways. Most obviously, essential communications between workers are facilitated. In addition, friendship ties can reduce or even remove the need for direct control mechanisms over workers.

A further reason why sociable colleagues are important for the company is that the social skills of workers can be transferred to interactions with customers. An ability to get on with colleagues is seen as evidence of an ability to get on with customers. Furthermore, happy workers may be assumed to provide 'better' customer service. Also critical is the use of workers' sociability as part of the image of the store. By recruiting people similar to each other – often people who were already known by other employees – companies can reproduce a workplace and shop culture through informal friendship mechanisms. The benefits are not universal, however, and in this chapter I have highlighted several ways in which either the social relations can break down or may work to the detriment of the company by excluding customers or certain workers, such as those on temporary contracts.

The implications of this for theorizing work are to point out how the strict division between work and non-work lives is unsustainable in the face of a blurring of boundaries, in particular the bringing in of notionally 'private' friendship relations into the workplace. Furthermore, those working in retail service work are in part employed for their sociability: one manager commented that 'you can't do the job if you're a wallflower' (Nigel). This means that the recruitment of 'people like us' that is facilitated by the pervasiveness of friendship relations at work assists companies in ensuring that suitable candidates are given work. The sociability of the workforce is a resource for the organization and hence is part of how private lives are marketized.

Notes

1 All stores and individuals have been given pseudonyms for reasons of confidentiality. Distinction is a mass market store selling men's, women's and children's clothing and homewares.
2 Shopper observation stores were: Amanda Jane (mid-market women's clothing); Canyon ('lifestyle', not high-fashion clothing for men and women); Cheap Chic (inexpensive fashion clothing for women); Fashion Junction (high fashion, design-led men's and women's clothes); Number 1 (market leader in young women's fashion clothing); Storm (more expensive women's clothes with distinctive design); Universal Provider (an amalgam of different variety stores).
3 This section draws on interviews with shopfloor workers.
4 'Real Men' is the menswear equivalent of Amanda Jane, a mid-market store which did not emphasize fashion.
5 Where menswear, childrenswear and home decoration were located.
6 This was in part because I did not have equal access to all social groups, getting closer to Luke's friends than to Jo's.
7 A part time, permanent worker with a young child.
8 Not wanting to be late for the staff party because of mistakes shopfloor workers made; not having had time to have a bath before work.
9 I too experienced the distinctions made between temporary (my own position) and permanent workers, and this affects the analysis presented here.
10 'Replen' involves taking products from the stockrooms to replace those recently sold.
11 The worker observation took place in a garrison town.
12 A strange thing to do on a busy Saturday afternoon.
13 For example, a young assistant at Cheap Chic had to ask a security guard to put something on a high rail for her; colleagues relived memories of the film 'Return to Oz' (Storm); a woman boasted her son had just passed a dancing exam (Universal Provider).

Interaction distance and the social meaning of occupations

Wendy Bottero

Introduction

This volume argues for a 'new sociology of work': to move beyond the confines of existing conceptualizations of work based on the dichotomies of paid and unpaid, public and private, which entail a narrow definition of work as either paid employment in the public sphere or unpaid domestic labour in the private sphere. Such conceptual models fail to engage with the complexity of people's working lives, and, in particular, with how work is embedded in other social practices. This chapter aims to explore a particular aspect of this: the embeddedness of *occupations* in broader social relations which shape their meaning in ways which have important implications for our understanding of 'class' and social inequalities.

What is the social meaning of holding an occupation? Conventionally, the meaning of occupations has been taken to rest in their economic or labour market characteristics – the skill, pay, and labour-market conditions of different jobs. All jobs, however, are embedded in wider social relationships, and the meaning of holding a particular occupation is strongly affected by the social identity, networks and life trajectory of the people in that job. This means that the distinction between jobs and incumbents, between work and non-work, and between the 'economic' and the 'social' is necessarily blurred. The analysis of occupations has been a central feature of stratification research and these blurred boundaries have created considerable difficulties for stratification theory. Stratification research has traditionally looked at occupations in an attempt to understand how labour-market relations create different social locations for workers, but we also need to consider how the embedding of 'work' in wider social relations affects the experience, consequences, and thus the meaning, of being in an occupation.

Since stratification refers to hierarchically organized social relationships, stratification theory entails the analysis of structured social inequality in all its aspects: material, social and cultural. Class analysis, however, with its focus on material inequality, has come to dominate stratification theory, generating models which see 'objective' economic conditions as logically prior to, and causative of, social relations. Conventional class analysis has been criticized for defining class in terms of employment relations, rather than as 'collectivities of people who share identities and practices' and for ignoring the influence of cultural and social resources on the 'micro processes by which classes are created and sustained over time and space' (Devine, 1998:23,33). Amid concerns that class analysis has 'attenuated' and become isolated from the wider concerns of sociology, there have been calls for a broadening of scope to address issues of cultural identity, gender, race and ethnicity (Bradley 1996; Crompton 1998; Savage 2000). A 'renewed' analysis would 'focus on how cultural processes are embedded within specific kinds of socio-economic practices' (Devine and Savage, 2000:193), exploring how inequality is routinely reproduced through *both* cultural and economic practices (2000:196).

This chapter explores a tradition in stratification that is founded on the idea that economic and social relations are embedded within each other. Relational or social distance approaches to mapping hierarchy and inequality theorize stratification as a social space of relationships. The idea of 'social space' is not treated as a metaphor of hierarchy, nor is the nature of the structure determined *a priori*. Rather, the space is identified by mapping social interactions. Exploring the nature of social space involves mapping the network of social interaction – patterns of friendship, partnership and cultural similarity – which gives rise to relations of social closeness and distance.

This gives rise to a very different view of stratification and the reproduction of inequality. Occupations are not seen as aspects of a prior economic structure which determines social identity and behaviour but rather are viewed as integral elements of a space of relationships. The *hierarchy* of occupations thus derives from the typical patterns of social relationships within which such occupations are located and take their social meaning. Similarly, when looking at patterns of 'social mobility', the emphasis is not on the movement (or not) across pre-determined labour market boundaries, but rather on the way in which individual trajectories are located within socially typical (or atypical) transitions. Social distance is not a measure of economic advantage or of labour market circumstances as such, since relationships of intimacy are affected not only by economic advantage or labour market position, but also by issues of cultural background, social networks, contiguity and opportunity of access, and so forth. The chapter explores how such an approach helps to rethink such issues as career trajectories and the social meaning of labour market change and social mobility.

Problems with class

Whilst class theory has always produced a diversity of research approaches, since the 1970s, 'class' has become increasingly identified with 'employment-aggregate' analysis (Crompton, 1998; Savage, 2000; Scott, 2001), characterized by 'an empirical focus upon 'class' (defined as employment) to the *exclusion* of other factors' (Crompton, 1996:59). But since the 1980s, this emphasis has come under increasing attack, amid broader claims that economic relations have become less important in shaping peoples' social and cultural destinies. Those who would defend the continuing importance of class processes in social life have been forced to admit that the narrowing focus of the 'employment-aggregate' approach is itself part of the problem. From within class theory it is suggested that the 'minimalist' nature (Devine, 1998) of employment-aggregate analysis has led to an 'attenuation' of aims (Morris and Scott, 1996), resulting in class analysis being seen as an 'increasingly arcane and technical specialism' (Savage, 2000:149). Critics make three main points: (1) that class analysis has increasingly sidelined issues of cultural identity and the subjective meaning of class location (2) that too great a priority has been given to economic relations in explanations of stratification, downplaying the importance of status, gender and ethnicity (3) that the 'economic' cannot be rigidly demarcated as an independent factor determining stratification position, since it is inextricably intertwined with social and cultural factors. These charges all relate to problems with the conceptual separation class analysis makes between, on the one hand, economic relations as underlying causal structures and, on the other hand, subjective and cultural identity as causal 'effects'.

Nuffield 'employment-aggregate' researchers insist on this distinction between the economic and the social because 'class concepts must be as sharply defined as is operationally feasible, in order to avoid any confounding of class with other factors of possible relevance' (Goldthorpe and Marshall 1992:385). In practice, this means that the class structure is defined quite *independently* of the education, status, prestige, lifestyle, gender or ethnic composition of occupations, even though these factors are acknowledged to affect an occupation's overall position in the stratification order. Critics, however, now see this as unduly restrictive, and a series of writers have questioned whether this conceptual separation is desirable, or even feasible. Such writers advocate a transformation of class analysis which would explore economic positions and processes in terms of their wider social locations and meanings.

It has been argued that what is required is a 'closer investigation of interests and identities' (Crompton and Scott, 2000:5) to give issues of status, culture and identity a more prominent place *within* class analysis. Crompton, for example, recommends approaches based upon '*social* class analysis which, rather than seeking to distance themselves from the status concept, are premised upon the interrelationship of the "economic" and the "social"' (1998:119). For Crompton, class analysis must move beyond the investigation of class *effects* to explore instead processes of class *formation* in which prestige, association and lifestyle, and status claims are entwined with, and help to shape, the class structure. This, of course, raises related issues of subjective meaning. Arguing that there is a major difference between class formation and the construction of class schema, the Nuffield approach first defines class in terms of 'objective', external criteria and only then explores subjective meanings as a class 'effect'. Social mobility, for example, is defined from the 'outside', with no reference to whether or not people themselves believe they have changed location. But the experience of mobility (or inequality) depends in large part on how we *perceive* that experience. Critics question whether it makes sense to relegate subjective meaning to such a secondary role, since 'to talk about subjectivity as only an "effect" – a dependent variable – is to ignore the way in which subjective processes are tied up with the strategies and actions which produce mobility itself' (Savage, 1997:317).

For a number of writers (Skeggs, 1997; Reay, 1998a and b; Savage, 2000; Devine, 1998) these concerns can only be addressed by rejecting the Nuffield analytical model in which economic class structure *gives rise to* status (or cultural) differences. Instead, they define class in cultural and lifestyle terms, in effect fusing 'economic' and 'status' elements.

> 'Rather than seeking to isolate the two so that the interaction between separate spheres can be determined, we might instead focus on how cultural processes are embedded within specific kinds of socio-economic practices . . . It is not especially useful to isolate the economic from the cultural but to show their embeddedness within specific kinds of social contexts'. (*Devine and Savage*, 2000:194–5)

These writers place a much greater emphasis on processes of culture, lifestyle and taste in the reproduction of inequality, arguing that both cultural and economic relations are central in processes of stratification. There are important conceptual differences in the positions of such writers and they cannot be regarded, in any simple way, as a distinct 'school'. All, however, advocate a new and expanded form of analysis which amount to a deliberate and substantial broadening of the scope and the analytical basis of class theory (Bottero, 2004). They reconfigure the causal model that historically has underpinned class analysis, questioning the centrality and distinctiveness of the 'economic' and stress the fusion of economic, cultural and symbolic elements in (individualised) hierarchical differentiation (Bottero and Prandy, 2003).

This recent work has a renewed concern with issues of subjectivity, agency, and meaning, as writers seek to investigate the way in which 'economic' processes are embedded within social and cultural processes. Reflecting these concerns, there has been an emphasis on the need for qualitative analysis to provide 'ethnographic examinations of how class is "lived" in gendered and raced ways to complement the macro versions that have monopolized our ways of envisaging social class for far too long' (Reay 1998a:272). A number of writers have combined qualitative and quantitative methods (for example, Mike Savage) but most recent work in this area has adopted a qualitative case-study methodology, providing a re-invigoration of the qualitative tradition in stratification and a valuable corrective to the hegemony of employment-aggregate approaches.

In this 'qualitative shift', however, there is a danger of effectively ceding the arena of quantitative analysis to the 'employment-aggregate' paradigm of class analysis. There is an alternative tradition of quantitative stratification research – social distance analysis – which starts from a fundamentally different set of premises about the nature of stratification, and which incorporates issues of culture and the socially embedded nature of economic positions much more directly and explicitly into the categories of analysis. In these approaches, stratification is not an influence on patterns of association (in the sense that we might investigate the extent to which economic position affects friendship, or 'class' location influences 'status' relations), rather differential patterns of association and lifestyle *constitute* the structure of stratification, which is conceived (and measured) as a social space of relationships.

Social distance approaches

Exploring the nature of social space involves mapping the network of social interaction – patterns of friendship, partnership and cultural similarity – which gives rise to relations of social closeness and distance. Differential association has long been seen as the basis of hierarchy, but the usual approach is first to define a structure composed of a set of groups and then to investigate social interaction between them. Social distance approaches reverse this, using patterns of interaction to determine the nature of the structure. Differential association is thus a way of defining proximity within a social space, from the distances between social groups, or between social groups and social objects (such as lifestyle items). Such approaches give a 'reproductionist' account of how stratified social relations are generated. That is to say, rather than identifying a set of criteria, such as employment relations, and deriving a stratification structure from them, they concentrate on the way in which a structure of inequality – identified from patterns of association – persists over time (Bottero and Prandy, 2003).

Bourdieu's work is the most famous in this tradition, but whilst an acknowledged theoretical influence on recent 'culturalist' approaches to class, his quantitative methodology has been less widely adopted. The 'social space', which Bourdieu describes as a 'space of relationships' (1985:725), is made up of various economic, social and cultural, and symbolic elements, and his empirical work explores how access to these different sorts of resources positions individuals and groups differently within this space.

> 'The conceptual space within which Bourdieu defines class is not that of production, but that of social relationships in general. Class relations are not defined by relations to the means of production, but by differing conditions of existence, differing systems of dispositions produced by differential conditioning, and differing endowments of power or capital'. (*Brubaker*, 1985:761)

Using correspondence analysis, Bourdieu identifies two main dimensions to the space of relationships, which he interprets as the *volume* of capital (the overall level of resources) and the *composition* of capital, (the relative degree of economic and cultural capital. The overall space, however, is defined by the distances between groups given by the similarity (or difference) of their lifestyle as represented by cultural items (Prandy, 1999; Bottero and Prandy, 2003). Bourdieu's approach to social analysis is *relational*, rather than *substantialist*. He rejects seeing social location in terms of the content of social positions or practices, arguing that the meaning of any particular social position emerges out of the relations of opposition and proximity to other social positions. Just as we can only make sense of the overall quantity of the material or cultural resources of a given location by comparing them to the resources of others, so the meaning of social location does not inhere in membership of given categories, but in the *relations between categories*.

Bourdieu makes an explicit link between issues of taste, in terms of cultural and lifestyle preferences, and taste more widely conceived, in terms of *interaction choices*, arguing that 'Taste is what brings things and people that go together' (1984:241). The implication is that 'those who are similar in terms of lifestyle prefer to interact socially and those who choose to interact socially tend to be similar in terms of lifestyle' (Prandy, 1999:229); however whilst Bourdieu makes this as a theoretical argument, he does not empirically address it. An independent – but closely related – set of approaches, however, uses interaction patterns to directly map the social space (Bottero and Prandy, 2003).

The use of social interaction to analyse stratification has been most fully explored by the Cambridge Stratification Group, who have developed a series of interaction scales, using friendship and marriage choices to identify the social ordering of occupations (Stewart *et al.*, 1980; Prandy, 1990; Prandy and Jones, 2001; Prandy and Bottero, 1998, 2000a). Differential association – the fact that who we associate with is affected by our social location – is the starting assumption behind social interaction distance approaches:

> 'Differential association can be seen as a way of defining distances within a social space: social interaction will occur most frequently between persons who are socially close to one another and relatively infrequently between those that are socially distant. It is possible to reconstruct this social space from the information about the set of distances. The social space determined in this way will reflect and represent the structure of stratification arrangements. The space is inherently social structural, not an aggregation of individual or group characteristics; it does not deal with each occupational group taken separately, but with each in relation to all of the others'. (*Prandy*, 1999:215)

The Cambridge approach is based on the analysis of patterns of social interaction (such as friendship, marriage and cohabitation) to determine the relative distances between occupational groups (as indicated by higher or lower levels of interaction). These different types of social association are used to produce a hierarchical scale of stratification: an 'ordering of occupations on the basis of social similarity as defined by the extent of social interaction' (Prandy, 1999:231). This, they argue, is a scale of 'shared experience' which measures material and social advantage, which they see as 'indivisible concepts' (Stewart *et al.*, 1980:28).

The central theoretical argument is that social interaction, lifestyle and the hierarchy of advantage that constitute social stratification are intimately inter-linked: 'our conception is one of stratification arrangements that involve differences in generalized advantage (and disadvantage) and hence in lifestyle and in social interaction related to level of advantage and lifestyle' (Prandy 1990:635). This is a similar approach to Bourdieu, the only difference being that instead of tracing distance between social groups and *lifestyle* items the social space is identified by mapping *social interactions* (Bottero and Prandy, 2003). The logic is simple: by investigating social relationships of social *closeness* – patterns of friendship and partnership, social similarity and contiguity – we can identify which groups interact at a *distance* or in terms of dissimilarity.

This 'social distance' method 'puts social relationships at the heart of stratification analysis' (Bottero and Prandy, 2001:6.1) using 'information about real social choices, telling us about the frequency of relatively high, relatively low and all intermediate levels of social interaction' (Prandy, 1999:230). It examines social hierarchy and differentiation by focussing on choices that are *socially meaningful to the people concerned*. Bourdieu's very similar method, using lifestyle choices, has been criticised (Longhurst and Savage, 1996) for not exploring how important such choices are in people's lives. By contrast, social interaction approaches are based on close and intimate social relationships – such as friendship and marriage – which, by definition, are important and meaningful in people's lives. To the extent that people limit their intimate social interactions with each other we can argue that hierarchy (or 'class') is 'recognized' and acts as an important force in people's lives, whether they are aware of it or not.

The social interaction approach orders occupations in terms of the differences regarded as socially meaningful by the participants of stratification processes (as these emerge in interaction). This is a departure from *objectivist* approaches, which impose observers' categories and ordering criteria. Neither is the method *subjectivist*, however, since it is does not directly access subjects' *perceptions* of the worth, prestige or social location of different occupations. Distance scales do not aggregate subjective perceptions of the social esteem of different social locations, in the manner of prestige scales, since they map actual social relations of intimacy and similarity. In that sense, they tap the social ordering of occupations as it is *concretely embedded in social practice*.

Occupation is the *tag* by which the social interaction distance method locates an individual's place in the social hierarchy. The emphasis is not on labour market location *per se* but rather on patterns of social distance in relationships. Occupations are not seen as aspects of a prior economic structure which determines social identity and behaviour but, rather, are viewed as integral elements of a space of relationships. The hierarchy of occupations is thus not given in their typical pay, skill or employment conditions but instead derives from the typical patterns of social relationships within which such occupations are located and take their *social meaning*. Social interaction measures use finely disaggregated occupational units but if differences in the pay, skill or employment status of occupations are not reflected in typical patterns of social interaction, then they will receive the same position in the social ordering, which measures general (rather than just labour market) advantage. Within this method, the dif-

62

ference between a skilled and a semi-skilled fitter, or between a clerk and a personal assistant, only counts if it makes a difference in the important social relationships of the people involved.

In this approach, stratification position is not just a relationship to the labour market, but the sum result of the close social relationships in which individuals are located. This is important because how individuals react to the same working conditions or level of pay is likely to differ according to their wider social circumstances – their life course stage and social obligations, the family relationships they are engaged in, their social background, past experience and their expectations of the future. This leads to great difficulties for stratification schemes which attempt to place individuals in terms of their current labour market circumstances alone. The alternative, social interaction, approach focuses on the location of occupations within a network of wider social relationships and influences. Because the background and network of close social relationships in which every individual is engaged strongly influence their position in the social hierarchy independently of their occupation, and also act to constantly modify and mediate the effect of their occupation, it is the social context of occupations which is key.

Social distance analysis – which is focussed on the *social relations* of hierarchy and inequality – gives a very different perspective on employment location and processes of occupational and labour market change from that of conventional stratification accounts.

Movement, change and the social meaning of occupations

Stratification analysis is concerned with the relatively stable nature of inequalities in social relationships, whilst mobility refers to the extent of movement between unequal positions. For many theorists, therefore, the extent of social mobility is a crucial test of the persistence of inequality. The more mobility there is – between generations or over the life-course – the less durable inequality seems. Total levels of social mobility in most western industrial societies, however, are strikingly high and 'Class mobility is the norm, not the exception, for both women and men' (Savage, 2000:80). The conclusion of many liberal theorists is that more mobility means less persistent inequality. This argument has been rejected by class theorists, who point out that inequality persists between generations even in the face of large amounts of movement.

The amount of social movement, however, creates difficulty for class accounts, whose analysis of inequality is based on fixed labour market categories. The problem in the conventional approach is that class formation is only seen to emerge out of 'stasis and continuity'. The assumption is that:

> 'The more the members of a class stay in its ranks (either between generations or over an individual's life), the more attached that people are to a class and the better formed is that class . . . However, by conceptualizing class formation in these terms, mobility and class formation are defined in terms of opposition. Rather than class formation

being itself a dynamic process, involving a particular way of linking pasts, present and futures, it is posited as being based on a static attachment to fixed positions'. (*Savage*, 2000:83–4)

The difficulty is that large amounts of social movement appear to be a stable feature *of* the structure of inequality. Indeed, routine patterns of movement make an important contribution to how patterns of inequality are reproduced over time. Yet conventional theories of inequality are rather poorly placed to address social movement on this scale.

This raises important questions about how movement and change are to be incorporated into theoretical and methodological accounts of inequality, given that such movement means that the *social meaning* of unequal social locations is constantly shifting. Conventional accounts of social mobility make a distinction between intergenerational mobility (the social location of the individual of one generation in relation to that of the individual of the previous generation) and intragenerational mobility (change in the social position of the individual throughout his or her working life).

'However, that distinction immediately raises a problem: if individuals move within their working lives, then what is the "social location" that is to be used for comparing one generation with another? The usual methods of analysis are unable to cope adequately with the additional complexities that this question raises. Because of the difficulties of combining inter- and intra-generational aspects, one rarely attempts to do so. On the one hand, there are numerous studies of individuals' worklife histories; on the other, most studies of social mobility are based on a "snapshot" of information collected at a single point in time . . . for the most part the comparison between generations is made on the basis of very limited information about individuals' work histories and taking particular points in their lives'. (*Prandy and Bottero*: 2000b:4)

There is a further issue. Treating mobility as movement between fixed social positions ignores the way in which movement affects the meaning of the structure itself. Take the way in which shifts in the pattern of movement between positions in the occupational structure *change the individual experience of occupying those positions* (regardless of whether or not the occupants are mobile).

'If we follow the usual practice of defining classes by constant sets of occupations we are faced with a steady drift upwards in the class structure; the top class has been growing and the bottom one shrinking . . . However, it is questionable whether treating class as fixed sets of occupations is theoretically meaningful. At the very least the social meaning of membership of a greatly enlarged top class must be different. More fundamentally, with the general upward movement of class membership there cannot be a corresponding rise in the relative social advantage bestowed by higher class membership'. (*Blackburn and Marsh*, 1991:203–4)

As occupations at the top of the hierarchy expand in numbers, they also lose their exclusiveness and relative social advantage. Similarly, as occupations at the bottom of the hierarchy contract in size, they become relatively more disadvantaged. To be a manual worker at the beginning of the 20th century was to hold a position shared by three-quarters of the population, but by the end of the century, manual workers were in a minority, with nearly two-thirds of workers in more privileged jobs. The obverse pattern holds for professional and managerial jobs. There are important differences, therefore, in being in the 'working class' or 'service class', between then and now, because the *relative (dis)advantage* of the positions has changed.

This has important consequences for how we measure social mobility over time:

'the idea of indexing a person's origin and destination by occupation is weakened if the *meaning* of being, say, a manual worker is not the same at origin and destination. Historical comparisons become unreliable'. (*Payne*, 1992: 220)

So, for example, the children of manual workers may be in a very different social position to their parents, even if they are manual workers themselves, because proportional shifts in occupational distributions (ie, the upward movement of *other people*) affects the social meaning of staying still. It is not enough to identify that someone has stayed in the same class 'box', because the meaning of the box itself is not fixed, and depends upon movement within the overall structure.

Class analysts believe that trends in absolute mobility are misleading because they depend, in part, on improvements in the general opportunities available. Class analysts have therefore attempted to *control* for shifts in the opportunity structure over time, by comparing the *relative odds* of children from different backgrounds in gaining access to the opportunities available at any given point. The analysis of relative mobility chances shows a pattern that has been called 'the constant flux' – the continuity of relative disadvantage in the midst of continual social movement (Erikson and Goldthorpe, 1992). Conventional approaches to the stability of inequality have therefore increasingly attempted to factor out structural change, by analysing differential patterns of access to fixed opportunities (using odds ratios), rather than the consideration of movement itself. But this leaves conventional accounts poorly placed to deal with one of the more interesting aspects of enduring inequality, namely how it is bound up in processes of change and movement.

Large amounts of absolute upward mobility have been a constant feature of the occupational structure for the 20th century, and before. This general expansion of opportunities has changed the meaning of structural locations, and has always been a problem for mobility analysis. The focus on social fluidity has tried to factor out the expansion of opportunities, in effect holding structural change constant. But 'The use of relative mobility (fluidity) measures . . . obscures the social significance of changing class composition' (Blackburn and Prandy, 1997:500). A similar point is made by Bourdieu, who attacks the 'positivistic naivety' of conventional social mobility analysis, which is:

'unaware that the reproduction of the social structure may, in certain conditions, demand very little "occupational heredity". This is true whenever agents can only maintain their position in the social structure by means of a shift into a new condition (eg, the shift from small landowner to junior civil servant, or from small craftsman to office worker or commercial employee)'. (1984:131)

Groups can improve their standard of living yet remain in the same relative position within the social hierarchy, because 'every group has moved up in terms of living standards (class situation), but the pecking order (class position) remains unchanged' (Swartz, 1997:183). Because large amounts of intergenerational mobility change the meaning of labour-market categories (by altering the balance of relative advantage/exclusivity between occupations), any comparison of the social position of different generations is potentially misleading if we focus on labour-market criteria alone. Bourdieu's disaggregated map of social space, however, does not permit direct investigation of his suspicions:

'It is one thing to dismiss the uncritical use of occupational categories in mobility tables and to counsel caution in determining the proper sociological significance in changing occupational titles, but quite another to offer a plausible empirical test of just what change in social structure might look like. This, Bourdieu has not sufficiently done'. (*Swartz*, 1997:184)

The shifting meaning of occupational categories, however, can be investigated by looking at relative social position more directly. Social interaction scales produce a hierarchical ordering of occupations through their relations of social distance. They look at the social location of the typical friends or marriage connections of the people in a job, and so order occupations by their relative social position. This means that social interaction scales are more sensitive to shifts in the social meaning of occupations (through composition changes, or expanding opportunities) than schemes which class occupations on labour market criteria alone. If the social meaning of an occupation changes, we would expect this to be reflected in the typical social relationships of the people in the occupation. So, for example, if we think the social meaning of being a 'clerk' changed from the 19th to the 20th century (because so many more people became clerks, and because the social composition of the category shifted from predominantly male to predominantly female), we would expect the social associates of 'clerks' to have also changed. In fact, social interaction scales do show 'clerks' slipping down the social order over the course of the 19th century, which corresponds to the declining exclusivity of the job.

Social interaction distance scales measure the relative advantage of finely differentiated occupations. They thus offer a different framework to analysing social mobility from either class or status attainment approaches. The social distance approach to analysing 'social mobility' doesn't look at mobility flows between class categories (because the meaning of class categories over time is not fixed) but instead looks at the extent to which relative social position within a hierarchy of advantage is passed on (or not) from generation to generation.

What do social interaction scales tell us about social mobility over time? The study which looks at the longest time period is Ken Prandy's research on the social reproduction of advantage, comparing (male) birth cohorts from 1790 to

1909. This study found 'a remarkable degree of stability of social processes of reproduction throughout this period, although there is an extremely slow shift towards a weakening of family influence. This process appears to have accelerated for those born in the last quarter of the 19th century, a period of both educational reform and major change in Britain's industrial organization' (Prandy and Bottero, 2000a:265). This confirms Bourdieu's suspicion that – even in the face of substantial occupational change and movement – there is considerable continuity in relative social location:

> 'The social reproduction of hierarchy involves the transmission of position and advantage from generation to generation. Yet the ability of parents to hand down social advantages to their children obviously depends on the changing nature of the "currency" of advantage and position. The period investigated in our study witnessed significant shifts in that currency – the decline in the importance of agriculture, landed property and 'family' firms; the rise of education, bureaucratic careers, white collar employment and credentialism. Yet family influence on social position has remained remarkably buoyant in the face of these changes . . . Children have continued to find their own place in the world, but a position closely associated with that of their parents.' (*Prandy and Bottero*, 2000a:276)

The issue of occupational change is not simply a question of labour-market re-structuring over time, since we also have to consider work-life movement as well. Savage argues that class identities can be formed by common patterns of movement, rather than through continuity of position, suggesting that, in particular, *middle-class* formation 'involves a dynamic relation to time, in which middle-class people expect prospective rewards, and in which work lives are embedded around ideas of individual progress, and advancement in the longer term (often . . . around the narrative of "career")' (Savage, 2000:83–4). There is a broader question here, however, because standard routes of work-life movement occur at *every level* of the labour-market:

> 'usually short-range, and along a limited number of main routes. People who start their working lives as apprentices become skilled workers. Others who are not formally trained become informally recognized as skilled. Some manual workers are promoted to supervisory and even management posts. [. . .] Another common career is from lower-level office and sales jobs into the middle class proper. Another is from the lower to the higher grades within the middle class. A further type of movement is from all other kinds of occupations into self-employment'. (*Roberts*, 2001:208)

Work-life movement is very common and often shifts individuals into slightly better occupations, even if the movement is only short-range. These patterns are complicated by gender, since women's working patterns do not always follow the male 'linear' career of continuous, rising labour market position and, even in female professions, low-status truncated career 'niches' have developed which show continuity of occupational position rather than progression (Crompton and Sanderson, 1990). Lifecourse shifts, however, mean that it is common for women to experience 'both upward and downward mobility, and . . . continuity of status, let alone monotonic career progression, is *not* the typical experience

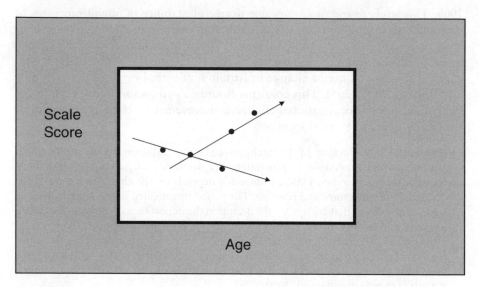

Figure 1

of women. *Our fundamental conception of mobility should therefore be not a move from one origin to one destination, but a profile*' (Payne and Abbott, 1990:165)

Work-life movement is so frequent that we need to take this into account when we consider people's overall occupational position. That is, we need to consider the entire work-life trajectory of an individual, rather than their labour-market position at any given point in time. This is because people at very different career stages are frequently to be found in the same jobs. But, of course, individuals travelling on different work-life trajectories are likely to react to the *same* labour-market conditions in very different ways. Take Figure 1. The two arrows are a representation of the career trajectories of two individuals, with the black dots representing the various occupations they hold at different points in their lives (the lines can be obtained by running a regression line through the scale scores of each occupation). We can see that the two career 'arrows' intersect, meaning that the two individuals hold the same job at a certain point in their lives. But the impact of holding the *same* job is likely to be different for the two individuals because of their very different labour-market trajectories. A student, for example, doing temporary work in a factory, is likely to see (and react to) the pay and conditions in a different light from someone who has been working there for twenty years.

How we view our current labour-market position partly depends upon where we have come from, and where we think we are going. But this means we need to see how jobs fit into an overall sequence.

'People's social location does not simply reflect their current experience. Their past, and even their anticipated future, experience also plays a critical part'. (*Prandy and Bottero*, 2000a:271).

This is difficult for conventional class approaches to accommodate:

'The conventional class approach puts considerable emphasis on the features of employment, which means that it inevitably tends to be restricted to a current job . . . because to consider more than one job involves taking account of the individuals through whom different jobs are linked. In other words, there would need to be a move from economic, employment relations to social relations'. (*Prandy and Bottero*, 2000b:4–5)

Social distance analysis focuses on the work-life trajectory, the sequence of jobs within which any single social location takes on a wider social significance. As Figure 1 indicates, using a regression line allows us to summarize the series of occupations held by an individual. Individuals on quite different trajectories may be in the same employment situation, but this does not mean they are in the same social location. What counts here is the way in which individual jobs fit into an overall social trajectory.

'The idea of considering individuals' worklife trajectories is an extension of the idea that their social location cannot be captured by a snapshot at a point in time. Their past experience and their anticipated future, particularly when based on understandings of normal processes, are essential parts of individuals' conceptions of themselves, their social identity, and their consequent behaviour'. (*Prandy and Bottero*, 2000b:6)

In the same way, proponents of social distance analysis argue that in comparing the class positions of parents and children it is better to compare entire work-life *trajectories* rather than taking snapshots at single moments in time (which may come at different points in the employment routes of parent and child).

Take Figure 2. The two arrows now represent the work-life trajectories of two individuals from different generations – parent and child – with the black dots representing the various occupations of the parent, and the white dots the occupations of the child, over the course of their working lives. But as the figure indicates, the child may experience work-life mobility yet experience the same career trajectory as the parent. Take an individual whose work-life progresses from a start as an apprentice bricklayer to becoming a builder, owning a business employing several workers. This route – to self-employment and small business ownership – is quite a common transition in craft trades, although in conventional class categorizations it is seen as mobility (from the manual to the intermediate class). It is also common for such transitions to be related to family firms, so that the father of our bricklayer may have made the same transition – from bricky to builder – himself. In that case, of course, our individual will have experienced upward worklife *mobility* but will have stayed intergenerationally *immobile*, having the same work-life trajectory as his father. Similar transitions occur in family shops, where children inheriting the family business transit from shop assistant to shop-owner, in the same way as their parents. In such examples, parent and child occupy essentially the same social position, but to correctly identify this we have to compare their whole work-life trajectories, in

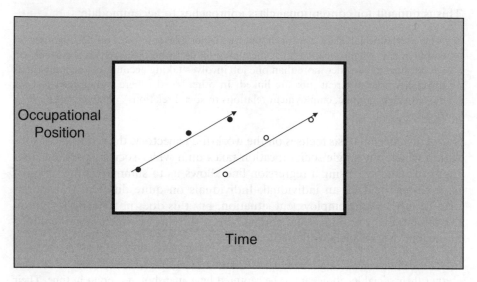

Figure 2

which both follow the same route. So, work-life movement may represent a very real improvement in labour-market conditions but it could be argued that this work-life mobility is more apparent than real. If work-life mobility brings about the *inheritance* of the parent's social position, then social movement is entirely consistent with the *reproduction* of position in a structure of social inequality.

Rather than focussing on fixed attachments to occupational positions, we should focus on an individual's employment trajectory to indicate their overall stratification position. This recognizes the way in which standard patterns of movement *within* generations need to be taken account of when we compare movement *across* generations.

> 'In comparing the occupations of two individuals at different points in time, there-fore, we also have to consider the network of social relationships – the influence of past history and future prospects – in which occupations are embedded and which give them influence and meaning. Focussing on work life trajectory is one aspect of a *social interaction* approach to stratification. Social class categorisations, which tend to abstract the individual from his or her social relationships and to classify them solely in terms of current economic location, cannot readily accommodate such an approach'. (*Prandy and Bottero*, 2000a:266)

Conclusion: The meaning of movement

In this chapter I have argued that the social meaning of occupations is better accessed through quantitative approaches which place social relations at the heart of analysis, and that such approaches can more directly address the shifting meaning of social location created by processes of change and movement. Whilst social distance approaches, however, are more sensitive to issues of social meaning than conventional quantitative accounts, they are, of course, no substitute for qualitative approaches which directly access the subjective experience of social location. Nonetheless, in exploring the subjective experience of social movement, we also have to consider how perceptions of difference are related to the level and nature of standard patterns of change.

The reason, for example, that sociologists have looked at the *amount* of mobility is to see how mobility flows affect the fairness of society, and whether the patterning of mobility gives rise to distinct demographic groups. Both these issues crucially depend on how people perceive their own social movement in relationship to others, yet 'how people feel about or experience changes in their class standing is an issue that has been almost entirely overlooked' (Marshall and Firth, 1999:29). The study of what people think about movement is much less developed than the analysis of the volume and rate of mobility flows. What little information we have on people's subjective perceptions of their own movement (whether of an absolute improvement of chances for all, work-life trajectory, or of intergenerational mobility) often don't correspond well with so-called 'objective' measures of their social location and mobility. So for example, measures of 'fluidity' or the relative odds of success bear 'little relevance to the experiential worlds in which most people live. The simple figures describing the proportion of working-class children who are upwardly mobile, for example, bear a closer resemblance to the worlds that lay people inhabit' (Roberts, 2001:195). Ken Roberts argues that the perception of mobility depends on the social context within which comparison takes place.

'Very few if any people live in neighbourhoods which are microcosms of the national structure. Very few children attend schools where children from different social class backgrounds are present in the same proportions as in the national population. The classes tend to live, and to have their children educated, separately, not necessarily consciously and deliberately, but because primary schools in particular tend to have local catchment areas, certainly in towns and cities. People are better able to compare, and are more likely to be conscious of, the differences between how they themselves have fared in life and the achievements of others from the same neighbourhoods and schools, than how their entire class's achievements compare with those of other classes'. (*Roberts*, 2001:199)

Such processes of comparison, however, drawing on different reference groups, again draw us back to the way in which individual movement is located within wider processes of transition and change.

Goldthorpe's classic study of social mobility showed that over two-thirds of the service class had started off in lower classes, but also indicated that these mass movements created less social dislocation for the individuals concerned than might have been expected. The reason that mobility did not lead to marginality was that *so many people* had experienced mobility into the service class that their experience was the majority one. So, even if the established middle class were standoffish, the upwardly mobile could 'provide *each other* with ample possibilities for relations of sociability' (Goldthorpe *et al.*,1980:200):

'in an expanding industrial society, in which rates of upward mobility are relatively high, the problem of assimilation facing the mobile person is far less severe than in societies in which such rates are low. It is not, or not necessarily, a problem of gaining acceptance, as a conspicuous outsider, into established social circles but rather, one may suppose, a problem not essentially different from that facing the stable individual – that is to say, one of forming relationships with, so to speak, his own kind, whom he can find about him in some number'. (*ibid*)

So the total amount of movement in a society affects the meaning of any individual movement. Put simply, experiencing social movement when large numbers of people are moving alongside you is very different from experiencing social movement as an isolated individual. A large amount of social movement, however – through routine work-life career trajectories, through the overall expansion of opportunities and through intergenerational advancement – appears to be a standard feature of the social order of modern societies. Immobility, rather than mobility, is the more unusual experience in modern life, and large numbers of people believe that they have experienced social movement of some kind. The ubiquity of social movement, however, inevitably changes the perception of that experience. In tracing out the social meaning of occupations, therefore, we have to be sensitive *both* to the contextual social relations and typical patterns of transition within which such occupations are embedded, and also to the individual perceptions and comparisons which help shape the subjective experience of social location. For that reason, it is important to pursue quantitative approaches to stratification which emphasize the contextual social meaning of location and transition.

Changing times: Flexibilization and the re-organization of work in feminized labour markets

Angela Coyle

Introduction

There is now not much that is 'new' about work flexibility. Employers' strategies for maintaining profitability in an increasingly competitive and 'global' economy have resulted in significant temporal and spatial changes in the organization of work and a much increased flexibility in how, when, where and by whom work is conducted. (See for example Benner, 2002; Beck, 2000; Beynon *et al.*, 2002; Felstead and Jewson, 1999; Felstead, Jewson and Walters, 2004; Nolan and Wood, 2003; Rosenberg and Lapidus, 1999). Although many of these accounts have emphasized the detrimental impact of labour flexibilization on employees and their experience of work, over the last decade a more positive construction has emerged in which work flexibility is promoted as a positive mechanism for reconciling multiple stakeholder interests, including those of women workers (Pillinger, 1998). Official policy discourses in Europe, North America, the Pacific Rim and even now India, support the idea that 'family-friendly' flexible working time can be the means by which businesses can increase productivity and efficiency; public services can achieve better value for money; individual workers can better reconcile the demands of work with other aspects of their lives, especially family and care responsibilities, and women can increase their opportunities at work.

Yet despite the rhetorical ubiquity of 'family-friendly' work flexibility and the idea that some form of 'work-life balance' can be achieved through flexible working, there is still little evidence of this positive construction in practice. On the contrary, work and the family seem increasingly in conflict (Hochschild, 2001); time outside of work is an ever scarcer commodity (Gershuny, 2000) and employers' flexibilization strategies more often intensify the pressures of work rather than diminish them (Green, 2001). What, therefore, is the basis of this discursive formation? In this chapter I am interested in exploring how the idea that work flexibility can also be 'family-friendly' has emerged at a time when employers are seeking to extend and intensify labour flexibilization in sectors, jobs and labour markets which are highly feminized and moreover when part-time work, employers' long-established route to securing flexibility amongst women, is proving to be extremely rigid as the requirement for 24/7 working expands.

The UK National Health Service (NHS) is one such feminized labour market, in which women make up 75 per cent of the workforce, making the NHS (and therefore the British state) the largest employer of women in Europe. The chapter examines how work flexibilization has become central to the state's effort to 'modernize' UK healthcare services. Alongside a massive restructuring and flexibilization exercise to increase labour productivity and to improve and extend service provision, the NHS has developed new forms of flexible working based on the assumption that this will help in the recruitment and retention of its predominantly female workforce. In this chapter, however, I argue that forms of work flexibilization intended to reduce costs and increase efficiency will not deliver the kind of flexibility that a feminized workforce, such as that of the NHS, might require. On the contrary, the overwhelming response of health care workers to the managerial effort to restructure their working time and intensify their work effort has mostly been one of resistance.

Recent scholarship on work flexibility provides some important insights into why this may be the case. Employers' universal and homogeneous employment policies in fact have different implications for a workforce highly differentiated by class, age, ethnicity and skills, as well as personal and family circumstances, terms and conditions of employment and pay. Those women workers who have scarce or marketable skills and therefore some ability to negotiate over their time – and they are few – may indeed derive additional benefits from work flexibility. Many others however are trying to limit the impact of flexibilization by retreating into areas of work which are not yet fully subject to reorganization and managerial control, or they are withdrawing their labour altogether. In the case of the UK public healthcare services there has been such an exodus of health care professionals, especially nurses midwives and doctors that the NHS has been forced to reconstitute this predominantly female labour supply. Officially this has been achieved through a massive new recruitment drive and training initiative, backed up by the introduction of new flexible working arrangements to improve retention. But there is every indication that the NHS could not have increased staffing levels without resorting to substitution and deskilling strategies, and the very significant recruitment of temporary and contingent workers, many of whom are minority ethnic women and migrant women from countries of the South.

Labour flexibility is now being extended into feminized labour markets, including and perhaps especially, women's full-time and professional work in the public sector and this is the context in which the construction of the idea of 'family-friendly flexibility' has emerged; at the conjuncture of temporal and spatial changes in the organization of work; the increased feminization of work; the incorporation of many more women into the professional workforce and the erosion of state provided welfare. It may be best seen as a discursive strategy to control, give meaning and secure consent for the re-organization of women's working time. In an epoch when the intensification of work is contributing to the rise of a raft of issues concerning social reproduction, not least questions about how we find time to care for our children and elderly parents, it helps construct the resolution as residing, not so much in social provision, but in the flexible organization of work itself.

This chapter is organised in two parts. The first examines changes in both work organization and the family to show how work flexibilization, far from reconciling work and family is giving rise to new sources of inequalities and stress, rooted in the varying capacities of different categories of workers to exert control over their working time. The second part of the chapter uses these insights to critically examine the impact of flexibilization strategies in the UK health care services.

Part-time and flexible work and the family

This idea that social reproduction and women's paid work can be reconciled through some form of reduced hours, 'non-standard' or 'flexible' work arrangement actually has its roots in the social democratic discourse of fordist welfare regimes constructed in Europe after the Second World War. As the demand for married women's labour steadily grew from the 1950s onwards, part-time work was represented as the means by which women could both contribute to family income and remain good mothers (Myrdal and Klein, 1956). The near universal growth in maternal part time working across Europe has inevitably consolidated this idea. Whether women 'choose' to work part-time or whether it is a choice structured by other factors such as the non-availability of childcare and other forms of flexible working, is endlessly debated (Fagan and O'Reilly, 1998; Hakim, 1996; Paull *et al.*, 2002). Clearly, however, it has been one way in which women could come to some individual compromise between the demands of work and family, and above all has enabled women to sustain both their paid work and their unpaid work of care and social reproduction.

It is widely acknowledged, however, that part-time work is mostly constituted as low paid, low status and gender segregated work, and in the UK in particular is based on very short hours (Beechey and Perkins, 1987; Dex and McCulloch, 1995). It can provide a useful secondary income, lifting low-income families out of poverty (Family Policy Studies Centre, 1995:12), but rarely does part-time work provide an independent income or acceptable standard of living (Fagan and O'Reilly, 1998). As a result most part-time work is confined to women who have a working spouse or partner. Part-time working does not usually generate an adequate income to be of help to the 23 per cent of families now headed by lone mothers (Office for National Statistics, 2002), nor the one in five households in which there are no wage earners at all (Taylor, 2002a). In this respect, part-time work does not much support official 'welfare to work' policies in which paid employment is posited as the route out of welfare dependency for lone parents. Nor for that matter does part-time work support women's increasing professional career aspirations (Walby, 1997). In the UK 69 per cent of women of working age are now in paid work (Taylor, 2002b:14). The fastest rates of increase occurring amongst women with children under school age (Taylor, 2002a:7), many of whom are returning to full time work after a period of maternity leave (Kozak, 1998; Reynolds *et al.*, 2003). Yet the absence of part-time work at higher skill levels (Hogarth *et al.*, 2000:15) means that an increasing numbers of working mothers in professional and management occupations have little choice but to work full time hours. In short, part-time work does not reflect changing patterns of family formation in which many women have become the sole, main or significant family earner.

Although part-time work is usually regarded as one form of flexible working, it is not rooted in the new forms of flexible work organization that employers have been driving through over several decades (Rosenberg and Lapidus, 1999, Beynon *et al.*, 2002) and which represents a fundamental change in employers' labour use strategies and organization of work. It is characterized by a shift away from modern 'industrial time' and fordist work principles that prevailed after the 2nd World War up to the early 1970s based on a hierarchical and specialized division of labour and full time, permanent and continuous employment contracts with fixed/ standard weekly and daily hours. Post-industrial time and post-fordist work organization emphasizes multi-skilling and continuous re-skilling rather than specialization, team working, and a variety of contractual and working time arrangements, often referred to as 'non-standard' or 'atypical' work. As the extent of flexible working deepens to become the new norm, the contrast with standard and typical work becomes less and less meaningful. There is now 'nothing normal about 'normal' working time' (Harvey, 1999:25).

As a labour use strategy, flexibility takes many forms and includes temporal, functional and spatial flexibility. Flexible working time concerns all those just in time arrangements that enable employers to adapt staffing levels to match peaks and troughs in demand. This includes a whole repertoire of practices including temporary contracts, shift working and annualized hours. Functional flexible working, on the other hand, may not be concerned with working time at all. It involves extending employee competencies and the range of tasks and jobs that an individual employee can undertake. Spatial flexibility is achieved through the sub-contracting and outsourcing of work to another organization, agency or self employed worker. It may also include teleworking and home-working. In itself flexible working is not indicative of terms and conditions of employment, status or job control. Working at home for example, can be a feature of the working arrangements of highly skilled workers who are able to negotiate flexibility in the places where they work, or that of a highly marginalized and excluded workforce (Huws and O'Reagan, 2001). The critical determinant of whether flexible working can be 'family-friendly' is the extent to which employees can exert some degree of choice over their working time, and in this respect there are vast differences and inequalities.

The inequalities of time

There is certainly a great deal of survey evidence to show that many people, both women and men, with and without children, are increasingly rejecting 'workaholic lifestyles' and support the idea of flexible working if it allows for some choice over working time (*Guardian* 17 August 2004). Despite this employee interest there is now much research evidence highlighting the big gap between rhetoric and practice (Bond *et al.*, 2002; Kodz *et al.*, 2002). Few employers offer family-friendly benefits beyond the legal minimum and most are resistant to government proposals to extend this. Many employers seem not fully to understand what new forms of 'family-friendly' flexibility might entail and have simply 're-branded' part-time working as flexible working (Work and Parents Taskforce, 2001). Most practices remain *ad hoc* and at the discretion of line managers who themselves work long hours, and often regard flexible working as inappropriate and difficult to implement especially in the context of staff/ skills shortages (Bond *et al.*, 2002).

It is increasingly evident that the *employee* benefits of flexible working are dependent on regulatory frameworks, the bargaining power of different categories of workers and whether employers are using flexibility to reduce costs and increase efficiency or as a retention strategy. Far from flexibility having mutual benefits for all, employers have 'segmented' or different strategies for different categories of workers with the result that some groups of workers benefit from flexible working more than others (Purcell *et al.*, 1999). High quality flexible working is more likely to occur when employers are competing for skilled staff in a tight labour market and use flexibility as a recruitment and retention strategy. The detail of such flexibility is highly localized. It will vary between employers, work places and even between individual employees (Dex and Smith, 2002). It is usually based on some form of negotiation in which, in exchange for working more flexible and unpredictable hours, employees work fewer hours overall, gain a degree of control over their working time and in the case of some skilled men, secure financial compensation as well. It is clear that it is those employees with the most scarce and marketable skills and expertise who have the ability to determine the terms and conditions of their employment contract, including working hours, who benefit from flexible working arrangements (Knell, 2000).

The dominant narrative of work/family balance has concentrated on professional women as increasing numbers of women have moved into the professional and managerial workforce and into jobs that place heavy demands on their time. The working patterns and working hours of professional women now increasingly converge with those of men (Taylor, 2002b). But, as relatively high income earners, they are in the strongest position to negotiate a reduction in their working time, to bargain with their partners over childcare and paternal support (O'Brien and Shemilt, 2003:26) and to pay for the time of others to provide childcare and domestic labour (Ehrenreich and Hochschild, 2003). The ability to trade less money for more time may be an option for relatively high earning two-earner family households but not for households dependent on one income or low incomes. And in this respect differences in working times reflect material inequalities. The lowest paid have to work the longest hours to make up their pay and a third of all employees who work extra hours do so to increase their pay (Taylor, 2002a:12–13). Unsurprisingly therefore it is part-time low-paid women, rather than highly paid professionals who report the highest level of work stress (Taylor, 2002b). Low income women very frequently boost their pay by working long hours, often in several different jobs (TUC, 2002:7).

Moreover, long working hours are only one source of the increased work related pressure. When employers have used flexibility to increase productivity, lower costs and shift the insecurity and risk associated with market fluctuations onto the employee, the outcome is often degraded, low paid and insecure work. It has also resulted in the increasing requirement to work unsocial and unpredictable (atypical) hours (Rosenberg and Lapidus, 1999; La Valle *et al.*, 2002; TUC, 2002) and a continuing intensification of work effort, especially for women (Green, 2001).

Flexibility is being used by employers to increase effort and raise the rate of capital utilization (Green, 2001). This can be achieved either by extending working hours or intensifying work effort. A range of 'just in time' techniques, including shift work, split shifts, reduced breaks and annualized hour contracts, designed to reduce the porosity of the working day and the 'waste' of employers' paid for time are familiar features of the flexible workplace. As a result both the duration and intensity of work has increased (Taylor, 2002c:10), along with an increase in those working both longer and shorter hours, as well as atypical hours. Atypical working hours can help overcome the lack of affordable childcare but in low income households atypical working is only 'family friendly' in so far as it is permitting of a system of 'shift parenting' where one parent takes over as the other leaves for work (La Valle *et al.*, 2002).

Flexibilization often takes different forms in different European countries (Felstead and Jewson, 1999). In the UK workforce there has been a significant growth in atypical work and shift working. An increasing number of employees now work over weekends and Bank Holidays, and before 8.30 am and after 5.30 pm. According to La Valle *et al.* (2002), in the majority of two-parent families one or both parents work atypical hours on a regular basis, as do more than half of working lone mothers. The majority of those working atypical hours, especially those on low income, have no choice about the hours they work (La Valle *et al.*, 2002; TUC, 2002). It is atypical hours combined with unpredictable shift working that is now especially difficult to reconcile with family life (Hatter *et al.*, 2002). Children, to a very large degree still run on standard time.

Work as a family policy concern

Rather than accommodating family life, the growth in flexibilization is seen as contributing to work related stress spilling over into home life for all employees, whether male or female, full time or part-time (Burchell *et al.*, 1999; Ferri and Smith, 1996). As paid work is increasingly feminized, so the organization of work itself is giving rise to new family welfare policy concerns, especially when demographic changes, including an ageing population, postponed fertility and increased divorce rates are all contributing to more fragmented and complex family life. Women and men in the 40–60 age bracket, in particular, are likely to find themselves sandwiched between the requirements of work, teenage children, older children still in higher education and elderly parents in need of substantial care (Deven *et al.*, 1998; Mooney and Statham, 2002; Phillips *et al.*, 2002; Warin *et al.*, 1999). The family now appears to be under pressure as never before (Hochschild, 2001; Gershuny, 2000) and it is long working hours especially that are now regarded as the enemy of family life.

The UK has the longest working hours in Europe with more than 16 per cent of all employees working more than 48 hours a week (TUC, 2002). Fatherhood increases men's working time rather than diminishes it and in 2001, 39 per cent of UK fathers with dependent children worked more than 48 hours a week (O'Brien and Shemilt, 2003; TUC, 2002). In the last decade in the UK, men's average working hours have increased 1.6 hours a week. Women, however, are catching up fast. Women's working hours have increased 2.1 hours a week, with the largest increase occurring amongst women in their thirties and forties; the time when family and child care responsibilities are often at their highest (Taylor, 2002b:15). Three quarters of a million women (6 per cent of working women) work in excess of 48 hours a week; a 50 per cent increase over the last decade (TUC, 2002).

Across the European Union (EU), a raft of new legislation on working hours, part-time and temporary working and parental leave has been introduced to regulate the growth and quality of flexible work and its reconciliation with family life (Pillinger, 1998:7–12). In the UK, however, the implementation of this EU regulation on flexible working is weaker compared to some of the other member states such as France, Germany or the Netherlands. Instead the UK has adopted a more voluntaristic approach based on the promotion of the idea that flexibility is of mutual benefit to both employer and employee. This approach can be found in many aspects of UK family and employment policy initiatives (see for example Work and Parents Task Force, 2001; Women's Equality Unit, 2001) and is widely advocated across government departments, including the Equal Opportunities Commission (EOC): 'How is it possible to argue that increasing access to flexible working can be anything other than positive for employers and employees alike?' asks Jennie Watson, Deputy Chair of the EOC (BBC News online, 23rd April 2003). Yet as will be seen later in this chapter, the extension of work flexibility in the UK healthcare sector suggest that employers' and employees' interests in flexibility are far from sharing a common purpose and may actually be in conflict.

Employers' flexibilization strategies in feminized labour markets

Employers' work flexibilization strategies may have their roots in the exigencies of labour markets in the new information technology industries (Benner, 2002; Perrons, 2003) but they are now at the centre of the EU wide reform of public services, especially the highly feminized sectors of health and social care. Faced with labour shortages, escalating demand and financial stricture, 'many of the issues concerning quality, funding and delivery of health and social care are either directly or indirectly related to working time and work organization' (Pillinger, 1998:79). Despite a shared policy concern however, the flexibilization strategies for reorganising public sector work and working time, are not the same in all EU member states. What is shared however is the push to extend the definition of working time so that employers are freer to schedule work across evenings and weekends and employees need to be available to work during those times. Not only has working time become flexible, but so has non-work time and which can no longer be planned on a fixed and regular basis (Beynon *et al.*, 2002).

This changing meaning of time has implications for feminized areas of work, where employers are increasingly requiring women, whether full time or part time, to work across a newly extended working day /week. While there is no evidence than men like working evenings and weekends, they are more likely to comply with this requirement of the new working time flexibility, if as is often the case, they are compensated by increased pay and reduced hours of work overall. Women, on the other hand, are less willing or less able to comply with employer redefinition of working time, which increasingly encroaches not just into 'family' time or 'private' time but into women's unpaid work of social reproduction. Where they are able, and amongst those who enjoy some legal and social protection, some women are resisting the flexibilization of their time. In France, where increased flexibility has been accompanied also by the extension of parental leave rights, there is evidence that women are using their new rights to limit or withdraw their labour altogether (Le Feuvre, 2004). In the UK, despite a weaker regulatory framework, there is also evidence of women workers using state welfare as a retreat from work intensification. (*Observer* 12 September 2004). While in health care services there is evidence that, rather than welcoming flexibilization, many women have experienced a degradation and intensification of their work and have responded with an exodus of epic proportions.

Health care and the flexibilization of women's time

In 2000, the UK government set out a panoply of new policy interventions intended to transform the National Health Service (NHS) from a bureaucratic public service regime to one based on performance and managerial control (Department of Health, 2000). Securing an increase in work flexibility was seen as necessary both to expand existing services and to respond to new and changing user needs. An increase in working time flexibility would help the NHS extend services beyond the standard day, with more services available at weekends, evenings and on a 24-hour basis, while more functional flexibility would enable nurses to take on more of the tasks of doctors and facilitate the expansion of many more nurse led services (Department of Health, 2000).

As a provider of hospital services, the NHS has always included an element of 24/7 shift working but new services are being introduced which require both functional and operational flexibility. Such new services have included a nurse run 24-hour telephone help line known as *NHS Direct* and *Walk in Centres* which are open from early morning to late evening to provide immediate treatment for minor injures and health problems. In both of these services, nurses have replaced doctors as the first point of contact. The intention is that they will ease the demand on General Practitioner (GP) surgeries and hospital Accident and Emergency (A&E) departments, while increasing users' access to health care services by operating outside of the standard working day. In some instances nurses may be trained to perform tasks previously only carried out by doctors. For example, new clinics have been set up to provide routine surgical treatment for carpal tunnel syndrome. Surgery is carried out by specially trained nurses. Waiting lists have been reduced from up to two *years* to four to five *weeks* and patients are able to choose the day and time, including evenings, of their operation (*Guardian*, 17 July 2002). Elsewhere, nurses have started to run mobile health clinics for farmers who were found not to be using mainstream services (*Guardian*, 17 April 2002). On the whole, nurses' and doctors' professional bodies have welcomed these developments. They offer nurses new opportunities for skill enhancement and professional upgrading and doctors the opportunity to reduce their heavy workloads and long hours of working.

The effort to expand and introduce more flexibility into UK public health services provision has been impeded however by staff shortages. New services such as the *Walk in Centres* are often competing with other services within the NHS over the same shrinking pool of nurses (Mountford and Rosen, 2001). Not only do staff shortages limit the services that can be provided, but it can be enormously expensive. The Audit Commission estimated that 10 per cent of nursing shifts are covered by temporary and agency nurses costing the NHS over £800 million a year (Audit Commission, 2001). Other estimates are higher and indicate that in London and the South East in particular, agency nurses are covering up to 40 per cent of shifts (*Nursing Times*, 2 January 2002). As with other health care providers world wide, the NHS is struggling to meet escalating demands while experiencing acute labour shortages especially amongst doctors and nurses, most of whom are women. (Buchan, 2002).

Nurses and their discontents

Women make up around 90 per cent of the NHS nursing workforce. Successive surveys over the last decade have indicated that large numbers of women have been leaving nursing with nurse vacancies continuing to increase, despite increases in the number of nurses in training (Robinson *et al.*, 1999; Smith and Seccombe, 1998). Not only do approximately twenty per cent of student nurses drop out of training, one in ten nurses leave the NHS within one year of qualification (Smith and Seccombe, 1998; Ball and Pike, 2004). In 2001 it was estimated that 90,000 nurses will have left the NHS by 2004 unless there was a significant effort to retain them (Audit Commission, 2001).

There is not one single reason for such high levels of attrition. In part it is due to the fact that the nursing workforce is an aging one. Whereas once nurses were predominantly young women, single and childless, they are now typically older. Only one in ten is under 30; a third are aged 40–49, while a quarter of nurses are aged 50 or over (Ball and Pike, 2004). Nurses are now more likely to have dependent children or responsibilities for elder care, and find shift patterns and long hours difficult to reconcile with home life (RCN, 2001). But there has also been a five fold increase in early retirement since 1988 with some evidence to show that this is due to work related stress and heavy workloads (Nuffield Trust, 1998).

The most common reasons nurses themselves cite for leaving the NHS are dissatisfaction with pay, occupational downgrading and excessive workloads (Robinson *et al.*, 1999; Nuffield Trust, 1998; Smith and Seccombe, 1998; Ball and Pike, 2004 p6). Pay is not only the main source of nurses' discontents but also the reason given for having to work long hours. Three fifths of nurses work additional hours to supplement their pay, often in second jobs. This is also the case for so-called part-time nurses, most of whom are working more hours than they would ideally like with one in three working more than 30 hours a week (RCN, 2001). There have been successive efforts to improve nurses pay but these have frequently been undermined by local managers' cost saving strategies which have not only suppressed pay overall but have contributed to a truncation of nurses career structures and a dilution of their skills (Coyle, 1995; Robinson *et al.*, 1999). Higher grade nursing posts have been cut while the proportion of nurses bunched up in lower grades has increased (RCN, 2000). Part-time work in nursing is rarely available at higher grades so that as many as 30 per cent of nurse who take up part-time work after maternity leave experience occupational downgrading (Lane, 1998).

Nurses' resentments have been simmering for years (Davies, 1995) but now find expression through mobility of one kind or another, at a time when nurses have many new employment opportunities. Although the majority of nurses will spend the first five years of the nursing careers in the NHS, 20 years after qualification, more than half will have left the NHS, to work for other health service providers in the private sector, in residential and nursing care homes and in GP practices (Ball and Pike, 2004).

The feminization of medicine

Medicine has not suffered the same exodus as nursing but widespread dissatisfaction with pay, working conditions and long hours of work has contributed, in the last decade, to the increasing numbers of UK trained doctors leaving the NHS to work abroad, in the private sector and outside of medicine altogether, where the pay and working conditions are far better and where they do not have to work such excessively long hours (Health Policy and Economic Research Unit, 2003). A third of doctors surveyed in the late 1990s claimed they would not enter medicine if they were starting their careers again and in the view of one consultant, 'the medical profession is now a poor career choice for an intelligent, aspiring young person' (BBC News Online 1 February 1999). At the same time large numbers of doctors are also leaving the NHS through retirement, especially GPs, and including the 18,000 doctors who were recruited into the NHS from the Indian Sub Continent in the early 1960s.

But the most significant factor now affecting the labour supply of doctors is that medicine is well on its way to becoming feminized. Women now take up 60 per cent of medical school places in the UK and make up 75 per cent of GPs under the age of 30 (Department of Health, 2002a). The proportions of female hospital medical staff in England have also increased and women make up over half of all House Officers and 44 per cent of Senior House Officers and over a quarter of consultants (Department of Health, 2002b). Large numbers of women in medicine highlight a concern over doctors' working hours which can be excessively long and one of the main reasons why doctors, male and female, leave medicine (Cooke and Chitty, 2004:4). At the same time, doctors' professional training and career development requires a long term commitment over many years. The 'standard' hospital consultant's career path requires 'fierce dedication and stoic endurance' as well as long hours at a life stage normally associated with family formation (McManus and Sproston, 2000). If doctor shortages are to be addressed through flexibilization strategies there will need to be substantially more opportunities for part-time professional training as well as reduced hours of work.

A feminized human resource management strategy?

Since 2000 the NHS has had to make a very substantial effort to reconstitute its largely female labour supply, by recruiting many more nurses and doctors and by developing an approach to its human resource management that is intended to appeal to women. The *NHS Plan* and the *Improving Working Lives* (IWL) initiative set out a very comprehensive range of new policy initiatives intended to improve working conditions and overcome staff shortages (Department of Health, 2000; 2001). Along with a new performance related pay system, these plans have included providing practical help with child care and other caring responsibilities, providing employees with affordable housing and the extension of flexible working arrangements. These include self-rostering shifts, annualized hours agreements, reduced hours options of different kinds, career breaks and flexible retirement, as well as flexible forms of training and professional development.

Nurses' working patterns have always included a wide variety of shift work and part time work. Through swapping shifts with each other informally they have also had some degree of work flexibility of their choosing. Ensuring adequate daily staffing levels however has long been a major anxiety for nurse managers (Allen, 2001), who have spent much of their time cajoling staff to work extra hours or extra shifts. Now a system of annualized hours and 24 hour shift rostering provides health managers with new 'just in time' staffing mechanisms. Commonly used by health care employers in Europe and North America, new shift rosters are based on hour by hour assessment of the staffing and skill levels required to meet service delivery needs at different times of the day and night. Staffing levels can be higher and working hours longer when required in busy periods and this can be offset by shorter hours and/or taking time off in quieter periods. This system is especially helpful in enabling managers to cover the busy winter months when demand rises steeply and staffing the less popular night time, early morning and late evening shifts.

Potentially this 24 hour shift system has benefits for the workforce too. It can better integrate part time working, as reduced annual hours can be incorporated into a 24 hour roster, blurring the boundaries between those in the team working full and part time hours. Rotating shifts means that the sometimes unpopular shifts, which cover the nights and unsocial hours, are more equitably shared. Combined with annualized hours, it gives employees the ability to vary their work patterns and hours across the year, while receiving a regular monthly salary based on a monthly average. It enables employees to take time off in the summer months, which is especially helpful for those with school age children.

For medical employees a flexible *Careers Scheme* was introduced in 2001 for hospital doctors and for GPs in 2004. As for nurses, it offers doctors some degree of choice over their hours of work and working patterns; enables them to take a career break and return, or to reduce their hours prior to retirement.

The intention has been to make the NHS an 'employer of choice' for health service professionals and especially for women. It is a management led programme of reform that places at its centre the flexible working, training and development that women health care professionals highlight. Time bound targets were set for implementing this very substantive programme of reform and the intention is eventually to reward those NHS Trusts and local employers who have successfully introduced 'modern employment policies' (Department of Health, 2001). Success in this instance includes such measurable criteria as reductions in staff turnover and doctors' working hours and a decrease in the use of agency staff. It is a monolithic but highly feminized model of change which shares many of the characteristics of public sector equal opportunities policies developed in the 1980s and 1990s: modernist, based on an undifferentiated category of 'women' and with universal and uncontested goals set by actors who behave as if they are achievable (Forbes, 2002).

Plus ça change?

The project on which the NHS has embarked is still in its early stages. Timescales for implementation have slipped (*Nursing Standard*, 4 February 2004) and there is little tangible evidence that flexible working arrangements are helping to reconstitute the female labour supply. The NHS has recruited many more student nurses but newly qualified nurses are experiencing difficulties in finding entry level jobs because of the 'logjam' of nurses already clustered in lower grades (*Nursing Standard* 21 July 2004).

Far from diminishing, nurses' discontents remain, 'pay and workloads are still viewed negatively and show little or no change in the last five years' (Ball and Pike, 2004 p6). The proportion of nurses in higher nursing grades is decreasing, suggestive of continuing career degradation. A third of nurses employed in lower grades have been on the same grades for ten years or more. Meanwhile male nurses continue to progress into nurse management more rapidly than women and white nurses more rapidly than black and minority ethnic nurses. Black and minority ethnic nurses are more likely than white nurses to feel that their grade is not appropriate to their qualifications and current role (Ball and Pike, 2004:4). There continues to be little opportunity for reduced hours of work in higher skilled nursing grades or nurse manager grades (Edwards and Robinson, 2002), so that women are still held back in the nursing profession relative to men, and prevented from accessing some of the new opportunities arising from increases in functional flexibility and nurse reskilling. Meanwhile nurses continue to take on extra hours to make up their pay. A quarter of all nurses have an extra job and almost half of minority ethnic women have an extra job (Ball and Pike, 2004 p5). On average full time nurses work 44 hours per week, and many still work well above the 48 hour limit demanded under the EU working time regulation (*Nursing Standard*, 28 January 2004).

And nurses are still leaving. Twice as many UK trained nurses left the UK in 2002–2003, as in the previous year, to work abroad in the United States, Australia, New Zealand and Canada where both pay 'perks' are better (*Nursing Standard*, 28 January, 2004). The most recent national survey of the nursing workforce shows that nurses over the age of 50 have not been persuaded to stay on despite a new flexible retirement scheme. They are still planning to retire at 58, and would in fact prefer to leave sooner. One in ten student nurses leave the NHS after qualifying to work in other sectors. A third of all nurses are planning to leave their current employer, eleven per cent are planning to leave nursing and nearly a third say they would leave nursing if they could. The nurses most likely to want to leave their jobs are hospital nurses working on the new rotating flexible shift patterns (Ball and Pike, 2004)

In medicine the 'New Deal' which promised to limit the working hours of junior doctors to 56 hours a week and to enforce the European Working Time Directive (EWTD) which limits doctors hours to 58 hours, is yet to show substantive results. As many as three quarters of junior doctors still work in excess of these limits in 2004 (Health Policy and Economic Research Unit, 2004). And while there are schemes for providing flexible working and part time medical training schemes for hospital medicine (Goldberg and Paice, 2000) they are not extensive and do not even begin to address doctors' (both women's and men's) overwhelming demand for reduced hours of work and part time training (Health Policy and Economic Research Unit, 2004).

Yet flexible working *is* what women health care professionals want, but on their terms. One in five nurses returning from a career break takes up work as temporary agency nurses or 'bank' nurses and, although this will usually result in occupational downgrading, it does enable nurses to have some control over their hours of work; while jobs in GP practices, hospices and school nursing are also much sought after. In these services nurse attrition levels are very low, even though there is limited scope for professional development. What they offer are opportunities for part time work within the framework of a 'standard' day (Ball and Pike, 2004). Women doctors are also seeking refuge in similar standard time 'spaces', in fact women doctors are now moving out of hospital medicine to work part time in general practice in such large numbers that this is fuelling new patterns of gendered occupational segregation in medicine, between feminized general practice and the concentration of men in hospital and academic medicine (Health Policy and Economic Research Unit, 2004).

Whether the NHS has achieved its staffing targets is much contested. The Department of Health claims it has achieved its recruitment targets, especially of nurses, while doctors' and nurses' professional bodies claim that staffing numbers still need to increase substantially in order to take account of the increased demand for reduced hours of working. What is clear is that increased staffing levels have not been achieved through progressive flexible employment policies alone. Deskilling and labour substitution has been one response to the problem of labour shortages and the NHS plans to recruit up to 144,000 unqualified nursing assistants (or health care assistants) to help cover the shortfall in nurses. The other is the increased recruitment of migrant labour. Initially a short stop gap measure, the employment of migrant labour, or 'international recruitment' as the NHS prefers, has become key in enabling staffing targets to be achieved: 'Without it, all the resources being allocated to returners, to improving retention and to increasing the numbers of student nurses would have done little more the maintain the number of nurses on the register over the period 1999–2002' (Buchan and Seccombe, 2003:9).

Since 2000, 40,000 overseas nurses have registered in the UK and the NHS could not have achieved its staffing targets without them. The numbers of internationally recruited nurses on the Nursing and Midwifery Council register now exceeds the number of UK newly qualified nurses, and make up over a third of the workforce in both NHS and private sector. All nursing employers using migrant nurses to plug their staffing gaps (Ball and Pike, 2004:2). In medicine the picture is not dissimilar. One quarter of all hospital consultants working on the NHS has trained overseas, as have more than half (58 per cent) of all doctors registered with the General Medical Council.

NHS employers have resorted to labour substitution in the absence of other alternatives but it is hard to see how such short term measures will contribute anything to the NHS' 'modernization' project. The large increase in the employment of unqualified nurses will significantly increase an area of work distinguished by low pay and in which minority ethnic women are disproportionately over-represented (Thornley, 2002). Migrant nurses employed on temporary contracts, clustered in the lowest nursing grades, make up a large but still marginal workforce, with few entitlements to social protection. Low pay and long and atypical hours look set to stay.

Conclusion; the power to choose?

In this chapter I have discussed how temporal and spatial changes in the organization of work have given rise to more flexible and individualized work organization. These changes have created the potential for individual workers to have more flexibility to choose the time and place of their work, while employers can use work flexibility to attract and retain labour. On the whole however, there is not much evidence that the majority of workers are deriving much benefit from flexibility. Despite official discourses which promote flexible working as a mechanism for the better reconciliation of work and family life, there is now considerable research evidence to show that employers' flexibilization strategies are intensifying work effort, extending the definition of working time and increasing work related stress rather than diminishing it.

While many European states have sought to regulate flexible labour markets, to ensure that flexibility has been accompanied by a reduction in working time overall, the British state has relied on a more voluntaristic approach which seeks to persuade employers and employees alike of the benefits of flexible working. This approach has been adopted in the UK National Health Service and where work flexibility has been promoted in an effort to reconstitute the predominantly female labour supply. However many women have proved resistant to the extension of their working time and their long term exodus from the NHS workforce continues. Rather than increasing its labour supply through 'family-friendly' flexibility, public health services in the UK have addressed staff shortages through an increase in marginal and temporary work. 'Family-friendly' flexibility is less of a material practice and more a discursive intervention to give meaning to and secure consent for the restructuring of employment. In this restructuring however new inequalities of time are manifest: between those who have some power to bargain over the definition of working time and those who do not; between those who are able and willing to comply with the requirement to extend their working time and those who are not; and those who can resist flexibilization and intensification and those who cannot.

Part 3
Privatized work

Time and labour: Fathers' perceptions of employment and childcare

Esther Dermott

I do enjoy my work, I do see a lot of my children and I don't think they need a parent with them every day all day . . . They're very happy and I think the balance is just right (Ken)

The impetus for this chapter comes from an unexpected finding that emerged while interviewing fathers; contrary to what had been anticipated, competition over time was not a dominant theme in the accounts of their lives. The initial prediction was that the difficulties of achieving an acceptable 'work-life balance' would be to the fore, with paid work and family activities placed in opposition to each other. However, the relative absence of such comments was stark and the fathers felt that they were able to achieve and maintain the status of 'good father' and 'good worker' simultaneously.

An explanation of this finding requires an exploration of how the labour associated with being a 'good father' and 'good worker' is viewed. This necessitates careful consideration of the perception of time in relation to different forms of work. Commonly, when time is considered in relation to work it is thought of in an additive way, with hours and minutes being equitable whatever the activity, allowing comparisons to be made across various forms of labour. This, however, ignores the fact that the same amounts of time may not be interpreted similarly by participants within different spatial and social contexts. It is argued here that, for fathers, the time required to be a 'good parent' may be qualitatively different from the formulation of time that is required to be a 'good worker' and it is this that leads to a more complementary relationship between work and family than has been previously acknowledged.

This chapter aims to extend the sociological analysis of work through an examination of temporality; a rather strange aim, given that both empirical and theoretical accounts of work, from E.P. Thompson onwards, have commented extensively on the structuring of work-time. Yet 'work-time' has usually been synonymous with time spent in employment and the labour market has been seen as foundational and dominant especially for *men's* relationship with time. Empirical studies that have used a more expansive definition of work, which includes unpaid labour such as housework, childcare and voluntary work, and have discussed the negotiated and contextual nature of time, have usually drawn on the lives of women (Glucksmann, 1998; McKie *et al.*, 2002). This discussion concentrates on how fathers think about the childcare they perform and contrasts this with the other forms of work in which they are involved. It uses their accounts of time in order to suggest the gendered and spatial complexity that must be recognized in order to develop ideas of temporality and to highlight an ignored marker of difference between forms of labour. Using the participants' perspectives also raises the issue of how particular activities become classed as work.

The data comprises interviews conducted with 25 fathers[1]. The men interviewed were all currently in employment and held professional/managerial positions. They had at least one child of primary school age – using a subjective definition of 'father' – and were cohabiting with their female partner. Principally the research was concerned with exploring how the men managed the roles of 'worker' and 'father', and documenting the benefits and constraints they felt existed between the two.

Fathering time versus employment time?

Recent research on fatherhood suggests some increased involvement in childcare activities by men (Gershuny, 2001; Sandberg and Hofferth, 2001) and, to a greater extent, the expression of the desire by men to participate more fully in a nurturing role (Cohen, 1993; Burgess, 1997). There is a growing cultural prescription that fathers should be more involved with the 'taking care of' children (Griswold, 1993; La Rossa, 1997). At the same time, there has been no dissolution of the doctrine that to be a full member of society one must be engaged in paid work (Levitas, 1998). Indeed, the emergence of debates over flexibility and the reorganization of employment relations have highlighted the increasing pressure that workers may encounter in the labour market (Purcell *et al.*, 1999; Beck, 2000). In order successfully to manage the developing demands of these different forms of labour, individuals can expect to face a difficult balancing act. Certainly, in accounts of modern motherhood, the terms 'juggling', 'managing' and 'coping' are testament to this problem (eg, Hochschild, 1989; Brannen and Moss, 1991). The question is why then did these fathers *not* speak about major tensions in achieving a balance between employment and family life?

Studying the interface between employment and family 'invites a focus upon time and upon time in its plurality of meanings' (Brannen, 2002). Despite the possibility of 'plurality', time in sociological writings remains most prominent in discussions of time management; concerned with the rationales and methods adopted by individuals and households in order to balance and negotiate the time demands they experience. The emphasis on the deployment of clock time has, more recently, been supplemented by recognizing patterns of time-use across the life course and generational time (Brannen, 2002). Yet while study in this area acknowledges the significance of time and attempts some degree of engagement, it does not seem to fully capture its dynamic quality. Although it is accepted that our perception of time varies depending on the context – 'Our experience of time rarely if ever coincides with what the clock tells us' (Melucci, 1996:11) – this experience of time is only occasionally brought into analyses of empirical studies.

Adams suggests that timed social life is 'fundamentally embedded in an understanding of the structural relations of power, normative structures and the negotiated interactions of social life' (1990:109), but that we should only be interested if investigation can further our sociological knowledge. In accordance with this, an examination of time in these accounts of fathers aims to make a contribution to disentangling the meaning of involvement in relation to employment and parenting and understanding how the 'complex inter-weaving of caring and working' (McKie *et al.*, 2002) is managed. Following Glucksmann (1998), a concern is to use the temporal dimension as an additional tool with which to explore gendered differences in labour.

The 'good worker'

Being in employment involves a time obligation, which, necessarily, restricts the hours available for any alternative activities, along with the amount of energy and enthusiasm expendable on them. This demand is often given especial significance as a way of explaining why men's apparent eagerness for involvement in fathering is not matched by their childcare activities, 'Because work has first claim on men, it limits the time men can spend with their families' (Blackstone *et al.*, 1992:12). The employment contract, which identifies the relationship between employer and employee, generally specifies both a wage and a corresponding number of contracted hours. While a close association between time and money exists, the correlation is less precise for those on salaries rather than wages. For members of the salariat, contracted hours operate as an estimate of the approximate amount of time the individual should need to get the work done, but this is a guideline not an absolute figure. For most of the men interviewed a set number of hours was formally contracted, but often this operated as a minimum figure with additional hours of work unpaid. It has been argued that the way in which employers operate to enforce longer working time in these circumstances is less through formalized systems of set hours and more through appeals to employees' feelings of responsibility. Taylor (2002) found that among higher professionals 90 per cent gave 'deadlines' as the reason for working long hours, compared to 68 per cent who said it was a 'requirement' of the job. A greater degree of freedom with regard to the organization of tasks or the location of employment activity may be gained but, through mechanisms of obligation, can also result in longer hours spent working.

'Feeling responsible' was voiced in two ways by interviewees: either to other people, be they colleagues or clients, or to the job itself. William, who is a lawyer in a large city firm, sees his responsibilities as being towards both his clients and to the more junior employees who look to him for assistance.

> Part of one's job is being available to clients, it is a service industry . . . And part of the job is when someone [a colleague] wants to wander in and say, 'I don't really understand this section, can you help me?' (William)

As a teacher, the 'clients' towards whom Jack feels his responsibility lies are his pupils.

> As a teacher, leave is very detrimental on the class and on the kids you are teaching, in a sense it is kind of irresponsible to them. (Jack)

Responsibility to the job itself was expressed as being accountable for 'getting the job done', emphasising that for these men, as documented for other professional workers, work is primarily experienced as task based rather than by duration (O'Malley, 1992).

> Basically if there is work to be done I will make sure that it gets done. I have a job, and what I do is quite self-contained, it is just me that does it really, so I have to make sure that it is done. (Raj, editor)

> The expectation is a very general one that I will just get the work done. We don't really have that many deadlines . . . it's more of an ongoing job, a work in progress if you like. (Phil, personnel manager)

The self-employed in the sample tended to present the most extreme version of this, as complete control corresponds with complete responsibility. Marcus, the director of a small company, had devised the rule that offers of work should never be refused but he also had to fulfil this obligation. Marcus used the phrase 'the buck stops with me' to explain how the consequences of this decision would at times result in undesirable demands from clients.

> I am normally the last person out of the door and if someone phones – we never turn down work as a policy – so if it has to be done, then it will be done . . . If it absolutely can't be done tomorrow I'll get it done at home. (Marcus)

Responsibility and time

In practice there was a hazy relationship between employment and time in terms of the formal contracting of an individual's time to their employer. Despite this, the perceived association of time with work *commitment* was strong. For employers, an employee's willingness to offer time above that which is formally required is taken as sign of trustworthiness and commitment (Sirianni and Walsh, 1991). The idea that time in itself signifies value, whether or not it is accompanied by any achievement, has its ultimate expression in the culture of presenteeism. Presenteeism is the term invented to describe the necessity of being seen to be present in the workplace (Cooper and Williams, 1994). The ethos is that employers reward those who show their commitment to work by spending long amounts of time in the office, preferably longer than their boss or colleagues. Although it may be impossible to judge whether the person at their desk is being productive, simply being present in the office from early in the morning to late at night is taken as an indication of the correct, responsible attitude towards the job. In Adam's (1995) terms, clock time is the yardstick that measures the positive attribute of busyness. A further example of this is the characterisation of part-time and full-time workers. The frequent implication is that part-time equals not merely fewer hours spent in paid work (a shorter quantity) but also lower levels of commitment and responsibility (a reduced quality) and therefore an, entirely justifiable, lower value in the eyes of the employer. The opposition between full-time and part-time is neatly encapsulated by Hakim's description of women workers as either 'self-made women' or 'grateful slaves' (1991).

While fathers in the study saw their paid work in terms of responsibility rather than a simple exchange of hours for money, they also accepted time as a proxy measure for responsibility. Alan (an accountant) commented that while it is theoretically possible to choose your own hours in his office, with the proviso that all the work is completed, 'if you walked in at eleven it wouldn't be acceptable'. Another interviewee mentioned how not adhering to the dominant schedule was just unacceptable,

> If you piss off at 4 o'clock in the afternoon or half past two in the afternoon . . . it is someone who is not quite playing the game (William)

The majority of the fathers tended to concur with the suggestion that responsibility equates with time and did not seek to challenge this association. Outlining how long hours are an implicit demand of employment that operates through the filter of responsibility rather than an explicit requirement is important because it allows for the possibility of a mediated response by the employee – the worker has some agency over choosing the way in which he transforms the demand for responsibility into behaviour. The requirements of jobs are dependent on the occupation, employer and culture of the workplace, in conjunction with the perceptions of individuals themselves, as decisions about what constitutes acceptable levels of time commitment are open to a degree of interpretation. The culture of workplaces encourages a certain approach to time and therefore sanctions about appropriate involvement may be difficult to challenge (Kaul, 1991; McDowell, 1997). Yet since employing organizations would ideally have their workforce donating all of their time and energy to paid work, individual employees do have to make decisions at some stage. Marcus could have decided not to take on all the available contracts offered to him and Jack (quoted earlier) acknowledged that other teachers took a different view to him; that there would be no great loss if a teacher took a day off work as colleagues or supply teachers would cover classes. William's previous comments illustrated how he is aware of a responsibility to be available when his clients and colleagues expect him to be. This involves being around at his office for the duration of the working day and accepting that he is unable to make any guarantees about always being at home at a certain time, even for one evening a week to allow his wife to take up an offer of part-time work. Although he states these restrictions, he also recognizes that he has to manage the demands made upon him.

> I say that work is a very jealous mistress. In the sense that, clearly management would like me to work twenty hours a day. Objectively what they want me to do is to work lots and lots and lots, and bill lots and lots and lots, and then we can all have Maseratis. And in a way work will take whatever I am prepared to give it, and my responsibility is in fact to make sure that the mistress in this context, work, is kept in reasonable proportions (William)

There were other examples of fathers recognizing that boundaries could be placed on the amount of time spent at work while not necessarily adopting these limiting practices themselves. One interviewee made a comparison between himself and a female colleague, illustrating how his style of working is not the only way to approach his job.

> If you are producing a programme you have to be at the front, you can't slide off, I think you have to work reasonable hours . . . My colleague round the corner, she is curious because she is much more of an auteur filmmaker than I am. You know she really has to have projects into which she can pour her heart and soul and express herself through the subject matter, whereas I think my approach is more anonymous, I try and serve the subject . . . but yet she is much more ruthless in protecting her time with her children, so she will leave at 5.30 . . . so people have very different attitudes to the work (Greg, television producer)

The conclusion he reaches highlights how, due to the advantaged nature of their employment positions, these men often have the ability to decide how to get their work done and could if they chose, challenge, to some degree, the status quo of their work environments.

The good father

In recent decades fatherhood has become a 'hot topic' (Marsiglio, 1995) and the body of research on fathers, fatherhood and men in families has increased exponentially (Dienhart, 1998). Fathering is alleged to have undergone dramatic changes, with proclamations of 'new fathering' and debates over what this phrase means, dominating the literature. Terms such as 'involved' and 'participatory' have been invoked to suggest that more 'traditional' ideas of fatherhood centred on breadwinning have been replaced by a more active emotional relationship between parent and child (Cohen, 1993) although arguments have also been made for the continuing importance of the provider role (Warin *et al.*, 1999). Other authors have contended that any discussion of fatherhood should accept its contested and ambivalent nature (Lupton and Barclay, 1997). Newer images of fatherhood have been associated with alternative fathering behaviour with men taking on a greater amount of childcare and participating to a larger extent in significant child centred events and children-related activities than in previous decades (Gershuny, 2001; Sandberg and Hofferth, 2001); the implication is that adapted forms of fatherhood will necessitate men spending a greater amount of time with children than previous configurations of fathering.

In response to questions about what kind of fatherhood they envisaged for themselves, the majority of interviewees' comments corresponded with the ethos of minimizing income generation and instrumental leadership as aspects of fathering identity and prioritizing involvement with children.

> I wanted to be really involved in what they do and kind of, really to enjoy seeing them growing up (Gareth)

The salient dimensions of this 'involved fathering' can be distinguished more precisely. It encompasses openness of emotions, expressing affection, and building a close relationship.

> One of my primary functions as a father, as a parent, is to let my kids know that, at the beginning of the day they are vital, important, independent beings . . . who know they are absolutely solidly loved and adored and appreciated (William)

> I didn't want to be loud and bullying and oppressive in any way . . . I'm not an austere, distant figure (Phil)

> I didn't want to be distant. I wanted to be around, wanted to do things with the child (Jim)

The description of involved fathering which the interviewees have produced corresponds closely to recent sociological definitions of intimacy (Dermott, 2003). Jamieson defines 'disclosing intimacy' as necessarily including 'close association, privileged knowledge, deep knowing and understanding and some form of love' (1998:13) and for Giddens 'it is the quality of the relationship between parent and child which comes to the fore' (1992:98). In a similar way to 'responsibility', the term 'intimacy' does not immediately equate with a time commitment. Time has to be fashioned and interpreted so as to permit these attributes to be read from it.

Intimacy and time

Unlike for paid labour, there is no formal contract laid down which specifies the number of hours that someone should spend engaged in the care of their own children. As noted with respect to paid work, however, cultural expectations exist outside of official prescriptions. It might therefore seem logical to conclude that the apparently heightened desire of fathers to develop an intimate, involved relationship with their children would correlate with a greater time commitment. Jamieson (1998) suggests that this connection with time is inherent to the idea of intimacy. She states that, as a relationship takes time to develop, a separation between knowing and understanding on the one hand and practical caring on the other seems unlikely.

Yet the fathers interviewed here were much less willing to accept that time was a useful measurement of responsibility and commitment in relation to the nurturing of children than they had been to embrace the idea that time represented a way of gauging an individual's commitment to employment.

> I knew that it was unlikely that I would be around all day, but I knew that at the end of the day, I should put work behind me and should throw myself into whatever is left of the day for the children . . . given that I have a long journey home from work (Greg)

While Greg is referencing the restrictions which a full-time and demanding job place on him, he is also stating that long periods of time are not necessary in order to be classed as an involved, intimate father. The assertion that whatever time is available is directed towards his children emphasizes his commitment to family life but also strongly implies that quality of fathering cannot be read off from a measurement of time and that good fathering can be achieved within severe time limits. Many of the fathers did speak about marginal time conflicts and certainly not all were as satisfied as Ken (quoted at the beginning of the chapter) with their work-life balance. Yet despite the time management that was required in light of competing desires and expectations, it was clear that time did not indicate commitment *per se*. Fathers who spent less time with their children did not express feelings of guilt about being worse fathers (in contrast to evidence from research with mothers eg, Brannen and Moss, 1991). The dominant impression is that a good father-child relationship is possible as long as *some* period of time is given over to it, although this cannot easily be quantified.

The complexities of different understandings of time are perfectly illustrated by another interviewee talking about the relationship with his own father, who he held up as a role model.

> I don't see, in any sense, that I did not have time with my father. You know, if I think back to my childhood I have what seems a lot of time with my father. But I'm sure it can't have been because I was at boarding school, apart from anything else, and he was in the Navy. Yet I don't feel any lack of involvement from him as a child (Hugh)

Hugh begins by implicitly supposing that time can be taken as an indicator in defining whether a father is involved with his child or not, with more time read as more involvement, but his personal experience does not support this formulation. The quotation again suggests that the desired father-child relationship, based on 'intimate fathering', can be achieved within a restricted time frame in a way that is not possible with the role of responsible worker.

Extensive and intensive fathering

From the responses of the interviewees it seems that the total length of time spent with children is not viewed as a way of measuring good fathering. This, however, does not mean that time is irrelevant to men's parenting; the way in which it is necessary to think about the work of parenting and time is simply different to the way in which labour market participation and time can be explored. While for these men the extent of time spent in childcare activities was not viewed as centrally important, it was key that some amount of time was available and that times of special significance could be accommodated.

All of these fathers were able to spend some amount of time with their children on a daily basis, even if it was restricted to a few minutes and did not necessarily involve a period of one-to-one interaction. This was possible because the fathers were co-resident with their children and so could be engaged in 'secondary' parental care where they were accessible even if not engaged in the 'primary' parenting of carrying out a child based activity (La Rossa and La Rossa, 1981)[2]. Tony says that in the evenings he and his wife may not actually be engaged in what their children are doing but says that, 'we'll both be around really' and adds that a central aspect to his image of fatherhood was being somebody 'who was there'. Patrick, another interviewee, listed the kinds of activity he does with his children on weekends, such as shopping, cooking and gardening but even when he is not interacting with the children he remains available.

> I am around the place . . . I don't do a hugely ridiculous amount of activities with the kids but I am often here. (Patrick)

One of the fathers highlighted how this secondary level of engagement held the possibility for greater interaction between father and child.

> It [is] important for me to make sure that I am there at the time [in the evening], so she has half an hour, 45 minutes of time and I am there available for her to question if need be, or to badger (Michael)

This secondary engagement in childcare may follow a format, as in Michael's case, but for the most part there is a degree of unpredictability. In one sense it is very elastic, as when fathers are in the home 'being available' opens up the possibility of more active childcaring. At the same time accessibility may not impose on the father's primary pursuit, if a child is thoroughly engaged in something else or the principal activity is complementary with availability (for example, if father and child are watching television together). Demands are also managed over a longer period and often in negotiation with another carer.

The role of father as expressed by these men would, evidently, be impossible to fulfil if they had no time with their children but also might be difficult to maintain if time with children was extremely curtailed. For fathers in other circumstances, when there are additional controls on the time available for involvement with children, the interpretation of time might be viewed differently. Intense concern has been ignited over some fathers' lack of contact time with their children after separation or divorce from a partner, whether by the choice of the father or by the actions of law courts, as the displays of protest by fathers' rights organizations such as Fathers 4 Justice bear witness. In these cases, when no time is permitted, the focus of men may turn towards a more quantitative calculation of involved fathering and childcare. Even when fathers do share time with an ex-partner, as it has been quantified at the outset and is restricted by external factors, the imposed division may still lead to an 'hours and minutes' assessment of involvement. Given the limitations of the data in this respect, this suggestion must remain speculative except to note that personal relationships may influence not only the negotiation, but also the perception of time.

When Adams wrote that 'not all times are equal' (1995:94) she was referring to the power relations that exist in the workplace governed by industrial time, but this phrase can also be applied to the childcare time of these fathers. Most of the fathers participated in a range of 'engaged' activity, from ferrying children to parties to making sure they brushed their teeth to attending school plays[3]. However, specific tasks were mentioned more often than others. Making breakfast for children was often mentioned as an activity that was the preserve of the fathers before they left in the mornings and in the evenings reading a bedtime story was a regular task. Certainly the way in which individuals recall activities and time is likely to make a difference to what was mentioned. When asked to recount a typical day it is easier to mention those tasks that are fixed in a routine and bounded; those that exist at a particular time, for a regular length of time, on a regularly timed basis. These forms of work may have been cited frequently simply because they take up relatively short periods of time and are easily memorable.

On interrogating the interviews it became clear that while some child centred tasks were merely listed, others were imbued with a deep significance for the fathering role. A father's presence at events that were seen as significant markers of a child's development and life experience were held up as a strong indication of involved fatherhood. These were often events in the school calendar – school plays, sports days and parents' evenings – or associated with children's hobbies – attending a swimming gala – and presence at these occasions was accepted as a basic obligation of parenting. They occurred infrequently, perhaps only once a year, but had a symbolic value which meant they were more highly regarded than the total amount of time committed to them would imply.

> I have already got down in my diary the dates of the school Christmas play and when I go somewhere and they say, 'let's sort out the date of the meeting, how about the 16th of December?'. I say no, I am busy (Derek, interviewed in September)

> I would say I had been to most but not all sports days. Fundamentally I pitch up (William)

It is not the case that fathering could be dismissed as taking up an insignificant amount of time; the concept of intimate fatherhood does have behavioural consequences and specific times were referenced. It is also not true that the work of fathering is entirely unfixed and could simply be coordinated around other activities. Preparing breakfast, bathing children, reading bedtime stories and attending football matches were strictly routinized, having a specific form and occurring on a frequent basis at the same time of day or week. Attending child-centred events, although they occurred much more sporadically, could not be timetabled by fathers themselves but were scheduled in advance. In addition, there were occasional mentions made of care requirements that were both irregular and entirely unpredictable such as dealing with a child's illness. A consideration of childcare labour in terms of time would therefore produce a typology based around length/extensiveness, the degree to which it is bounded, ability to schedule the time in advance and intensity of time use. The total length of time spent in fathering work, however, was not used by these men to calculate the quality of their fathering. (This may be in harmony with children's perspectives as one recent study found that there was very little difference in the scores given to resident and non-resident fathers by children in terms of involvement where there was at least some contact (Welsh *et al.*, 2004)). Further, comparing the length of time spent in individual childcare tasks does not help in assessing how important each is considered in contributing to the overall role of 'involved father'. The time that each of the interviewees spent making breakfasts was considerably longer than the time they spent attending school plays, but the latter was credited with much greater significance for the accomplishment of good fathering. In some ways, this is not radically different to the variable importance of time in paid work; some meetings are more important to attend, some tedious, routine items take up considerable amounts of time and are less productive and significant to the job than other tasks which take up relatively short periods. Yet in commentaries about employment it is the totality of working time that is highlighted and this is patently different to the complicated commentary on time and activity by these fathers in relation to the work of childcare.

Discussion: fatherhood, work and temporality

The way in which this group of fathers viewed time in relation to labour was not consistent; labour that was associated with their professional employment and conducted in the public sphere was viewed as having a different relationship to time than labour that was associated with childcare and carried out in the private sphere. In attempting to integrate forms of labour conceptually and avoid the somewhat tired dichotomies of paid/unpaid, public/private and men's work/women's work it has been noted how many boundaries have become blurred; for example with respect to work within the family and work in the public sphere (Brannen, 2002). Their limitations as useful divisions have been highlighted as awareness of the permeability of work has come to the fore. The old demarcation between private and public is not valuable *per se*, but does, in this instance, encapsulate some meaningful dimension. As Glucksmann (1998) has suggested, differences in the structure and experience of temporality is one aspect of the division between public and private as a strong split between temporalities may be indicative of a marked division between public and private. The fathers interviewed here had radically different ways of thinking about time depending on the location of the activity they were assessing.

The spatial context of the work is one component, but variations in the meaning of time also occur within categories of labour and distinctions within childcare were evident here. Childcare crosses the boundaries between paid and unpaid work and also between work and non-work, as the different kinds of time in the men's accounts of fathering highlight. Childcare is bought and sold on the market and unpaid childcare has increasingly been recognized in definitions of work. However, care for an individual's own children is included in relatively few empirical accounts (even descriptions of domestic labour have had a tendency to disregard it) and through exploring the narratives of the interviewees, it becomes clear that the classification of childcare as a work activity is also problematic for them. The aspects of parenting the fathers viewed as most significant indicated that 'caring about' was more important than 'caring for'. Childcare does not operate as a unified entity and fathers concentrated on the aspects of parenting that were least 'work-like'. Although acknowledging their existence, they downplayed the requirement to perform regular child maintenance activities. Instead they focussed on the negotiation and development of a strong relationship with their children and the activities they cited were representations of this. Previous studies have found that not only do men spend less time in childcare than women but that the time fathers do spend with children includes a higher proportion of play than child-related domestic tasks (in contrast to mothers) (Parke, 1996; Lewis, 2000) and these emotional and pleasurable elements of parenting may also be intrinsically tied up with the self-identity of the fathering role.

There is a gendering of time in that there are different valuations of men's and women's time and tasks together with different physical realities of time (Adams, 1995) but a broader temporal perspective provides another way of thinking about how the categories of 'good father' and 'good mother' diverge. Accepting that the concept of involved fathering should correspond with men spending more time with their children fails to recognize that the role of fathering may not follow the model of motherhood. The tasks that women tend to take on are time intensive, with the role of 'good mother' defined similarly to 'good worker', where time equals commitment. The same association may not apply to men. Understanding men's perceptions of the work/non-work of childcare may be informative in better comprehension of the construction of fathering identity.

Time-use surveys have become a popular and fashionable research tool. Detailed time diaries such as the UK 2000 Time Use Survey and its international counterparts have provided more exact pictures of how people really spend their time. They have contributed to attempts at deciphering how tasks are divided up within households and the multiplicities of work that may be going on at any one point in time. In particular, time-use data has raised awareness of unpaid activities and presented a way of thinking about the totality of labour. Statements such as 'men's leisure time is longer than women's' or 'women working part-time in employment do less total work than women working full-time in employment' have been made possible by calculating 'paid work time +

housework + childcare'. Because additive models necessarily imply that all time is equal, however, by reducing all activities to a calculation of hours and minutes an important aspect of how we think about time is lost. We may have an intuitive sense that this is not correct, but the dominant method of handling time in empirical analysis leads us to treat units of time equitably; any one hour is the same as any other. It is therefore important that studies of time are not restricted to quantitative analysis but combine this with a qualitative understanding of the meanings of times. Experience may not be all there is to temporality (Glucksmann, 1998) but by including perceptions of time another dimension is added to our understanding.

Exploring how fathers think about the work they perform and particularly the construction of childcare work by men highlights that in broadening the sociology of work it is necessary to take the issue of time seriously. A recognition of the importance of temporality means not only an awareness of time in the narrowest sense of time management but also, more expansively, in terms of how the association between labour activities and individuals' identities influences how time is understood. Including an awareness of how time is perceived and the way in which time is viewed differently in gendered, spatial contexts provides some insight into how activities may come to be deemed 'work' and permits an additional focus in our thinking about the organization and meaning of work.

Notes

1 The research was funded by the ESRC.
2 Lamb's (1985;1987) typology of involvement defines engagement, accessibility and responsibility.
3 The age of children influenced the kinds of childcare activities in which fathers participated.

Doing the dirty work of social class? Mothers' work in support of their children's schooling

Diane Reay

Introduction

A major achievement of feminist research has been the broadening of the concept of work to include 'the invisible labour' of the home and neighbourhood (Glucksmann, 1995; Ungerson, 1997). A growing, but still relatively neglected, aspect of domestic labour is the educative work increasingly expected of parents. Over the past twenty years there has been an increased emphasis on the accountability of parents for their children's learning, but more recently expectations that parents become 'home educators' have grown exponentially. Since the early 1990s, parental involvement has been officially recognized as a key factor in school improvement and effectiveness (Reynolds and Cuttance, 1992), and in 1994 became a requisite part of a school's development plan (OFSTED, 1994). OFSTED guidelines issued the following year (1995: 98) encouraged inspectors to explore how well schools help parents to understand the curriculum, the teaching it provides, and how this can lead to parents and teachers working together to provide educational support at home.

Miriam Glucksmann (2000a) argues that the boundaries between household and market economies, and what is produced in each, varies over time and between places. Educational activities have always gone on in middle class households and a significant numbers of working class ones. However, what has changed is the intensification of this work within the home. The educational workload of families has grown apace and school work is now seen to be the responsibility of the family as well as the teacher. Glucksmann has developed the notion of the 'total social organization of labour' which refers to 'the social division of all of the labour in a given society of whatever kind between institutional spheres' (Glucksmann, 2000a:19), and we need to deploy such an understanding of work in order to grasp both the shifting balance in relation to educational work between family and state schooling, and the current high expectations and delegated responsibilities imposed on families.

In Britain, we have reached a point at the beginning of the twenty-first century when parental involvement is no longer optional. Under the Labour Government, elected in 1997, there has been an intensification of the move from parental rights to increased parental responsibilities initiated under the previous Conservative administration (Whitty *et al.*, 1998). Edwards and Warin (1999) go as far as to argue that collaboration between home and school seems to have been superseded by the colonisation of the home by the school. Certainly, schemes like PACT and IMPACT, devised to ensure parents support their children's reading and numeracy development, are widespread (Merttens and Vass, 1993), while in 1999 home-school agreements became a statutory requirement, despite considerable disquiet from both educationalists and parent groups. According to the Government White Paper 'Excellence in Cities' (DfEE 1998a):

> 'all schools should, in discussion with parents develop a home-school contract. These agreements will reflect the respective responsibilities of home and school in raising standards, stating clearly what is expected of the school, of the parent and the pupil.'

With the home-school agreement policy, the expectation that all parents will engage in 'home-school work' with their children has become normative and part of common sense understanding about what being a parent involves (Crozier, 2000). Parents are expected to carry out a range of tasks, for example, supervising homework, attending school meetings and providing the correct equipment, as well as offering unconditional support to the school (Vincent, 2000). As Stephen Ball (2003) argues, the range of recent educational policies which emphasize parenting roles and empower parents in relation to schools have made the boundary between the private domestic sphere and the public sphere of schooling increasingly porous. Currently, we have a paradoxical situation in which the public sphere, including education, is increasingly being privatized, while the private sphere of the home is increasingly being publicly regulated and activities within it held up for scrutiny and judgement. According to Brannen (2002) family time is today's symbol of proper family life. Yet, family time is increasingly transformed into work time. As Kay Standing asserts, parental involvement in schooling has become:

> 'A form of unpaid household labour that breaks down the public/private divide by taking the work of the home into the school and that of the school into the home.'
> (Standing, 1995:2)

Now that the prevailing dominant discourse is one which sees education neither as an entitlement nor an end in its own right, but as a means to enhancing economic growth and proficiency, a case could be made that parents' work in support of their children's schooling should increasingly be viewed as an economic as well as an educational activity. What is uncontestable is that supporting schooling has a substantial economic impact on families. In 2003 for the first time in the history of state schooling, parents were spending more per annum than their children's schools on textbooks (Townsend, 2003).

This simultaneous redrawing and blurring of the boundaries between household economies and the new developing market economy in state schooling potentially increases the workload and the spending of all families. It also compounds existing educational inequalities between families. The current political preoccupation with parental involvement in education is underpinned by an assumption that all parents share an identical experience of involvement in their children's schooling. We have a discourse of parenting in which gendered, racialized and classed notions of parent are not acknowledged, rendering inequalities existing between parents invisible. The actual processes of parental involvement are very different. I want to examine these processes of supporting children's schooling more closely and develop a gendered and classed analysis of parental educational work in the home by drawing on two qualitative research studies, one of mothers' involvement in their children's schooling in two urban primary schools conducted from 1992 until 1995 (Reay, 1998b), and the second, an ESRC project on the transition to secondary schooling carried out from 1997 until 2000 (Reay and Lucey, 2003).

A gendered division of labour: Close up engagement or helping at a distance

In both research studies, within a majority of families there was a clear division of labour in which children's schooling was seen as primarily the mother's responsibility. There was little evidence in any of the women's accounts of men being closely involved in monitoring or supporting their children's educational performance. Intense daily work with children was very much the province of the mother. They were the ones with 'the finger on the pulse'. Men occasionally helped out with school work, particularly in middle-class homes and would find time to attend parents' evenings in school, but what came across very clearly was that parental involvement meant very different things to mothers and fathers. So the vast majority of fathers 'helped out', while the main responsibility lay with their female partners. 'Helping out' comprised a wide spectrum of different types of support from Janice's husband 'who'll maybe sit with them and read once in a while if I haven't got time to' to Christine's husband 'who helps a lot. He'll pick the kids up one or two nights a week, hear them read and always goes to Parents' evening'.

Fathers, and in particular the middle-class ones, were better at public prominence than private home-based support with school work, and hardly any of them got involved in the practical maintenance work that involved physical rather than mental labour, ironing school blouses or preparing packed lunches. As Evans asserts in his research into primary schooling in Australia:

'In equating parenthood with these forms of school activity, fathers are able to shift their parental responsibility from the home, to the more masculine territory of maintenance work at school or attending meetings. Within their families such fathers are

106

able to absent themselves from what little parenting they do at weekends or during evenings, in order to perform what are recognized as important tasks' (Evans, 1988:87).

As one father explained when turning down my request to interview him 'Well I suppose I'm typical of most dads in that I'm only involved at a distance'. Mothers, however, rarely had the option of being involved 'at a distance'.

Mothers as educators: 'Doing what comes naturally'

There was very little difference among women, regardless of their social class[1] or ethnicity, in either the importance they attached to education or the mental energy they devoted to their children's schooling. Where they did differ was in the types of involvement they engaged in and the level of difficulty they had to negotiate in order to be involved. Particularly in relation to involvement in academic work, mothers' own educational histories continued to exert a powerful impact on their involvement in the present. Many of the working-class women had had negative experiences of schooling, which undermined any sense of expertise in relation to academic work and left them feeling disempowered in relation to education. Cultural capital weaves itself through women's accounts of their own schooling just as much as it does in their tales of involvement in their children's schooling. The working-class women invariably talked about having mothers who were too busy working a double shift in the home and the labour market to devote any time to their educational progress. In contrast, the middle-class mothers were far more likely to refer to positive educational experiences and parental interest in their schooling. Schools may not have been making educational demands of mothers in the 1950s, 60s and 70s when these women were growing up, but that did not mean that many middle-class mothers were not independently undertaking educational work with their children in the home. This class difference was facilitated by home circumstances and the much greater availability of mothers in middle-class homes. While three-quarters of the women from working-class backgrounds had mothers who were working full time in the labour market while they were school children, more than half of the women from middle-class backgrounds had mothers who were full-time housewives while they were at school.

Inequalities resulting from the past were compounded by those in the present. Working-class mothers, particularly if they were bringing up children without the financial and emotional support of a partner, were very hard-pressed, and talked of how little free time they had after finishing paid work. Cathy's comment below was typical:

'When I get in in the evening the first thing I do is cook them something, get them to eat, a little bit of schoolwork or whatever. You see by the time I pick them up at half five or six o clock it hardly leaves you any time to do the schoolwork. You are kind of thinking about getting them ready for school the next day, you know, making sure they've got clean underwear, something ironed, sorting out something they may need to take into school the next day. Straight away I need to start thinking about what needs to be done, meals, washing up, cleaning, ironing and on top of that the spellings and the reading – it's hectic.'

Other working-class mothers were also likely to stress the physical and practical care aspects of supporting schooling – the emphasis was on sorting out clothing, making packed lunches, the trials and tribulations of getting children out of bed and into school on time – the practical maintenance work of involvement in schooling (Smith and Griffiths, 1990):

'I'm trying to get him to be more independent, but I suppose behind that I've organized everything. It all has to be organized for him so for instance his clothes are always laid out in the same place for him ready to put on. I've got a list in the kitchen of the things he needs for school and what day he needs to take what in.' (Carol, working-class mother)

It was mainly working-class mothers who spelt out the details of the practical maintenance work involved in supporting schooling. Middle-class mothers stressed other aspects of support in their interviews which nearly always stopped short of 'doing the dishes'. Here the emphasis was more on the academic: helping with curriculum assignments, doing maths cards with children, helping with vocabulary, giving support with essay writing etc. Laura is an extreme example because whenever I asked her about practical activities she invariably responded by describing a learning activity:

'You asked me about breakfast that's when I'll go over his spellings but it's hard to squeeze in. You see all three of my children learn the violin by the Suzuki method in the morning. They have to listen to the tape so at breakfast the cello tape goes on so that's when they have their practice time'. (Laura, middle-class mother)

Here the practical maintenance work disappears behind a middle class emphasis on educational and cultural support work in the home. What was striking was that for a significant number of these middle-class mothers in both research projects there were no boundaries between home and paid work. A significant number of the middle-class women worked in the education sector of the labour market as university lecturers, teachers, educational psychologists, advisors and educational administrators. Consequently, educational work in the home with their children was an extension of their paid work in the labour market.

There was a similar extension of paid work for many of the working-class women. It operated in a very different way, however, and without the returns of educational and cultural capital that the middle-class mothers' input generated. Many worked in the service sector or in servicing jobs. They were employed as cleaners, care workers, shop assistants, child minders, dinner ladies and waitresses. Here too a close correlation could be seen between the types of activities women engaged in the labour market and the activities they emphasized as important in relation to their involvement in their children's schooling. This is not to say that working-class women did not engage in academic work, they did.

Similarly, middle-class mothers undertook practical maintenance work. Rather, there was a difference of emphasis with mothers seeming to stress what they were familiar and comfortable with. This differential emphasis was supported and reinforced by a further gendered paid labour carried out in the homes of a majority of the middle-class mothers (Gregson and Lowe, 1995; Anderson, 2000). Over 60 per cent of the middle-class mothers had cleaners, au pairs, nannies or a combination of the three. Coincidentally, one of the working-class mothers in the second research project turned out to be the cleaner of one of the middle-class mothers that I interviewed. While she complained that she never had time to hear her daughter read, her employer timetabled a half hour reading slot with her son every evening. So middle-class mothers' focus on academic work was facilitated by the paid domestic labour of working-class women in middle-class homes. Maybe part of the reason why middle-class mothers did not stress the practical maintenance work of supporting children's schooling was because for a considerable number of them it was other women's work, not their own.

Conversely, many of the working-class mothers resisted a construction of themselves as their children's teachers. Their ambivalence about assuming a teaching role was rooted in mothers' differential access to dominant cultural capital and what women saw as appropriate educational work for 'people like them'. As I have argued earlier, this was linked to their paid work in the labour market, and the skills and competencies they saw themselves as possessing. As a consequence, despite all the time and energy mothers like Carla, Lisa and Cathy devoted to their children's schooling, they could not compete with their middle-class counterparts. I am not trying to create a binary between working- and middle-class women, but to describe a strong tendency across the data for women to concentrate on utilizing the skills and competencies they have developed in the labour market when engaging in involvement in schooling in the home. The working-class women's transcripts were saturated with references to 'supporting' and 'helping out'. Carol articulated this most clearly but many of the working-class women used the terminology of support and servicing to describe their involvement in children's schooling:

> 'I see my job as 'backing the teacher up'. I don't see it as being my job to teach her. I leave that to the teacher.'

In contrast, the middle-class mothers used a far more directive language in which they could be seen to be 'taking control', exercising initiative, and 'laying down the rules':

> 'I had to really push to get things done. Richard was having problems and I wanted him assessed but school couldn't really see the problems so I had to keep on going in, talk to the teacher, go and see the Headteacher. If I hadn't kept on going in nothing would have happened. I had to make them see there was a problem and do something about it.' (Jane, middle-class mother)

> 'I spent hours talking to the Headteacher and she wasn't doing anything so I went to the Borough authority and asked for support. The Head didn't like it but they sent

someone and she assessed him. That's why he has a special support teacher because I got him assessed. It was recognized as a school assessment because even though I initiated it, it was done through the school.' (Lilian, middle-class mother)

In all of this we can see the importance of temporality and spatiality that Glucksmann (2000a) emphasizes in her concept of 'the total social organization of labour'. Work in very different times and places impacts on contemporary mothers' work in support of schooling in the domestic sphere. But there is a further issue about the work this work does. There is a sedimentation of levels of privilege; an accumulation of advantage/disadvantage from work in other times and places – the contemporary labour market as well as the homes these mothers grew up in.

Complementing, compensating or modifying: differing roles in relation to schooling

Similar class differences to the ones that I have described in relation to the work of parental involvement were also evident in the roles mothers adopted towards schooling. While the largest group of mothers, predominantly the working-class women, conceptualized their relationship to schooling as one of complementing the education their children received, a further group, in particular middle-class mothers, saw their role as a compensatory one. Other mothers, also predominantly middle-class, spoke about their efforts to modify the school provision. These three roles were by no means mutually exclusive. Middle-class mothers moved in and out of different positions with regard to schooling. They could do 'the supportive work' but also, at times, saw a need for being directive and 'taking charge'. For these women 'supporting the teacher' could rapidly transmute into 'being the teacher'. Manju employed a tutor for her daughter but also took on a teaching role in the home:

'Education starts at home, starts from her time after school actually. She is in year five now and I feel she has to do some serious work at home because she hasn't covered a lot of the stuff at school. I find I'm having to compensate despite the fact that according to the school she's doing quite well.'

Similarly, Claire sent Sophie to Kumon Maths classes and oversaw her practice every evening, as well as setting Sophie additional educational work:

'We go over the Kumon maths techniques every evening, that takes about half an hour. But then I've been worrying about her writing standards so I've been setting her essay writing so we can concentrate on writing techniques, grammar, spelling, punctuation, all that sort of stuff.'

Parental involvement is gendered; it is also powerfully classed. Mothers were investing time and energy in the types of school support that 'came naturally'. And for working-class mothers, neither taking control when there are

110

educational problems nor intense academic drilling and emphasis on high status cultural activities came naturally. I am not arguing that it came naturally to all the middle-class mothers, there is an issue of degree here. But academic work was far more likely to be 'what people like us did' for the middle-class mothers than it was for working-class mothers. Economic capital also had a contributory and compounding impact, and not just in relation to the ability to pay for domestic help. A few of the middle-class families I interviewed were spending over £100 a week on private tuition and cultural activities such as music and drama for their child – more than some of the working-class lone mothers on benefit were getting in total to live on. The norm. however, among the middle-class families was to pay for at least one out-of-school activity, while a sizeable minority paid for their child to attend two or three.

Being able to afford culturally and educationally enriching activities added to middle class educational advantage. Many of the middle-class parents had themselves done very well at school and this educational success translated into self-confidence and a sense of entitlement in relation to parental involvement. So cultural capital is powerfully implicated in mothers' ability to successfully support their children's schooling. Financial resources, the requisite skills and competencies, confidence in relation to the educational system, a previously history of being supported educationally in the home, educational knowledge and information about schooling all had a bearing on the extent to which mothers felt empowered to intervene in their child's educational trajectory and the confidence with which they embarked on such action. For Angie, a white, working-class lone mother, whose account stresses over and over again the importance of education, her personal feelings of incompetence and lack of confidence mitigated against her embarking on any action with a sense of efficacy:

> 'I have tried, I really have. I knew I should be playing a role in getting Darren to read but I wasn't qualified. Therefore it put extra pressure on me because I was no good at reading myself, it was too important for me to handle and I'd get very upset and angry at Darren.'

Attempting to modify the school's offer also had unpredictable and upsetting consequences:

> 'I always found if I went to the classteacher, she'd take it very personal and think I was attacking her. I wasn't. I was just bringing it to her attention in case she didn't know, you know, that in my opinion he's not progressing. The way I see him and from what I expect of him I don't see the progress. But I'd say 'I'm not saying that it's because you're not teaching my son. I do realize you have a class of thirty and you're only one person and you do so much and you're expected to do a lot of other things because the National Curriculum expects so much of you. I do understand about that. But what can I do about his reading?' But when I did go to the classteachers I think they took it too personal and felt I was attacking them when really it was that it is so important I couldn't let it go.'

It is important to reiterate that there exists a significant minority of parents whose own negative experiences of schooling makes involvement in their children's schooling difficult, even painful (McNamara *et al.*, 2000). Working-class mothers invariably cited the pitfalls, dangers and misunderstandings they encountered in their own education. Working-class mothers who feel ill-equipped to engage in repair work in the home and lack financial resources are reliant on the school to get the job done. For Josie, in particular, the school had come to be perceived as 'the last and only resort'. Her personal history of immigration, working-class background and academic failure resulted in a sense that there were no other options:

> 'When I went to see his teacher I was pretty upset about Leigh not reading and it may have come across like 'how come Leigh's not reading. If you aren't hearing him read what are you doing then?' I was maybe coming across like that but what I meant was can he possibly have some extra time. Can someone hear (sic), for God's sake, give him some extra reading and let him get on because it's making my life harder. I was getting so anxious about him not reading cos I couldn't really help him. I'd get upset and frustrated and it wasn't doing Leigh any good because if he can't read what was happening.' (Josie).

Within the sphere of parental involvement, a potent cocktail of personal educational history, labour market position, paid domestic labour support or its absence, and the skills and competencies developed both inside and outside of the labour market generate powerful reproductive tendencies that shape the relationship between class groupings and education. Women were mostly reproducing their classed position in the labour market in their educational work in the home and this work contributed to and intensified educational inequalities. The ways in which inequalities are exacerbated by the intensification of parental involvement in schooling are made clear in Maria's words:

> 'You need parental involvement, you need parents to be able to complement what you are doing but that's all it should be. It shouldn't be any more. You see not all parents can do it. Not all parents speak English, not all parents read and write so how can they help their children at home. They're at a disadvantage anyway so when they come to school they've got to have the help there. You should be able to say to the teacher 'Look I can't do it. You're qualified, can you do something about it?' without the teacher getting all upset. There's a lot of parents who can't, just can't do it.'

Supporting children's schooling was an easier process if mothers had access to material and cultural resources and the opportunity to develop educational skills and competencies. Women need to feel confident about tackling educational work in the home and to have access to material resources to support such work. Without these other essential ingredients of cultural capital, the time of mothers like Angie, Maria and Josie did not count to anything like the same extent as that of the more privileged women. Yet, it is mothers like Maria, Josie and Angie who are being targeted under current educational initiatives despite the fact that they are the mothers with the fewest resources with which to meet government demands for parental involvement.

Conclusion

The work of social reproduction is located in the interlinking of the domestic sphere with public institutions. The self-production of class collectivities (Wacquant, 1991: 52) goes on in the home and is predominantly the work of mothers. Mothers, not fathers, are the target of policy moves to improve home-school relationships, while the redistribution of responsibility for education away from schools and towards parents (Mayall, 2002) has disproportionately increased the workload of women in relation to that of male partners.

The last twenty years has seen the transformation of women's domestic labour to include extensive educational work in the home. As I have tried to demonstrate through data from two research studies on home school relationships, in the sphere of parental involvement, the division between the public and the private has started to collapse in on itself. For a majority of mothers in both studies there is a continuation rather than a separation of their paid work with work in support of their children's schooling. This is not to posit any causal link. Rather, women's waged work generated particular tendencies in relation to the nature of their involvement in children's schooling. The type of paid work they undertook did not determine the sort of involvement they had but it did help to explain what were largely class patterns of involvement.

What is key, however, is the work that this mainly maternal work does. The research studies, discussed above, of mothers' work in support of children's education within the state system suggests a very different relationship between women and social class from orthodox perspectives which view their activities as largely peripheral. Over twenty years ago Basil Bernstein suggested that changes in the composition of the middle classes were transforming the mother 'into a crucial preparing agent of cultural reproduction who provides access to symbolic forms and shapes the dispositions of her children so they are better able to exploit the possibilities of public education' (Bernstein, 1975:131). The mothers in both these studies, in particular middle-class mothers, are at the front line of social reproduction, heavily investing in terms of time and mental and emotional labour. Mothers have a different relationship to the generation of cultural capital and, concomitantly, social class than fathers. It is mothers who are making cultural capital work for their children. And it is they, more than men, who appear to be the agents of social class reproduction. In particular, mothering work bridges the gap between family social class and children's performance in the classroom. Maternal practices demonstrate that class is much more than materiality (Reay, 1997). It is played out, not only in mothers' activities in support of children's schooling, but also in women's attitudes, assumptions and levels of entitlement in relation to their children's education. It is mothers who are the arbiters of taste (Bourdieu, 1984) and the home based educators of their children. And the work they do as mothers is often more important than the work they do in the labour market in maintaining social hierarchy and the class inequalities that underpin it.

Class practices are historically specific. At the beginning of the 21st century, class processes within families are integrally linked to the operations of the wider marketplace. An analysis which conceptualizes mothering work as strategically located in relation to schooling systems allows for an understanding of mothering work as social reproduction in action. Within a capitalist society in which market forces are ascendent (Hutton, 1995; Jordan, Redley and James, 1994), 'acting in their child's best interests' inevitably means middle-class mothers are simultaneously acting against the interests of the children of other, less privileged, mothers. As I have pointed out earlier, this is not to blame middle-class mothers but rather to see all mothers as caught up in educational markets which operate on the (il)logic of 'to her who has yet more shall be given'. Educational success becomes a function of social, cultural and material advantages in which mothers' caring within the family is transmuted by the operations of the wider marketplace to serve its competitive, self-interested individualistic ethos. Mothers' practical maintenance, educational and emotional work underpins the workings of educational markets contributing to a culture of winners and losers within which one child's academic success is at the expense of other children's failure.

Theorizing such social inequalities has become increasingly problematic within a contemporary educational marketplace underpinned by a rhetoric of classlessness. Current discourses of classlessness perpetuate the fantasy that ungendered parents only have to make the right choices for their children for educational success to automatically follow. As the words of the women in both research studies illustrate, the reality is far more complex. It is one in which gender, 'race' and class continue to make significant differences. In Britain class infuses everyday practices and social interactions. As Beck argues:

> 'It is evident in speech . . . in the sharp class divisions between residential areas . . . in types of education, in clothing and in everything that can be included under the concept of 'lifestyle'' (Beck, 1992:102)

Implicit within the concept of 'a classless society' are more equitable social relations and enhanced mobility. However, despite all the talk of classlessness and increased social mobility, in the 2000s British class differentials in educational attainment remain the same as they were fifty years ago (Blanden and Gregg, 2004; Stewart, 2005). Parental, and in particular, mothers' involvement in children's schooling contributes to the maintenance of this inequitable status quo. This is not the same as asserting that reducing parental involvement will result in the reduction of educational inequalities. Rather, I would argue, that within the contemporary individualistic, competitive, educational marketplace with its rhetoric of 'doing the best for your own child', the middle classes will always utilize their economic and cultural resources to ensure the continued

114

reproduction of their children's educational advantage and it is mothers who are at the front line, ensuring the hard work of reproduction gets done.

Notes

1 The social class attribution of mothers was based on a composite of socio-economic categorization, both their own, their partners and their parents, their own level of educational qualifications and that of their parents, housing tenure, and how they self-defined in class terms. The intention was to work with three groupings, the unambiguously middle-class, the unambiguously working-class and a third grouping that I have called elsewhere (Reay, 1998b) women on the boundaries of class. However, in both samples this latter grouping was small, being less than 10% of the total.

Part 4
Challenging the boundaries of the public and private spheres

Part 4

Rethinking voluntary work

Rebecca F. Taylor

Introduction

There is an enduring stereotype of the volunteer as a middle-class 'lady' juggling church jumble sales and charity lunches. The reality is that voluntary work – unpaid work outside the home – takes a wide variety of forms in contemporary British society. It includes activities as diverse as manning a lifeboat or refereeing a youth club football match, and the work takes place not only within voluntary organizations and charities, but also in commercial companies and arts organizations, statutory social services departments and informally in local communities. Neither are the numbers who engage in this work insignificant. A survey in 1997 by the National Centre for Volunteering, found almost half of the population engaged in some form of formal (organization based) voluntary work in the previous 12 months and almost a third volunteered regularly every month. These figures increased if informal work by an individual (such as helping a neighbour) was taken into account, with 74 percent of the population having taken part in the previous year (Davis Smith, 1998).

Survey data reveals other important characteristics of those who volunteer. Despite the gendered stereotype, men are as likely to volunteer as women. According to the 1997 survey, 48 per cent of men and 48 per cent of women volunteered. Other elements of the stereotype are more accurate. Volunteers do tend to be white, middle class, middle aged and well-educated. For example 54 per cent of those who left school at 16 had done some volunteering compared to 80 per cent of those who left education at 21+ (Davis Smith, 1998: table 2.7). In relation to socio-economic groups, 37 per cent of unskilled manual workers undertook voluntary work compared with 58 per cent of skilled manual workers and 72 per cent of professional managerial workers (Davis Smith, 1998: table 2.5). Socio-economic position affects not only whether someone volunteers, but also the nature of the unpaid work that they do. For example, 52 per cent of volunteers from professional backgrounds sat on committees compared with 22 per cent of volunteers from an unskilled manual work background, and women were more likely to be fundraising while men were more likely to be engaged in sports-related activities (Davis Smith, 1998: table 2.3).

The volunteering statistics are based on surveys that tend to assume people define themselves as 'volunteers' and what they do as 'volunteering'. They are less likely to capture informal activities which are more likely to be conducted by those from manual and unskilled social groups (Davis Smith, 1998). Despite these issues, however, they reveal that different forms of unpaid labour are undertaken by different social groups, within different social contexts. The questions this chapter seeks to address are concerned with understanding these differences and examining what motivates people to do unpaid work in the public sphere and how this work is meaningful in terms of their social practices, priorities and norms. The substantive content is based on a qualitative research project in which 29 depth interviews were carried out with paid and unpaid workers in two voluntary sector organizations (Taylor, 2002). In the context of a new sociology of work, the empirical research raises important issues about what counts as work and how people's working lives are understood. The chapter highlights how different types of labour in different domains are organized at a social structural level.

The existing literature on volunteering within the domain of social policy that formed the backdrop to this research, provides little insight into the social aspects of voluntary work, lacking both a critical perspective that acknowledges the role of structures of power, and a rich qualitative body of research data which could be mined for meaningful accounts of unpaid work in people's working lives. The first part of the chapter provides a brief critique of this literature and, by going on to historically examine unpaid work, sheds light on the way certain culturally constructed assumptions continue to inform policy understandings and research methodology. Focusing on five interviewees from the research, the paper then examines how their education and upbringing shaped their priorities and expectations about their working lives. Their class position is understood through Bourdieu's concept of habitus (1990) and the chapter explores how this habitus provided them with an orientation to work: a taste for particular types of work and strategies for organizing their work. Their work practices are embedded in their class identity and their class identity is defined and represented through their work, paid or unpaid, public or private.

The choices and decisions people make about their work over the course of their lives, however, are also shaped by the structure of the labour market, and the value and type of capital they posses. The final section of the paper goes on to explore how unpaid work in the public sphere is organized, the nature of the field for different types of work, and the methods of recruitment and promotion within and between paid and unpaid positions. It explores changes in the balance of paid and unpaid positions in a particular field, such as health care or community work, in relation to the impact of shifts in social practice or policy initiatives and the effects that these have on the options available to the individuals in the research. In particular it highlights how political and monetary priorities of the Conservative government in the 1980s and early 90s opened

120

up particular configurations of paid and unpaid positions and closed down others.

The literature on voluntary work

Research on voluntary work and volunteering has been shaped by policy makers' interest in the nature of the voluntary sector and its relationship with the state, particularly in terms of the provision of services (Kramer, 1990). Successive governments have viewed voluntary work as a cost-effective weapon in the fight against particular social problems such as 'juvenile delinquency' and 'unemployment' (Sheard, 1992). The 'Millennium Volunteers', a New Labour initiative, aims to encourage young people to get involved in activities to help their community. Whilst voluntary sector organizations have, in response to these initiatives and a drive towards contracting out public services, been encouraged to increase their use of volunteers, a perceived dearth in numbers volunteering has created a particular climate for research. The result has been a largely organizational and managerial literature that sees volunteers as a group who are interesting in as much as they need to be recruited, supported and retained. Although policy research in this area may start from the question 'why do people volunteer?', the answers are sought primarily in Human Resource management strategies (see, for example, Hadley and Hatch, 1981; Billis, 1989; Handy, 1988; Knight, 1993; Marshall, 1994; Kramer, 1990). Nor are these answers provided by rigorous qualitative research. Instead open and closed questions in large social surveys or, occasionally, focus groups produce uniform and un-illuminating findings regarding motivations for volunteering. Davis Smith notes one problem of these surveys being that '. . . confronted with a checklist of reasons for volunteering it is possible that people might choose the one most socially acceptable, that is 'wanting to help others''(1992:84). Other common reasons for starting volunteering given by those surveyed are: 'being asked by friends or relatives', 'association with an organization', or 'having time on their hands'. The real problem, Roger Sherrott has argued, is that 'these studies have sought simply to categorise the statements of motive uttered by volunteers while giving little attention to the circumstances and life histories of which these motives are a product'. These statements are taken as the end rather than the start of the research process and as Sherrott goes on to point out there is no indication of why 'having time on their hands' led someone to volunteer and not do something else, or why they said yes when someone asked them to help. (1983:62).

More problematically the policy literature rests on the assumption that volunteering is by definition a positive activity, 'beneficial' for the volunteer, those they help, and society at large. Groups such as young people or black and minority ethnic communities who find themselves under-represented in the volunteering statistics are assumed to be 'missing out'. Their volunteering becomes the focus of various initiatives aimed at increasing participation (see, for example, Obaze (1992) and Gaskin (1998)). However, despite the social inclusion agenda and the visibility of class, ethnicity, level of education and gender in the surveys as characteristics that define who volunteers, these categories are strangely absent from attempts to understand why people engage in voluntary work. Nor are any links made between what these survey/focus group participants do – the particular form their voluntary work takes – and their motivations for doing it. Neither the type of activity engaged in, nor the social characteristics of the volunteer are explored in relation to statements of motive. It is the equivalent of asking a sample of people in paid employment why they work and attempting to make sense of their answers without any reference to the particular job that they do, or to their social position.

These problems are not simply a product of narrow policy-driven research questions. A more critical approach is difficult given the conceptual underpinnings of these studies. In the first place voluntary work has been entirely separated from the concept of work itself, with research into these two activities differentiated from one another within disparate academic domains. Whilst the concept of work has been reduced to paid employment and assumed to be a self-interested search for economic reward, voluntary work has in opposition been defined as a selfless activity motivated by rewards that must be disinterested and so by definition, not actually work (Taylor, 2002). Thus voluntary work has been reduced to a policy/morality issue embedded in debates around citizenship (Howlett and Lock: 1999), or reduced at a conceptual level to the individualized study of psychological propensity (Bales, 1996) or altruism (Griffiths, 1979; Horton Smith, 1981). In explaining volunteering these texts often resort to the language of needs and urges that are perceived to be 'natural' (see for example Griffiths, 1979; Titmuss, 1970). Jos Sheard provides an example of a common motif in the voluntary work literature.

> 'volunteering clearly taps into a natural urge that people have to help their fellow citizens, at the same time it enables individuals to place boundaries around their involvement and thus provide a safe structured outlet for their altruism and social concern' (1992:122).

The point being made in this chapter is not that psychological motives are invalid as explanations, but that they do not define the difference between paid and unpaid work outside the private sphere. For example, studies of the professions or those who hold salaried positions within the welfare state and the civil service have also argued that altruism is a key factor in explaining their work (Page, 1996). Altruism does not define the volunteer anymore than self interest defines the employee, and it cannot render other social, economic and cultural factors irrelevant to understanding what people do. By psychologizing voluntary work, the policy literature has effectively erased its history. Voluntary work is regarded almost as a permanent feature of British society, part of the national psyche and as such beyond the reach of a social critique. Prochaska, for example, argues that:

'whether they call their work voluntarism, community action, or the
of philanthropy or charity, the possibilities in self-help and helping
today in a manner reminiscent of a hundred years ago.' (1988:7)

Reducing all unpaid work in the public sphere to a model o
enacted by the middle classes, however, does not help us to
people do unpaid public work in contemporary society. In fact it obscures class
and gender differences, and the (changing) relationship between paid and
unpaid forms of work in different spheres. Perhaps most worryingly, it has
enabled researchers to make moral judgements about the legitimacy of their
respondents' motivations for volunteering: such as criticising those they interviewed who saw voluntary work as a route into paid work on the basis that it
'inverts the spirit of voluntary work which by its very nature is based on the
desire to help others . . .' (Britton, 1999).

A brief history of voluntary work

A more critical reading of history reveals how 'the volunteer', and the symbolic
meanings assigned to unpaid work, are a product of the social relations and
organization of labour in particular historical periods. In the first place, voluntary work is essentially unpaid work in the public sphere, therefore there needs
to be a clear distinction between public and private spheres as the location of
work in order for it to exist. It can be argued that in Britain this was not the
case until industrialization had enforced the divide between home and work.
Secondly, it is not possible to have a concept of voluntary work until there is an
opposing concept of employment where 'work' signifies paid work in the public
sphere. The latter half of the 19th century not only saw the creation of the phenomenon of 'unemployment', referring to those not in paid work (Kumar,
1988), but it also saw the adoption of the term 'volunteer' to refer to those in
charitable and philanthropic associations who were working but not employed.
The term 'volunteer' had, until this point, referred almost exclusively to men in
the unpaid militia – a product of various crises during the 18th century
(Cunningham, 1975:18–33). Prior to industrialization such distinctions in relation to workers were not meaningful, because employment as it is understood
in contemporary Britain did not exist. The 'volunteer' is a product of industrialization and the attendant distinctions and divisions in social class that
characterized the period of its creation.

The 19th century saw the rise of the middle class and alongside this a surge
in the establishment of philanthropic institutions and voluntary associations
that created a new world of civic and professional power dominated by the
middle-class urban elites (Morris, 1983: 96; Owen, 1964). Historically there was
a visible shift in the late 18th / early 19th century from informal and individualized charitable acts to organized formal volunteering under the guise of philanthropy. This is exemplified by the process whereby the informal charitable

ing of gentlewomen to tenants on their estate was replaced by the scientific charity of middle-class Victorian visiting societies which in turn gave rise to social workers and health visitors – that is, paid professionals. The projects of professional closure embarked on by various middle-class occupational groups built on the symbolic and cultural capital they acquired through philanthropic work. For example, the unpaid work of physicians and surgeons in the expanding voluntary hospital system provided them with access to operating theatres, laboratories, training material in the form of the diseased and injured poor, and the management committees of the hospitals themselves. In this way they acquired the knowledge and power necessary to transform themselves into a medical elite and secure their position near the top of the middle-class social hierarchy (Owen, 1964).

The term 'volunteer' applied to a distinct category of unpaid worker in these organizations. It did not refer to those at the top of philanthropic associations, such as chairmen or secretaries whose roles were already legitimized by a job title and attendant power and status. Rather its usage became necessary to distinguish the mass of unpaid 'helpers' in the field who constituted the lower levels of the graded structures of voluntary and philanthropic organizations from the newly emerging semi-professionals: social workers, nurses and health visitors, who were starting to be employed by these organizations. Thus it was the introduction of paid workers in formal employment relations in these organizations that lead to the creation of the volunteer.

These categories of worker were also inherently gendered. The Evangelical doctrine that informed many middle-class Victorian practices defined women as guardians of the domestic sphere and their role as providing the spiritual education of their children, caring for their family, encouraging their husbands' religious sensibilities, and setting an example to servants and neighbours (Hall, 1992; Davidoff, 1995). Paid employment was regarded as the antithesis of women's nature and duty and tantamount to prostitution. Unpaid charity work, however, tied as it was to the agenda of setting an example to those lower down in the social order, was a highly desirable activity for middle-class women and became one of the only legitimate roles open to them outside their domestic positions as wives and mothers. Sarah Ellis noted in 1869:

> 'As society is at present constituted a lady may do almost anything from motives of charity or zeal . . . but so soon as a women begins to receive money however great her need, . . . the heroine is transformed into a tradeswomen.' (Cited in *Prochaska*, 1980:6)

The increasing circumscription of women's access to paid employment, and the new public domains of middle-class civil and political power (Hall, 1992) lent philanthropy its distinctive gendered nature. The Victorian 'volunteers' tended to be women, since men were less likely to be merely 'helpers' and more likely to reside in the upper echelons of these organizations. Thus it was middle class women that came to characterize the 'volunteer'. The term volunteer, however, does not capture **all** those engaging in unpaid work in the 19th century, as the example of the unpaid public work of the working class highlights.

124

The 19th century saw working-class membership of cooperatives, friendly societies, temperance societies and other self help associations explode, as did membership of labour organizations and trade unions. Estimates put membership of friendly societies at 4 million, trade unions at 1 million, and co-operatives at half a million by the late 19th century (Davis Smith *et al.*, 1995:30). Like the philanthropic associations, these organizations were run by committees and required not only members or subscribers but those who were prepared to contribute their skills and time unpaid in positions such as secretary, shop steward, administrator, treasurer, collector and, in the case of friendly societies, 'father' who guarded the funds. In the highly democratic structure of the friendly societies, unpaid officials were usually elected or chosen in rotation (Finlayson, 1994:68). Although the positions were unpaid and in many cases similar to the work done by middle-class volunteers in philanthropic organizations, those who held them were not defined as volunteers.

Working-class participation in these organizations was driven by a rather different set of material circumstances and cultural values to those that encouraged philanthropic activity amongst the middle classes. Working-class societies, whether they were benefit, campaigning or labour organizations, were concerned primarily with protecting members in the case of death or illness or providing their members with a living wage. They also carried out an important function organizing social evenings and events (Harrison, 1971:141). Their central tenets were of mutual aid rather than helping the less fortunate, and they were guided not by goals of scientific progress or professionalisation, but by the need to survive the insecurity and poverty of industrial capitalism. David Zeldin has argued that friendly societies, trade unions, co-operatives and community groups, were nurtured by labour politics and working-class notions of 'solidarity' (1983:115). It was not only formalized working-class unpaid labour that was not defined as voluntary work. Historical social research has touched on the existence of informal mutual support networks within working-class communities, particularly the role of reciprocal domestic labour arrangements between women (Anderson, 1971; Tebbutt, 1995; Glucksmann, 2000a). These working-class forms of reciprocal labour and community support, however, were never defined as voluntary work and efforts to unpack these labour relationships are hampered by the lack of both contemporary and historical research in this area (exception of Parry, this volume).

The meanings contemporary researchers and policy makers attribute to voluntary work are not free from its history. The political drivers to this research area mean that authors continue to attempt to understand all unpaid work activities in the same terms despite the significant differences in the origins, nature and meanings of the work. The distinctions between working-class and middle-class unpaid work, formal and informal work and between those who call themselves volunteers and those who do not, are crucial in understanding contemporary narratives of unpaid work. Issues of power, privilege and respectability on the one hand, and community support, solidarity and reciprocity on the other, are likely to be embedded in the meanings and practices that exist today. As in the Victorian era, unpaid work in the public sphere in contemporary Britain is inherently bound up with the wider social organization of labour and the nature of relationships between public and private, formal and informal, paid and unpaid work. This chapter goes on to explore these issues in relation to people's experiences of doing unpaid work in contemporary society.

The research and the interviewees

The research was conducted with paid and unpaid workers in two organizations chosen to capture very different ends of the spectrum of voluntary organizations, from local and informal to national and highly organized. The names of the two organizations and interviewees, and any identifying details have been changed to provide anonymity. 'North End Community and Refugee project', located in an inner London borough, worked closely with local asylum seekers and other ethnic minority groups, providing services that included education outreach, English classes, housing advice, and a range of cultural groups and events. 'Care Aid', a national health care charity founded at the end of the 19th century, focused on the provision of emergency first aid cover and training, and also ran a number of services such as 'hospital after care', staffed by volunteers, and domiciliary care, staffed by paid care assistants. Care Aid also ran a refugee centre in central London that provided a befriending service staffed by volunteers.

The 29 who were interviewed were purposively sampled to represent a cross section of workers in each organization. They worked in paid and unpaid positions that reflected the social characteristics of each organization's workforce. They ranged in age from 19 to 68, with slightly more women than men, and covered a range of socio economic groups, from professionals to unskilled staff. They included individuals from Somalia, the Philippines, Chile and Ethiopia, reflecting North End's broad community base, although the majority of the workers at Care Aid were white British. The interviews, which lasted between one and two hours, covered topics such as the nature of their work, their education, work history, family and parents' work. The questions were designed to explore how these individuals understood the different forms of work in which they engaged, their priorities and the decisions they made with regard to work, and the various ways they organized and juggled different jobs. The majority of those interviewed were involved in regular voluntary work, most of which was formal and over half were doing more than one job, often juggling a mixture of paid and unpaid work. It was not possible to characterize and distinguish 'paid workers' and 'unpaid workers'. Those who worked paid for one organization often worked unpaid for another or the same organization and vice versa.

The many differences (generational, cultural, social, etc.) between the 29 research participants meant that their work histories and their understandings of these histories were incredibly diverse. This chapter focuses on 5 cases:

Elizabeth, in her 50s, President of the Care Aid branch; Maria in her 40s, fundraising officer at North End; Sophie in her early 20s, acting unit manager at Care Aid's refugee centre; Tony in his early 40s, vice president of the Care Aid branch; and Diane in her 40s, assistant care services manager at the Care Aid branch. These interviewees were chosen to represent a range (although by no means all) of the experiences and issues that were highlighted by the wider sample. The next sections explore why and how these individuals undertook, or in some cases did not undertake, unpaid work in the public sphere.

Family, education and orientation to work

The interviewees' descriptions of their upbringing and family life made it possible to explore the transmission across generations of cultural values, priorities and practices, in particular those that shaped orientations to work, defining appropriate jobs, areas of work and ways of making a living. For some, their orientation to work was so embedded in their habitus that they naturalized these practices, describing their work as driven by particular personality traits inherited from their parents. Those who rejected their parents' values and choices with regard to work and career saw themselves as 'breaking the mould' or 'going against the grain'. The different ways voluntary work was framed within individuals' work narratives highlighted the different meanings it had for those with different social and cultural backgrounds, and echoed the historically constructed class differences touched on earlier. Elizabeth, Care Aid's unpaid president who also ran a smallholding with her husband and bred and sold livestock, provided an interesting contrast to Diane, Care Aid's paid assistant manager, a qualified nurse and also a lone parent. These two women's class positions and their parents' work ethos gave rise to their very distinct orientations to work and attitudes towards unpaid work.

Elizabeth's upper-class family of were of 'independent means' and she stressed the non-economic character of her parents' work, describing how her father, who began his career in the navy, went on to hold several unpaid directorships and 'unpaid positions in several charities'. Her mother raised the children and undertook extensive charity work that included St Johns Ambulance, Church of England Children's Society and the Parish Council. Diane's parents, on the other hand, could be defined as *petit bourgeois*, coming from what she described as 'self-made', 'well to do' families. Her maternal grandfather owned a garment factory and her paternal grandfather owned a haulage business, although both enterprises eventually failed. Diane's own parents became publicans and this enabled them to continue the family's ethos of self employment.

For Elizabeth's parents, unremunerated charitable work was an integral part of their working life the importance of which was passed on to their children. Elizabeth and her siblings were all heavily involved in charitable work. As she put it: 'volunteering was very much the ethos we were brought up with'. It was a practice supported by a family narrative of moral obligation and social duty to those less privileged, which echoed the Victorian philanthropic tradition. Elizabeth explained that 'giving something back' was regarded as a requirement of those who were 'lucky enough to have all they needed'. This involvement required little effort on her part. Although she had had no formal education (she had never been to school) and no qualifications, her extended family's social networks in the charity world provided what she described as 'a real old boy's network' through which she could access public positions of power. As she herself acknowledged, she had very little choice in the matter; her recruitment to Care Aid and subsequent career can be seen as a product of the expectations, obligations and recognition attendant on her social position and relations:

> 'The president of Care Aid twenty years ago was Lady Summerville and she was at a presidents' conference and my sister, then I think she was deputy president of Cheshire, and she said, "Surely, you've got three sisters, one of them must live in Berkshire?" and Anne said, "Yes." So I got asked to dinner and Lady Alice is a wonderful lady, very frightening, and said "I'm about to give up and I want to hand over".'

In this context, just as it had for many upper- and middle-class Victorian women with little formal education, unpaid work provided Elizabeth and her sisters with a career with considerable social status for those who otherwise would have few ways to access public power. Like the Victorian volunteers, the power inherent in this work comes not only from the social capital required to access the positions but also from the symbolic capital signalled by its moral aesthetic, the apparent 'disinterested' nature of the work and the distance of their (labour) practices from necessity. Although such work was impossible without a private income, its economic foundations were effectively disguised by its claim to moral legitimacy and disinterest. In this sense, as a form of symbolic capital, the unpaid work of women like Elizabeth was crucial in the reproduction and maintenance of class structures and practices.

Diane's experience and understanding of work, and voluntary work in particular, provides an interesting contrast. Her family's working life was shaped by a concern with self sufficiency, respectability and independence from what they regarded as an over-intrusive state, characterized as 'paying your own way' and not relying on the state or charity for support. It was not voluntary work that provided status for her parents but demonstrating their self-made wealth through such practices as membership of the Masons, which was felt to be 'really only for the elite'. In contrast to Elizabeth's family, any association with 'those less fortunate' was to be avoided, as this description of her mother's attitudes to charity makes clear:

> 'her family always paid their way, it would be everything private and, you know, if there's someone begging in the street . . . "Oh you don't want to go near them dear, you might catch something", that kind of attitude. They wouldn't rely on anyone's charity, they had to be self-made and, obviously, if you hadn't made any money you were a lazy wotsit and, you know, useless.'

Unlike Elizabeth, whose voluntary work was embedded in her habitus, within Diane's family's orientation to work, voluntary work was unthinkable. Diane herself had never done any and she explained in a rather embarrassed way that she probably never would as she was 'too lazy', thus naturalizing her choice as a character trait. Indeed, although Diane's position at Care Aid was in a paid role she noted that 'it goes against the grain what I do,' adding that her mother was only really impressed by her Care Aid uniform and had little interest in her work. 'It's alien, especially for my mother (. . .) she doesn't really believe in charity.' Whilst Care Aid was a part of Elizabeth's social world and networks, it was not a part of Diane's. Her family's resources – economic, social and symbolic – were invested in the Masons and she trained as a Registered General Nurse (RGN) at a Royal Masonic hospital. Most of her early nursing career was in private hospitals and nursing homes and she explained she 'didn't know where the Care Aid centre was':

'. . . I couldn't have told you that there were centres, probably walked about with my eyes closed . . . we never had Care Aid mentioned in my hospital work at all or even in homes.'

In a rather different vein Tony, deputy president of Care Aid, partner in an accountancy firm, school governor and unpaid auditor for several local charities, came from a working-class background. His father was a steel worker who was made redundant in his 40s and remained unemployed for the rest of his life after suffering a heart attack. His mother was a housewife. Like Diane, neither of his parents engaged in voluntary work and he too described them as not coming 'from a terribly well disposed to charity background'. He explained that his brother did not understand why he did voluntary work. Unlike Elizabeth and Diane, Tony's account of his family's work was brief and highlighted the differences between his life and work ethos and theirs, rather than the connections. Tony volunteered briefly whilst at college, where he fell in with a group who were engaged in fundraising for local disadvantaged young people. It was his professional work, however, that provided him with access to high status unpaid roles in various charities, Care Aid in particular. Tony's social mobility from working-class boy to middle-class processional was underpinned by his unpaid roles and the status they endowed. After working his way up the ladder at the accountancy firm he joined as article clerk on leaving college, Tony was invited to become a senior partner. This invitation came with a particular set of expectations and obligations, which initially involved taking on the role of Care Aid Treasurer vacated by the senior partner in his firm. 'I had a lot of respect for him and if he had lived with it for 25 years it couldn't be all bad'. Tony adds 'I could have said no but I didn't.' Interestingly, despite the fact that this unpaid work was an expectation of his position as partner he preferred to understand it as a disposition, noting how 'the people that are more likely to, shall we say, 'get on' here, are more likely to have the same disposition as the ruling body or the partners if you like'.

What these very different orientations to work demonstrate is the variety of class based meanings ascribed to voluntary work that define it as 'something you do' or 'something you don't do'. Unpaid work played a different role for

Sophie's educated middle-class parents, and she grew up in a family environment where juggling paid and unpaid positions was a central feature of working life. Her father was a retired solicitor who volunteered for a homeless hostel and the National Trust. Her mother, with a degree in archaeology, did 'bits and pieces' of unpaid archaeological cataloguing work while her children were growing up, moving into paid freelance work when they had left home. Sophie noted that both her parents were 'always like involved in the village fairs and stuff'. Like Elizabeth, her understanding of her parents' work made reference to a moral code of social responsibility, but there was a crucial difference. These notions were not tied to the idea of unpaid work exclusively, but were values required of all work in the public sphere, paid or unpaid. In much the same way as the Victorian middle classes, philanthropic endeavours were entwined with professionalisation projects, Sophie's parents' work prioritized the acquisition of skills and knowledge that had both economic and symbolic value.

Sophie's own orientation to work was shaped by a rigorous formal education that, through such strategies as taking a year off before university, membership of clubs and societies, and doing voluntary work, echoed her parents' concern with skills and knowledge. For Sophie, three months spent teaching English to refugees as part of her 'year off' initiated her voluntary work in a refugee project during university holidays. She defined her motives for doing this work in instrumental terms as 'getting experience', 'getting a foot on the ladder' and as a useful source of material for her final year dissertation. Voluntary work at this stage in her working life was not an end in itself as it was for Elizabeth. It was part of the work of 'acquiring capital', both cultural and symbolic, needed to achieve educational and career goals. It was a successful strategy because Sophie soon moved into a paid administrative position, before become the acting unit manager. Again the economic basis of her unpaid labour was hidden by the symbolic narrative that appeared to define it. Sophie's initial full-time unpaid role, which enabled her to gain enough capital to move into paid employment, was only possible, she admitted, because she lived rent free with her aunt's family. Although Sophie relied on her family who were well able to support her financially whilst she was working unpaid, other graduates interviewed were at that time (late 1990s) able to claim an additional ten pounds on their unemployment benefit if their voluntary work was under 15 hours a week.

Maria, a Philippine woman in her 40s, was engaged in paid fundraising work at North End as well as a plethora of unpaid positions working for the Philippine community in London. She had encountered first-hand the impact of living under repressive political regimes and the experience of migration, and her class position was harder to pinpoint. Unlike Sophie, Elizabeth or Diane, whose family lives were relatively stable, she described many differences between her parents' lives and work and her own. Neither of her parents had engaged in voluntary work, yet it had played a significant part in Maria's working life and career trajectory. She was bought up in a 'religious and conservative' middle-class family in the Philippines where her father was a pharmacist and her mother a housewife, and she had an uncle in the army. The situation in the Philippines, however, led to her politicization when she was a young girl and this in turn formed the foundations of her orientation to work. Despite her parents' wishes for her to enter a profession, it was the political activities that she engaged in whilst she was a student, as part of the radical political movement against the Marcos regime, that shaped her orientation to work and provided her with the social capital in the form of networks and connections that set her on a path of unpaid Non Governmental Organization (NGO) work in the Philippines. Although, like Sophie, university provided a (liberal middle-class) context to her initial voluntary work (and like Sophie her parents supported her financially while she engaged in this work), her community development work was not an arbitrary career choice but arose out of her experience of grass roots activism and the oppression suffered by those living in a dictatorship. Although she no longer lived in the Philippines she continued to work unpaid for her community in the UK as the director of a Philippine community organization.

For Maria her priorities in relation to work were driven by notions of community, and a perception of the importance of supporting and serving her community was closer to working-class notions of solidarity and mutual aid than to moral notions of helping the less fortunate. Her unpaid work in the UK was paid for by her paid employment which she saw as driven by the same motives and priorities. What was important for Maria was the nature of the work: the fact that it was helping her community, rather than whether she was paid for it. Maria explained that she could not imagine a time when she was not doing unpaid work for her community in addition to her paid work:

'Even if I don't want to do it I would feel very guilty if I don't because the work is already in my blood and I would feel guilty because if I think about what is happening in the Philippines . . . can you imagine how hard their life is?'

Structures, markets and the organization of labour

These five individuals had different priorities in relation to their work, different understandings of unpaid work, and different motivations for engaging in it. Whatever their motivations, however, the actual unpaid positions and roles they inhabited were created and maintained in relation to the organization of all forms of labour, paid and unpaid, domestic and public, formal and informal. In this final section the focus is on the wider organizational and institutional structures that have shaped the options available to these five individuals. Exploring Elizabeth, Tony and Diane's careers in different areas of the health care field and Sophie and Maria's experiences in community and refugee work, highlights how voluntary work has a particular logic within certain fields, and the way positions are organized in a particular field in response to political, cultural and economic priorities.

Health care

Elizabeth and Diane make an interesting comparison as at the time of interview in the late 1990s both were working for Care Aid, although one was paid and one unpaid. Unsurprisingly, their experiences of recruitment to and promotion within the organization were quite different. Elizabeth's progress up the ladder at Care Aid from first aid volunteer to branch president mirrored the mechanisms of her recruitment. She was invited to take on more senior positions by those above her in the organization, who had deemed her to be appropriate for these posts. Elizabeth was, on several occasions, reluctant to take on more senior roles but found promotion was an obligation that was impossible to refuse and when the position of president became available, Elizabeth remembered that despite rejecting it 'the trustees all started to ring me up and put pressure on me saying "you've got to do it, you've got to do it".' Her decisions to do unpaid work were moulded by her habitus, but also shaped by the organizational mechanisms for recruitment to and promotion within Care Aid: a finely tuned system of social obligation and patronage. In addition, although Elizabeth was strongly focused on what she saw as her duty to husband and children these family responsibilities did not prevent her from working for Care Aid, because positions in the organization were structured around women's domestic role (and men's multiple directorships) and as such were part time and flexible, often specifying only the minimum number of hours required per year.

Diane's career move from the private nursing to the voluntary sector could be seen as contradictory given her habitus, and was guided by a very different set of mechanisms to those of Elizabeth. Like other nurses, her career ground to a halt when she had children (Halford *et al.*, 1997). On returning she found herself demoted from ward sister to ward nurse and forced into part-time low-paid shift work. Her situation was made more difficult when she become a single mother, requiring non shift work hours that would enable her to take care of her daughters, and which were hard to come by for nurses. Structural changes in the field of healthcare, however, brought about by the UK's then Conservative government in the early 1990s, meant many of the services previously provided by the health service were being contracted out to the voluntary sector (Leat, 1995). This created a new domain of work for professionally qualified nurses like Diane outside the health service. As the nature of the organization of nursing labour shifted in the 1980s and 1990s, many Care Aid branches professionalized their domiciliary services, opening their doors to women like Diane who had not been brought up to see charities as the location for paid work opportunities.

Like Elizabeth, Tony found himself on an inexorable climb up the Care Aid hierarchy as he followed in the footsteps of his senior partner. 'He (the partner) became deputy president of Care Aid at that stage, and two years ago he retired as deputy president and became honorary vice president.' However, changes occurred at Care Aid just prior to this research as a result of a unification process. The organization's attempt to consolidate their position in the market for contracting and the need to prevent possible litigation claims led to an exodus of older members and trustees who no longer recognized an organizational ethos that no longer recognized their social capital. Tony, however, adopted the new professional ethos with enthusiasm and as vice president described himself as 'representing the business interest', effectively securing his long-term position within the organization.

Community and refugee work

Sophie and Maria both worked in the field of refugee and community support and development (in different organizations). This field is not professionalized in the same way as health care, and it was experience and knowledge of these communities that were required to access employment positions. Voluntary work was a crucial currency in this process and both saw their unpaid work as the key route into paid work in the field. It is not only community expertise, however, that is crucial for accessing these positions. Like Elizabeth's experiences of Care Aid, community work recruitment is dependent on social networks. Maria was recruited from the Philippines via these networks to her first paid job in London, working for a Philippine community advice centre. She already 'knew the people' and described how the centre 'knew different organizations in the Philippines so they just sent the adverts and they talked to people "if you know some one who can fit the job . . . ?"' Her community expertise was in demand and this need for people with community experience in London coincided with the changing nature of the field of NGO work in the Philippines. The Marcos regime came to an end in 1986 and Maria was able to leave the work she had been doing in Manila. She described how many other Philippine activists utilized their community expertise and social capital in a similar way to find employment in the voluntary sector in Britain and Europe:

> you know, they were nurses before or medics in the hills. They were able to penetrate the NGOs here and they didn't need to train (. . .) in development work. You have to have the experience'

Institutionalized cultural capital (such as a degree) has little exchange value in this field. Maria pointed out that many Philippine migrant workers in the UK are forced into domestic slavery despite being professionally qualified teachers or accountants. Unlike the activists, whose social capital and experience were valued in the field, these professionals find their qualifications are redundant within closed professional fields in the UK. Sophie, with a degree from Oxford, had considerable institutional cultural capital but almost no community expertise or knowledge. She argued that she had to do voluntary work in order to gain this expertise and find employment: 'I really felt that I needed to get some experience, I don't know if that's just sort of my lack of confidence. I mean, it is how it works in this area, you have to'. Sophie acknowledged that voluntary work was the only entry point to the field for graduates like herself and added 'you have to assume that that's what you do', even giving up one voluntary position because she 'didn't see that it was going to be that useful really'. Her voluntary work with refugees was a strategic career move rather than being driven by a sense of solidarity or particular grass roots expertise. Sophie's entry into refugee work coincided with a period of growth in the field as significant increases in numbers entering Britain and the quick staff turnover meant that she only had to do unpaid work for a year before she was able to access a paid position. Unlike Maria, who saw unpaid work as a crucial and permanent element of her working life, something she would always do, Sophie did not see voluntary work as central to her future career or moral framework:

> 'I think probably the only thing that would make me do voluntary work again is if I felt that I needed to get more experience in a certain area. I feel like I've done that. I want my money now. It kind of makes you realize your selfish motivations for volunteering. Yeah, it's actually "thanks very much".'

Conclusion

These five individuals, with their varied backgrounds and orientations to work, provide the empirical focus for an exploration of the different meanings unpaid public work has for different people. The mechanisms through which individuals find themselves in a position to take on unpaid work, either within a voluntary organization or informally in the community, involve a complex interplay between social and symbolic capital and work ethos on the one hand, and the social organization of labour that makes those positions available on the other. The work histories of Elizabeth, Sophie, Diane, Tony and Maria provide richly complex narratives that highlight the inadequacy of attempts to explain people's participation in voluntary work in terms of statements of motive, such as, 'wanting to help other people'. Elizabeth and Tony's description of the obligation and social expectations that were part of the mechanisms that led to their unpaid careers at Care Aid undermine assumptions about altruistic choices.

The work ethos of each of these individuals, shaped as it is by their class, gender and cultural inheritance, provided them with a particular set of priorities and practices that made unpaid work 'something you do', even 'something you have to do', or 'something you don't do'. That Diane has **not** done voluntary work does not signify a lack of natural urges to do good, or support her own assertion that she must be 'lazy'. Volunteering is not part of her upbringing and orientation to work, and it is this, not to mention the financial pressures associated with her family circumstances, that makes sense of her work trajectory. Similarly, those that criticise workers such as Sophie, who undertake voluntary work as a route into employment, fail to recognize that unpaid work is a product of a particular configuration of social and structural circumstances. For Sophie it formed part of a strategy to embark on a particular career trajectory and was no more or less legitimate than the unpaid work of Maria or Elizabeth.

Within the wider project to contribute to a new sociology of work, this chapter touches on a number of the key themes. Most importantly, it has high-lighted the importance of rethinking definitions of work and re-examining forms of labour that have been excluded from the sociology of work. Taking a holistic perspective on a person's working life rather than simply focusing on their employment or their domestic labour gives rise to a more textured and complex picture of people's work practices and choices. It particularly raises the issue of remuneration and reward in how we understand work, suggesting that other forms of capital are as important as economic capital in defining and shaping work practices. Understanding a person's unpaid work in relation to their paid work and their economic and social position is crucial. Voluntary work, like domestic labour, has to be supported economically, whether directly through a person's paid employment as it was for Maria and Tony, through a partner's employment, through family wealth or inheritance as it was for Sophie and Elizabeth, or in some cases through state benefits. Crucial to the analysis of the data is the way that different forms of work are interconnected at both macro and micro levels. For example, Tony's employment is inextricably linked to his voluntary work, and in the community work field Sophie sees unpaid work as a crucial training ground for paid positions, whilst for Maria the two forms of labour sit side-by-side with little distinction being drawn in terms of status or importance. At the macro level, government policies in the health care sector significantly affected the nature of paid and unpaid positions available. Voluntary work cannot be ignored as a marginal form of labour. On the contrary, as this chapter has shown, it provides important insights into the nature of work in contemporary society.

Markets and politics: Public and private relations in the case of prostitution

Jackie West and Terry Austrin

'The occupational hazards of regular workers are not remotely similar to those faced by women in the sex industry . . . Rather than society pretending it is a career choice, prostitution needs to be exposed for what it is – violence against women. Unionization cannot protect the women in this vile industry . . . Women in the sex industry need human rights, not workers' rights.' (Bindel, 2003)

'One would have thought it self-evident that the best way to confront exploitation in the sex industry is to empower the women and men who work in it . . . Telling sex workers that what they do is so degrading that they are not entitled to a union helps perpetuate the stigma from which so many sex workers suffer . . . [Most] do not want to be saved – they want the right to do their work in a decriminalized industry, they want labour rights and health and safety rights. They want dignity and respect.' (Lopes and Macrae, 2003)

The above exchange follows the establishment in March 2003 of a sex workers' branch of a mainstream UK union, the GMB, in which Ana Lopes, herself a sex worker, played a key role[1]. Julie Bindel is an academic and radical feminist activist.

Prostitution is a special, but far from unique, case for understanding work and employment. Indeed its exceptionality helps to illustrate a number of more general 'rules' about the constitution of work. We have argued elsewhere that prostitution and mainstream work are analytically more similar than they are different, although dominant paradigms of service sector employment reduce these similarities to issues of (gender) identity, the performance of embodied labour and dyadic interpersonal relations. An alternative focus on the practices of work, what people actually do, along with the labour market and the regulation of work, permits an understanding of the wider relational context of occupations and the production of diversity and change (West and Austrin, 2002). Such an approach can apply to commodity trading (the mainstream case we used) as much as to prostitution, or to medicine (Pringle, 1998) as much as to tomato production and distribution (Harvey *et al.*, 2002). The case of prostitution, however, remains particularly significant because contemporary developments in the sex and entertainment industries are beginning to position commercial sex as 'normal business', while its continuing contested nature throws the very nature of work, the constitution of work itself, not just worker identity, into sharp relief.

We argue here that traditional approaches to prostitution fail to address these issues, concentrating as they do on debates about the essential properties of prostitution. These debates, echoing popular understandings, neglect the conditions and relations, social and technical, through which prostitution is constituted as illicit or legal work. The question of prostitution, whether debated by academics or activists, is conventionally posed in philosophical or moral terms, that is, in terms of its status as free labour or as abuse/exploitation, with attempts to move beyond such essentialist conceptualizations still comparatively rare. The chapter begins by outlining these divergent approaches showing that they tend towards irreconcilable differences of view about the rights and wrongs of commercial sex. A more productive and specifically sociological question is that of identifying the relations under which prostitution is produced as legitimate work or not. For there is considerable variety in this, notwithstanding the competing claims of sex work activists and abolitionists.

In reflecting on these relations through which prostitution or sex work are mobilized, there are some parallels with domestic work, to which we briefly allude in part two of the chapter: the intensely interpersonal nature of 'reproductive work' and its private rather than public character. But we argue that the private/public distinction in framing work and employment is about much more than the distinction between family and economy or household and market for it also concerns the social and technical relations involved in the establishment of illegal and legal markets. In our view, a more fruitful approach is one that more fully situates commercial sexual labour, and this requires appreciation of three distinct but interconnected dimensions: the influence of discursive struggles played out between different actors; relations with others over and above clients or third parties; and, finally, practices adopted to seek accountability (or secure 'space' to work, if only illicitly). We argue, that is, for understanding prostitution as 'practice' and embedded in networks, relational and discursive, whose articulation in (necessarily) local contexts produces given but never pre-determined outcomes.

More generally, our argument then, developed in the final part of the chapter, is about the need to embrace not only production and consumption in understanding work, especially service work, but also the intermediaries that link these spheres, along with the politics of markets and their regulation. We use examples of sex work 'normalization' to illustrate this relational approach, but we begin by summarizing the main themes in conventional approaches to prostitution and their limitations.

Autonomy or subordination?

Prevailing debates about prostitution as work centre on its status as free labour or as abuse/exploitation with questions about whether prostitution fundamentally entails autonomy (or at least the promise of such) or subordination (McIntosh, 1996; Chapkis, 1997; Shrage, 1994). The terms of this debate were shaped by the feminist controversies on sexuality, the feminist 'sex wars', of the 1980s and the rise of prostitutes' collectives[2]. But they have subsequently been aired in wider social discussion of the sex industry, especially in the mass media. And they have directly informed social policy in the form of competing initiatives for law reform, that is to say, those which favour decriminalization or legalization of prostitution on the one hand, and, on the other, those which favour abolition if not prohibition (West, 2000). As the dispute referred to at the start of this paper indicates, the case for one or the other rests primarily on moral grounds, a case of sex workers' employment and civil rights versus claims of victimization.

This is not an equal contest because the victimization view is very much more dominant, in the UK as in many other societies. This, however, is not universal. The discursive struggle over prostitution is played out among different players, to different audiences and with different effects in particular societies and locales. Looking at these specific cases enables us to begin to identify the relations through which prostitution is stabilized as normal work. This is necessary because most attempts to resolve the moral debate about prostitution fail to get beyond essentialist conceptualizations. But it is to these that we turn first.

In seeking to assess whether prostitution is simply a free exchange of labour, unfairly criminalized and stigmatized, or whether it is intrinsically exploitative, an ultimate expression of patriarchal power, a central issue concerns what exactly *is* being sold/exchanged and on what terms. Does the prostitute just sell a service or something more intrinsic to her (or his) person, their body, soul or self?[3]. At the core of this controversy is emotional labour, for prostitution is the epitome of embodied work, but the use to which Hochschild's (1983) concept is put reflects the different interests of the protagonists in this debate.

Liberal feminists and sex work activists tend to the view that emotional labour entails a clear separation between self and role, a clear sense on the performer's part of when they are acting and when they are not (Nagle, 1997; Perkins *et al.*, 1994). Emphasis is placed on the many professional skills deployed and the boundaries prostitutes draw (whatever their own identity) between their working and private lives: the way they seek to distinguish their dealings with clients from their relations with partners, by, for example, refusing to kiss the former, by insisting on condom use or by managing the encounter so that 'intimate' contact such as intercourse is reduced to a bare minimum[4]. As one Dutch window prostitute put it to Chapkis (1997:76), 'I don't think any whore totally reveals herself in her work. You just show a part of yourself, the part they can have sex with, but you keep the rest for yourself.' Some refer to selling their body, but not their soul. Others, however, are less convinced that the self can be split so effectively, especially in the work of selling sex. Here they identify a profound form of alienation. Prostitution is seen by radical feminists and many other abolitionists as inherently abusive, if not violent, a form of degradation arising from male domination (Pateman, 1988; Barry, 1995), in contrast to the liberal view which argues that criminalization itself is a, if not the, major cause of prostitutes' vulnerability to violence.

There is variation in the degree to which prostitutes are, in practice, subordinated (just as liberals concede variation in autonomy), and the work and personal relations of prostitutes are often deeply contradictory. Street work, for example, both allows and jeopardizes survival (Phoenix, 1999). It represents the search for economic and social independence, an escape from housing problems and abusive relationships, but it also increases poverty and dependence[5]. Violence from pimps may be understood as the price of 'business protection' or intimacy. Prostitutes working in parlours and escort agencies will experience varying degrees of control (Sanders, 2005). By contrast, independent prostitutes, who work legally from their own premises and who may enjoy good relations with the police, are not only far better remunerated but exercise a high degree of control over their clients and their work situation. Even O'Connell Davidson's 'Desiree', however, who has become iconic in this respect, is arguably subject to more complex relations of power.

The notion of prostitution as a free contractual exchange between equals is, argues O'Connell Davidson (1998), an illusion of liberal theory and ideology. The prostitute's livelihood depends on her becoming 'a living embodiment of the client's fantasies'. She thus always and necessarily sacrifices reciprocity, the right to make demands of the other, the client, and thus sacrifices a core component of personhood itself. She can be treated this way because she is a social outcast. Clients often attribute desire and pleasure to those they pay for sex but this allows for the illusion of emotional relationships, a false mutuality since it is without obligations (Plumridge *et al.*, 1997). Indeed prostitution precisely absolves the client from the 'tedious' demands of normal sexual relationships (Hoigard and Finstad, 1992).

O'Connell Davidson equates this lack of reciprocity or social recognition (the treatment of the prostitute as 'non-person') with 'social death' and its 'eroticization', since clients are really purchasing not a defined service or amount of time but rights of command over another's body. Independent prostitutes may have control in terms of how they manage this, but never power. However, in what respects, we might ask, does this really distinguish prostitution from other contractual/employment relations? A high degree of control may compensate for lack of power in many legitimate occupations. Moreover, any service sector work involves non-reciprocity – the plumber, hairdresser or therapist does not expect reciprocal recognition or acknowledgement as a person with demands to be met. It is precisely the commercial transaction which distinguishes this from ordinary social interaction.

O'Connell Davidson's argument, in contrast, is that the exchange in prostitution is premised on dehumanization. At the root of her critique, then, is the view that prostitutes' rights to social recognition are denied because they flout central elements of gender ideology, namely the view that women should not trade in sex at all, and hence become 'Other'. But that, of course, is exactly the point being made by prostitute and sex work activists who argue that this ideology over-determines their status, preventing a dispassionate and objective appreciation of the way in which their work is actually no different, or little different from other service sector employment.

There can be no final, agreed judgement on such essentialist and foundational controversies. To escape them we need to examine the social and technical relations of prostitution beyond the prostitute-client encounter, that is, relations *beyond* those of gender and embodiment. Most contemporary studies of prostitution, however, narrowly conceptualize a 'micro' level of dyadic interaction shaped by a 'macro' frame of economic, political and social inequalities. The impact of poverty, gender subordination and racism in both western and global contexts is immensely influential in accounting for routes into prostitution and conditions of work (Kempadoo and Doezema, 1998; Lim, 1998; Phoenix, 1999). Such 'macro' inequalities also broadly influence the organization of prostitution and forms of control/autonomy via relations with managers and pimps (O'Connell Davidson, 1998). But the organizational forms of prostitution are also produced by relations with numerous others beyond these actors who facilitate or impede the exchange with clients – relations and networks which are locally variable, not uniform, and political as much as social.

We turn to this wider and more complex relational context below (in the final section of the paper), for it is critical in understanding the constitution of prostitution as (il)legitimate work. It is necessary to an understanding of markets in prostitution and their regulation. We are arguing, therefore (contra Glucksmann, 2000a), that to *embed* the work of prostitution in social relations requires more than a recognition of market and household relations, or rather that to focus on the articulation of 'economy' and 'family' relations is to neglect the ways in which activities are established in the 'marketplace' as either private or public, illegal or legal practices. There are some parallels between prostitution and domestic work itself in terms of their location as market or household labour, to which we now turn, but the meaning of public/private boundaries is quite distinct and does not map isomorphically onto the question of legality. The regulation of prostitution as legal work also involves both social and technical relations and public agencies as intermediaries in ways that are critically different from the regulation of prostitution as illegal work.

Domestic and sexual labour

The role of both discursive and relational elements in the construction of prostitution as work echoes those in domestic work – to some extent. The parallel is useful in highlighting similar conceptual issues in the constitution of work across the private/public divide and the related matter of reproductive work. But the discussion also reveals the need to go beyond this domestic/sexual parallel to understand political and legal relations in the constitution of both 'private' and, especially, 'public' work.

140

Unpaid care and housework typically entails a personal relation between spouses/partners, or parents/children, and is performed privately, spatially isolated in the home. Additionally, reproduction (care work, mothering, sex) is ideologically equated with women's 'nature', so making domestic work a labour of love, notwithstanding feminist challenges to this and divorce settlements that recognize a wife's contribution.

Paid domestic work, while formally recognized as employment, is also equated with women's natural attributes, rather than as learned or technical competences deserving of reward, and the 'work identity' of those who perform it is often precarious or incidental. It is invisible and isolated labour, with little to separate work and leisure – in both space and time. The 'casuals' of Glucksmann's (2000a) study, for example, identified as wives/mothers/neighbours, reflecting the blurred boundaries between their 'little' domestic jobs and their role as women. In contrast, the 'cottons' identified as workers, equal with (not dependent on) men, reflecting their distinct skills as weavers and a clear separation of public and private domains. Paid domestic work is frequently undertaken by those whose own private domestic commitments, such as small children or elderly dependents, tie them to the home or their locality.

The oppressive and exploitative character of paid domestic work arises, however, from its relational rather than spatial or temporal context. The employer-employee relation does *itself* entail embodied, interpersonal labour, and this labour typically requires intense emotional engagement, as well as demeaning physical tasks, since long hours of child care and personal servicing are involved. For Anderson (2000), domestic workers, like prostitutes, sell their very personhood not their labour power. But her own analysis in fact suggests that the employer's power to command the worker's self, and the denial or non-recognition of her needs, is less a function of the work per se than the wider relations under which it is performed. Racism, the politics of migration and lack of citizenship make illegal or quasi-legal migrants acutely vulnerable to exploitative employment tied to personal interdependencies. As Anderson (2000: 167) herself also argues, NGOs' attempts to construct the domestic worker *as* worker, and to assert the relations of employment contract *over* relations of status, is very difficult, not only because of the ideology that equates reproduction with non-work but because it is conducted in the private sphere. What is of most significance here, however, is actually not the discursive construction of the private but the fact that the employer-employee relation is embedded in a private, personal relation: that is, there is nothing institutional or public to mediate it. We return to this below.

Prostitution does share some features with domestic work, particularly the difficulties of conceptualizing it as contractual labour given the kind and degree of personal servicing involved, especially the servicing of men, and the ideological construction of sex and intimacy in opposition to commodification. Hence the rationalization of informal prostitution such as sex tourism as an extension of non-commercial relations, as merely intimacy or even fun for tourists, which obscures the economic inequalities and those of race and gender which underpin it (Sanchez Taylor, 2001). There are, moreover, specific parallels in the way in which the performance of dishonoured and degrading labour confers honour, status and identity on the employer (in domestic work) or the client (in prostitution) (Anderson, 2000; O'Connell Davidson, 1998).

However, the issues of private/public in comparing domestic work and prostitution are very different. Most academic and activist discussion of prostitution emphasizes the symbolic significance of the way in which prostitution breaches the private/public boundary and its associated gender order. The commercialization of intimate relations transgresses the separation of sacred and profane, pre-market and market transactions, and is a key source of the stigma and vilification encountered by prostitutes ('whores') in contrast to the 'innocent madonna' (Shrage, 1994; O'Connell Davidson, 1998; Phoenix, 1999; Brewis and Linstead, 2000). But the public/private boundary also concerns the distinction between private (personal) and public behaviour. The principles enshrined in 20th century criminal law (in the UK both before and after the Wolfenden report[6]) ostensibly distinguish between the private behaviour of citizens, which is not the business of the state, and public order or decency. The state, that is, does not supposedly concern itself with private morality or immorality, providing that no corruption or exploitation is involved. These principles, however, do not fully extend to the private lives of prostitutes, as distinct from their clients (Self, 2003). Moreover, there are heated debates over whether prostitution itself is a form of exploitation, as we have already noted. The legal distinction between private and public is also overlaid by the symbolic meanings of this boundary in the sense that attitudes to public prostitution such as street work are particularly shaped by gender discourses (Hubbard and Sanders, 2004). Leaving these issues on one side, however, we focus below on the ways in which prostitution is legally framed since this has such practical implications for the conditions and relations under which prostitutes work.

Other than in societies where prostitution in all respects is banned, private prostitution is often legal, both spatially and commercially, while public prostitution is not. A distinction is drawn between prostitution within the private domain as opposed to public places, and also between dyadic personal exchanges and more collective or corporate forms. Abolitionist state strategies (that is, those intended to discourage prostitution but without additional victimization of women), do not make the sale of sex itself illegal providing it is exchanged between consenting adults, in private. Rather, there are a battery of legal constraints on its public promotion, such as those which apply in the UK – on advertising and soliciting custom, on recruitment ('procuring'), on benefiting from income derived from it (brothel-keeping, pimping), and on working with others. Sex workers' personal dependents, such as partners or children, are technically criminalized and this contributes to the difficulties sex workers have in separating their working and private lives. Contacting providers is also increasingly prohibited in the form of bans on kerb-crawling (and the as-yet more exceptional Swedish ban on the purchase of sex), although in general it is sex workers, not clients, who are subject to scrutiny and sanction.

A number of complex ambiguities arise from this legal framework. For example, the UK street worker does not commit a crime by selling sex, only by loitering and/or soliciting clients, but the scope of the criminal law in this respect is currently widening under pressure to contain street prostitution[7]. A highly successful 'entrepreneurial' prostitute like Desiree, working discreetly in the suburbs on her own, can only employ one receptionist but she enjoys good relations with the local police, for she is not breaking the law (O'Connell Davidson, 1998). Many arrangements for promoting prostitution are legal/quasi-legal by virtue of letting space or client access to self-employed workers, thus absolving the owner/managers of massage parlours, clubs, or escort agencies of technical responsibility. And there is often tacit police acceptance of illegal brothels through selective law enforcement and a focus, for example, only upon those where trafficking or under-age prostitution is suspected.

Criminalization actually increases risks for prostitutes, for example increasing vulnerability to violence, by having to work alone or lacking time to weigh up potential customers for fear of police action (Kinnell, 2004), while making third parties more necessary to put them in touch with clients, as O'Connell Davidson (1998) has observed. Sex workers are thus more vulnerable to physical harm and potential exploitation, yet they are more likely to experience police harassment than protection. Criminal penalties undoubtedly contain the scale of legal business operations, while at the same time providing for large-scale illegal activity. Indeed they may encourage organized criminal networks in order to procure workers. Since these networks will target the most vulnerable (the most easily controlled) – those desperate through poverty, age or citizenship – trafficking on a global scale is fostered, given the inequalities of international capitalism (Kempadoo and Doezema, 1998).

Thus while the mediation of exchanges with clients is crucial to the nature of prostitution work, they are over-determined by the legal/illegal context. And the constitution of prostitution as illegal or legal work is embedded in complex networks beyond the dyadic encounters between prostitutes and their clients.

The relations of prostitution

The organization of prostitution entails relations between workers and third parties which vary considerably according to market sector and workplace. But it is also contingent on relations with and between an array of other intermediaries from the police to sex worker collectives. We examine here some recent examples of the legalization of brothels and street work, highlighting the complexities of regulation, local variability and the political, social and technical relations that produce this.

Working conditions vary in different types of prostitution: street work, parlours (or brothels), escort agencies, clubs or independent working (Matthews, 1997; Perkins *et al.*, 1994). More useful analytic distinctions, however, are in terms of degrees of freedom/control – economic, personal and contractual

(O'Connell Davidson, 1998). There is clearly a world of difference between the independent escort who owns her own property and the illegal migrant who is forced to work in flats controlled by pimps under conditions of debt bondage. For O'Connell Davidson, third parties, whether brothels, agencies, clubs or individual pimps, are seen as necessarily exploitative since their income depends on the extraction of surplus labour, so a premium is placed on client throughput. But given this Marxist theoretical frame, the extraction of surplus is little different from any third party arrangement in the legitimate economy, that is, it is not unique to prostitution. All managers will have an interest in productivity unless quality is a greater priority. Indeed, productivity pressures are increasingly powerful in the service sector, even where embodied labour is required as in hospitality. Nevertheless, the exploitative potential of third party relations in prostitution is aggravated by illegality. Legally the parlour or club can only charge entrance and/or massage fees to clients, and laundry, receptionist and shift fees to its masseurs/prostitutes, while its actual share of prostitution income depends on the 'cut' of what the client pays in private. Though prices for different services are fixed (and workers may negotiate hidden extras), owners have an enhanced interest in maximizing client numbers. Owners' hold over workers is also increased where, given the illegality of advertising and running a business, they shoulder the risks of securing access to a clientele (see also Sanders, 2005).

There is an assumption in most studies that brothels tend to the lowest common denominator in terms of working conditions, but there is market segmentation, and this appears to be increasing (Matthews, 1997). Parlours, for example, do vary in terms of the degree of direct control exercised over selection by clients, working practices, scope for bargaining with clients and earnings (Perkins *et al.*, 1994; Perez-y-Perez, 2004). In the Netherlands, brothel differentiation is reflected in distinct employer associations representing window owners on the one hand and exclusive clubs on the other. Even 'relaxation businesses' require a probationary period of membership, quality inspections to guarantee 'safety and fairness for customers and workers', registered by an 'Erotikeurmark', and management courses for operators (IPI, 1998). Such market segmentation has been reinforced by the 1999 law reform which ended the ban on brothels: this decriminalized free (consensual) prostitution while increasing penalties for coercive forms (Outshoorn, 1998), so brothel owners who can comply with the costs of meeting regulatory standards have a clear incentive to distinguish themselves from the illegal sector.

So does legalization make a difference? Sex workers typically see conditions in state regulated brothels as little different, if not worse, than those in illegal brothels since licensing only adds direct police control to that conventionally exercised by pimps or madams and further restricts workers' mobility and flexibility. It tends to include technical features such as zoning, special rules of operation, police registration, compulsory medical examinations and social restrictions on personal autonomy. For example, in rural Nevada sex workers must hold individual licences, conditional on weekly medicals and compulsory condom use, and some owners impose restrictions on their visibility, even preventing them from having their families live in the community (Hausbeck and Brents, 2000). In Western Australia, similar conditions are found in 'containment parlours', so called because, as in Nevada, their purpose is to contain legal prostitution within confined areas.

However, what is adopted when prostitution is legalized is a contingent political and local matter. Australia in the 1980s initiated licensing by civil boards via planning permits rather than police control (in the state of Victoria), and normal business registration in place of licensing (in Canberra, ACT [Australian Capital Territory]). This distinction between civil and police registration is of considerable significance, even though electoral change in Victoria during the period of law reform overturned proposals to prevent council bans on brothels and to allow independent prostitutes exemption from licensing (Neave, 1994). In Melbourne, Victoria's capital, recent mainstream political action has forced the closure of many illegal brothels, while sex work organizations actively promote 'best practice', for example, in the form of occupational health and safety training for both prostitutes and owners (Edler and Scarlet Alliance, 1999).

Following law reform in the Netherlands, some municipalities want to ban prostitution altogether, most zone brothels, and some continue to regard improvements in health as the only consideration (Venicz *et al.*, 2000). But legalization can nevertheless limit corruption and bad practice: other Dutch city councils require owner responsibility for the technical matters of safety, hygiene and working conditions along with respect for prostitutes' rights to safe sex, choice of clients and no compulsory drinking. Activists have argued the case for applying ILO (International Labour Organization) standards to sex work (Bindman and Doezema, 1997) and while there are difficulties in tackling exploitative, low paid work of any kind and enforcing such standards, prostitution is not unique.

The regulation of street work is also subject to local variation. Some recent Dutch initiatives have been progressive in providing police protection and on-site sex work project support, while other 'street-walking zones' have been less well provided for, or poorly located for business (van Doorninck, 2003). In the UK, Edinburgh successfully operated a quasi-legal tolerance zone for eighteen years, resulting, activists argue, in substantial reductions in both violence and rates of HIV infection (Morgan-Thomas, 2003). But this was ended by the council in 2002 in the face of economic pressures (gentrification) and lack of mainstream political will to combat these[8].

Markets, then, exist within politically-influenced regulatory frameworks. They are also negotiated by prostitutes, albeit with varying degrees of freedom. Mobility between street work and indoor prostitution is increasingly difficult because the chaotic life-styles induced by extreme poverty and drug use militate against recruitment into much of the indoor trade where regular hours and conformity to working practices are required. But mobility between parlours, and between parlours and independent work is very common. Many sex workers construct careers in prostitution by moving through different markets with distinct services, locations, work practices, rules, methods of client contact and negotiation (Perkins *et al.*, 1994; Perez-y-Perez, 2004). This entails the development of specific knowledge, contacts and appropriate identities, allowing successful and experienced prostitutes to move, for example, to parlours where there is less direct control over practices or earnings. Independent sex workers must themselves promote their services and secure safe space to work. This requires negotiating relations with police, hoteliers, landlords or other intermediaries. These include health and social services, tax advisers and advertising media, which are locally variable. Access to health care may be via conventional medical routes, with fears of stigma and control, or may be mediated by sex work projects (Ward and Day, 1997). Opportunities for media self-promotion also vary. In Oslo parlour workers took advantage of television chat shows to present stories of successful professionals in opposition to accounts of victimization (Skilbrei, 2001). In Christchurch, New Zealand, mainstream newspapers exercise substantial control over the content of advertisements (Perez-y-Perez, 2004).

Prostitutes, therefore, negotiate different discursive contexts and regulatory regimes. So must those who own or manage a prostitution business. Self-employed prostitutes and operators must also themselves engage in practices of regulation. These practices are evident in illegal contexts, but are a condition of legalization, of public, legal identities – as sex workers seek recognition of their professional status and operators seek recognition as legitimate business.

Decriminalization of prostitution is often thought preferable to legalization but, beyond the removal of police jurisdiction, this is misleading for two reasons. First, because decriminalization at national level requires legalization at a local level for the principles of law reform to take effect (Visser and Oomens, 2000). Second, because decriminalization does *not* mean deregulation – indeed regulation may increase. Partly this is because, in normalizing any 'deviance', the state has particular interests in ensuring control and law reform is likely to have been wholly or partially motivated in any case by arguments that control is better secured through legalization than prohibition. This is also very clear in the case of gambling, which shares with prostitution a history, albeit uneven, of moving from 'carousal zones' to 'diversion districts', with government, including UK government support (Judd, 1995; Austrin and West, 2004 and 2005). In addition, however, normal business is subject to regulation, even though the forms this takes are highly variable. All legal transactions must be accountable so measures, mechanisms and procedures are required to make them transparent and secure or safe.

Occupations work to create their own markets, or protect and improve conditions for existing members (Larson, 1977). They do this through the control of competition: price setting and cartels; control of information (to potential customers, regulators, political bodies and also stakeholders); and control of producers and their product or service to guarantee quality. This is particularly important in the case of *labour* markets as distinct from standardized commodity or product markets (Paradeise, 2003). This is arguably of even greater significance, however, where embodied labour is itself the commodity. In legalizing prostitution, governments have a particular stake in securing sexual health, and sex workers rather than clients tend to be targeted. Where mandatory health testing is a condition of individual licensing, sex workers often refuse to register and are less likely to access health care (Ward and Day, 1997). Independent sex workers, however, also have a stake in public accountability in order to establish and maintain a clientele: parlour workers in Oslo chose to refuse condoms from sex work projects and purchased their own, as part of their strategy to distinguish themselves as professionals (Skilbrei, 2001).

A major impact on 'normalization' strategies has been the development of prostitutes' collectives. Their political ideology and commitment to total inclusivity may be in conflict with professionalization. They seek to speak for all sex workers (Kempadoo and Doezema, 1998), while professionals frequently seek to distinguish themselves from drug and criminal networks, from street workers in particular, in order to resist stereotypes of degradation (Poel, 1995; Skilbrei, 2001). Collectives' political influence is highly variable (West, 2000) but they may play an active part in the self-regulation of prostitution, in providing support and advice for sex workers if not brokering reform of employment and taxation law. Conventional trade union initiatives are less common but the GMB, which has recently passed a resolution in support of decriminalization and 'proper regulation of the sex industry', has an entertainment branch which is successfully recruiting lap dancers in clubs run by a proprietor who regards the union as a useful weapon in his struggle to legitimize this sector (MacErlean, 2002).

Conclusion

The new sociology of work centres on the public and private and divisions of labour within and across these two domains. We have argued that the diversity of public and private extends beyond conventional understandings to include legal and illegal markets, and that understanding work requires appreciation of the ways in which it is organized and markets formed and regulated. The analysis of prostitution has generally centred on moral controversies about its status as work, on gender and embodiment, or paid attention only to dyadic (micro) encounters (workers/clients, workers/third parties) and structural (macro) relations. An alternative and more fruitful approach examines how prostitution is mediated by others and produced as illegal or legal work. This approach focuses on how the performance of 'dirty work' is practically achieved (Hughes, 1971) in private and public contexts. Economies are, for the most part, 'instituted' through public forms (Harvey *et al.*, 2002) and prostitution is a very good case for showing both the differences between markets, the difficulties associated with their reform and the shifting nature of identities associated with them. Abstracted conceptions of economy and family do not approach these issues in the politics of work.

147

Notes

1 The GMB, the UK's general trade union, has 700,000 members nationally, with a number of specialist branches for occupational groups with distinct needs; these include mini-cab drivers, tatooists and festival 'roadies'.

2 These controversies centred on political and theoretical disputes about coercive heterosexuality, that is, about whether the exercise of male power and domination is intrinsic or not (see, for example, Jackson and Scott, 1996).

3 Although some of the following analysis applies to male and transgender prostitution, these sectors are very distinct and this chapter focuses only on women.

4 'I mean some of the women were making wads of cash with a string of regulars. They would brag that they wouldn't actually bonk the guy any more than six minutes at the most . . . it all came down to getting them so worked up by other means . . . that by the time you got down to it . . . well it would be just about over': a New Zealand sex worker on her induction training into parlour work, quoted in Perez-y-Perez (2004). *On boundaries and 'identity work'* see also, for example, McKeganey and Barnard (1996), Brewis and Linstead (2000, chapters 8 and 9) or Sanders (2005).

5 Economic costs include condoms, room hire, childminding, 'tied' housing – and fines. Moreover, illicit earnings encourage fast consumption rather than investment (see also Day, 1996; Perez-y-Perez, 2004).

6 The Wolfenden Committee, reporting in 1957, addressed both homosexuality and prostitution. It was associated with both the 1956 Sexual Offences Act, which criminalized procuring, brothel-keeping, living off 'immoral earnings' and controlling prostitutes, and the 1959 Street Offences Act, which dealt with loitering and soliciting (including by men for 'immoral purposes'). Persistent kerb-crawling was made a criminal offence in 1985 and arrestable in 2003.

7 A number of punitive measures against (even consensual) prostitution, especially street work, have been introduced in recent years such as ASBOs (anti-social behaviour orders). In effect, these bring back imprisonment for soliciting (abolished in 1982) since they include this penalty for breach of an order. UK government policy more broadly is focused on tackling trafficking and child prostitution. Key principles were embodied in legislative proposals to modernize the law on sexual offences, particularly with respect to homosexuality (Home Office, 2000) and they have since been developed into a comprehensive set of proposals on prostitution principally designed to address 'abuse' and 'exploitation' (Home Office, 2004).

8 At the time of writing (February 2005), Liverpool city council had agreed to set up a managed zone for street workers, but business objections in areas thought likely to be so designated were reinforcing the council's unwillingness to proceed without government endorsement in the form of primary legislation. For more detail on 'normalization' strategies see West and Austrin, 2004.

Care in the Community? Gender and the reconfiguration of community work in a post-mining neighbourhood

Jane Parry

'When our grandfathers founded this and that institute all over the valleys, what were they intending? They regarded them as instruments for raising the quality of the mental and social life of the valleys. Our livelihood is founded on coal and the object of getting coal is that we only achieve a life, a civilisation. There is no other point in blasting rocks and tunnelling under the earth. They saw the institute as helping to blast the rocks of ignorance, lighting the minds of men, and feeding the fires of fellowship. (An institute) Library is a translation into stone and wood and books and paper of the thoughts of those who had an ideal of a better civilisation . . . That surely was the goal of the institutes.'

Thomas Jones, founder of Coleg Harlech, a Welsh adult education charity

Introduction

Work geared towards supporting communities was a central, albeit taken-for-granted feature of coalmining cultures, and adhered to highly gendered formations (Massey, 1994; Williamson, 1982). Its public or institutional face, which comprised various trade union lodges and welfare clubs, community associations, sports and drinking establishments, was characterized by men's interactions and strongly linked to their employment in the collieries. By contrast, its private sphere, maintained through informal kinship and neighbourhood networks, was female-dominated. This distinction has otherwise been conceptualized as a formal/informal axis along which community work was organized (R. F. Taylor, 2004), and these spaces of interaction proxied for the public and private spheres.

The work performed by men and women within these different community locations took two qualitatively distinct forms. The first comprised the interactions embedded in the material structures of community, gendered male. These ranged from elected and sometimes paid positions, for example, as trade union officials or community councillors, to a multitude of less visible but nonetheless demanding unpaid work within the unions, working-mens' clubs, leisure associations and local Labour Party. This kind of labour is characterized in this chapter as **structural** aspects of community work, and represents the more formalized end of community life. Its counterpart was the matrix of interactions associated with the maintenance of local informal networks, gendered female, and described here as **relational** community work. This included keeping an eye out for neighbours' children, providing the intense practical and emotional support needed by family and friends during times of crisis, or helping a frail neighbour with day-to-day tasks, such as cooking, running errands and cleaning.

This diverse range of community labour was embedded within a spatiality characterized by a high degree of overlap between occupational, social and domestic experiences (Dennis *et al.*, 1956; Lockwood, 1975): to a large extent the work of coalmining structured broader social relationships and practices. Francis thus described the social organization of the Valleys in terms of '*a crucial triangular linkage between pit, union and community*' (1990: 112), and linked their socio-political focus to work. What such accounts imply is that work equates to paid work or employment, that is, coalmining. This risks overlooking the wealth of other forms of work, often manifested in communal forms, which underpinned the social organization of coalmining populations. Community labour is particularly interesting in this context, crossing public/private boundaries (in contrast to the voluntary sector work examined in Taylor's chapter, which focused on the public sphere), and while this work was largely unpaid, distinctions between economic and non-economic activities were sometimes permeable[1]. As the quotation at the beginning of this chapter illustrates, referring to one of the many institutions associated with the work supporting coalmining populations, community activities contributed to a unique quality of life. Involvement in their various forums cumulatively created and reproduced a sense of collective wealth and identity, which empowered residents and mitigated against some of the physical hardships of a life that revolved around the collieries. Historically, this kind of cultural self-determination has been a key feature of coalmining communities (Cope *et al.*, 1996; Williamson, 1982), and in the sense that the work necessary to maintain these solidarities constitutes productive labour, and is intertwined with labour in a range of spheres, there is a strong impetus for conceptualizing work for the community as *work* in its own right.

With the collapse of traditional industries in many parts of the UK, the heterogenization of experience and fracturing of gendered occupational aspirations among associated population groups, the mapping of their work has become more complicated and nuanced. In this context, and with talk of a 'decline of community' (Stein, 1971), it is often assumed that work geared towards maintaining community solidarities is on the wane. This draws upon the assumption, however, that the male employment of mining coal was unalterably connected to community work for coalfield populations, a dynamic without which their social similarities would collapse. This overlooks the reconfigurative potential of a broader matrix of social relations and their associated forms of labour. Glucksmann's 'total social organization of labour' (TSOL) framework (2000a) is valuable in examining whether and how labour activities geared towards promoting the interests of communities can persist in an environment where participation in paid work has become more diverse, and no longer necessarily offers a focus for shared experience. I argue that membership of particular communities, which is re-enforced by the work that people perform to support these solidarities, informs their broader decisions, and thus provides a central component in understanding local labour distributions.

This chapter draws upon a qualitative research project which examined the post-1984/85 Strike experiences of a South Wales coalmining population, and looked at how people engage in work for their communities, why this work is undertaken, and how it fits in with their other responsibilities, transgressing private and public, formal and informal boundaries (Parry, 2000). I argue that community work continues to provide a powerful occupation for local populations, and that the disruption of traditional solidarities in the coalfields has at once encompassed gain, loss and stasis. These have given way to a more diverse array of community activities, which reflect the increasingly variable socio-economic circumstances of people's lives.

Community work is related to paid employment for these populations in more complex ways. A TSOL framework is henceforth employed to explore how class and gender relations interact in the construction of its multiple forms of cultural practice and capital. Attention is drawn to the progressive potential of work in and for communities, and its role imbuing meaning and belonging upon people's lives, in addition to realigning, reconfiguring and consolidating social solidarities. Crow and Allen (1995) have argued that 'community time' offers an additional dimension in analysing communities, in facilitating an understanding of their interconnectedness to temporal events. Drawing upon this rationale, and following a discussion of the conceptual meanings of community work, this chapter draws upon my research to compare the dynamics of community work under coalmining with its current manifestations for a population who are only remotely tied together by the industry's institutions. Themes of continuity and fragmentation are employed to analyse the kinds of community labour that goes on, and the chapter moves to consider a series of 'new' formations associated with work for the community. It is argued that the latter act as bridges between the formerly analytically distinct gendered framework of the 'structural' and 'relational' aspects of communal interaction. New community formations represent an important context for reinvigorating and broadening communal participation within a restructured labour market, and offer particular insight in terms of developing a TSOL analysis.

In terms of its contribution to a new sociology of work this chapter gives space to work that is largely invisible in the mainstream literature: community labour. Specifically, it looks at the interconnections between this and labour in a number of different and overlapping spheres, drawing attention to the porosity and non-fixity of community work, and analysing its multiple meanings and their role in actors' negotiation of social inequalities.

Conceptualizing community work in the coalfields

Activities geared explicitly, but more often implicitly, towards supporting and reproducing communal attachments have rarely been conceptualized as 'work' in the sociological literature. Indeed, as Taylor's chapter has observed, community work tends to be dealt with as an aside to voluntary work, a perspective that overlooks critical differences in their forms and meanings. Further, the presupposition that community work is somehow apart from labour marginalizes the often considerable efforts involved in sustaining and reproducing communities, and neglects their contribution to local economic relations: a criterion which Glucksmann (1995) set out as central to definitions of work. So too individuals frequently fail to conceptualize their efforts to support communities as *work*, particularly when these are associated with shared or taken-for-granted expectations about community life. Countering these dominant assumptions, Mercer (1995) has striven to achieve recognition for 'community' as a *verb* rather than a noun, and Crow (1996) has drawn attention to the work of active sustenance necessary to reproduce communities. In the context of restructuring, this work has undoubtedly become more complex and worthy of study.

The former conceptualisation of communities as entities rather than social processes represents a failure to recognize the intricacies of the labour performed for communities, and a missed opportunity to analyse how community work relates to other types of labour performed by populations over a period of time. A focus upon community work necessarily also incorporates a class-based labour analysis, since the informal context of community work is potentially more accessible and meaningful for disadvantaged groups than the traditionally formalized sphere of voluntary work, with its more middle-class demographic (Barnes *et al.*, 2002; Midwinter, 1992; Taylor, this volume).

I approach these issues by analysing the various manifestations of labour performed on behalf of communities within a distinctive and geographically contained coalmining population that has recently undergone dramatic macro transformation of its expectations and institutions. In one sense, the fieldwork location[2] facilitated this investigation, since the physical distinctiveness of these communities offered conceptual clarity in documenting the work that supports them. My starting position is that community work is dynamic and variable, with a great many (changeable) boundaries, both real and imagined (Anderson, 1983). These range from the informal everyday interactions between neighbours and families, to involvement in traditional, developmental and ad-hoc community organizations, with a series of relationships linking the two – the different spheres of interaction within which an individual's portfolio of work interests simultaneously occur.

Community work's amorphous character means that it encompasses activities subjectively classifiable as leisure activities, but which also function to maintain or reproduce community attachments. The location of community work within leisure institutions belies the labour efforts which individuals may contribute, to the extent that they sometimes proxy for economic positions (for example, a sports coach). Community work then, transgresses public/private boundaries, and mirroring the disparity in the remuneration of employment/ domestic labour, its distinctive forms are differentially valued, gendered and visible. Recognition of this was exploited by the Conservative government's Community Care policy of the late 1980s, which made use of the social reformist philosophy of close-knit populations, paradoxically by stripping the community out of the equation and transferring the onus of care from the state onto the family (Sullivan, 1990). This devalued the traditional reproductive work performed by local communities in the provision of social welfare, and is likely to have been instructive in reducing public consciousness of community labour.

The lack of recognition attributed to community activities as work in their own right is a notable oversight, since failing to count these types of work risks overlooking the powerful resources they provide working-class communities. This is particularly important where paid work has become less capable of providing social or material assets, as may be the case under economic restructuring. Indeed, the transformation of local labour markets has been posited as detrimental to communal attachments for traditional working class populations. Yet this perspective overlooks the dynamic processes involved in the shaping of community relationships, and the complex interactive connections between places, social structures and meanings that unfold over a temporal continuum. For example, Warwick and Littlejohn's (1992) analysis of a post-Strike coalmining community, identified 'centripetal' and 'centrifugal' forces, propelling certain community members closer of the centre of local social life while marginalizing others, which were permeable at particular moments in time. Commentators (Crow and Allan, 1995; Sullivan, 1990) have also observed that expressions of community solidarity (conceptualized here as community work) are more explicitly crystallised and deployed in response to key external events, such as the 1984/85 Miners' Strike. These may be regarded as *peak* moments in communities' biographies, which require more explicit or measurable labour inputs.

This project upon which this analysis is based considered the longer-term effects of coalmining's decline, being carried out fifteen years after the dramatic events of the Miners' Strike (Parry, 2000). It drew upon eighteen months of fieldwork in the western part of the South Wales coalfield, when 50 qualitative interviews were conducted with individuals with a range of labour market positionings[3]. Using this data[4], community work is approached from an inclusive perspective, drawing attention to ways in which it has persisted and may be reconfigured in a context where coalmining's traditional institutions have diminished and offer less formalized labour settings. It is argued that individuals employ temporality in complex ways in relation to their communal experiences, invoking both dynamism and stasis in wrestling with the simultaneous pulls of social change and the explanatory power of tradition. In the following analysis, quotations are employed to illustrate trends within the data, and all interviewees' identities are disguised by pseudonyms.

Working-class communities have never been distinguished by a singular fixed pattern of communal relations; these have been diverse and shifting, variable with socio-economic factors. Individuals are differentially embedded in communal relationships, reflecting their levels of commitment and exchange potentiality (Crow and Allen, 1994) and shaped by their labour market positioning. This, in turn, informs the ways they mobilize localized expectations to frame their personal priorities. In unpicking the patterning of these experiences, it is possible to decipher the relationships between contemporous forms of community work and broader social relations. However, with the challenging of homogenized theories of community coherence (Strangleman *et al.*, 1999), so too it might be expected that within a restructured social environment individuals' participation in community labour will become less uniform. While for traditional coalmining populations, work for the community was fundamentally related to the gendered character of local employment and domestic labour, amid a reconfigured labour market it remains patterned by a multiplicity of work commitments. These are illuminated by adopting a TSOL framework.

In the aftermath of the 1984/85 Strike, a number of commentators (Francis, 1990; Rees, 1985) anticipated that subsequent transformations would diminish coalmining communities' cohesiveness. Women's relationships to the public and private spheres are critical in understanding whether this has happened. Warwick and Littlejohn (1992) recognized that for coalmining populations, women's responsibility for 'traditional social institutions' (the domestic sphere and local informal networks) entailed part of the 'local cultural capital' that helped sustain communal identity. Drawing upon a comparable working-class community, fishermen, Lummis (1985) described women's communal relationships as constituting their class experience, an observation that holds true for the way community work was organized within the TSOL of coalmining populations. Women's greater integration into the workforce in recent years is therefore likely to be reflected in a reconfiguration of their communal and class relations, and the labour forms in which these are manifested.

Community work and the TSOL in traditional coalmining communities

While there is a danger in over-generalising coalmining populations' homogeneity, community in the South Wales coalfields at the industry's height was highly gendered and synonymous with a specific set of class interests, described in the introduction. Gender distinctions, however, were not continuously or uniformly manifested in terms of separate spheres. For example, both men and women attended local chapels, yet gendered hierarchies included a largely male clergy, distinctive male and female voice choirs, and mainly female-fundraisers. In light of their distinctive involvement in community work, men and women placed a different value on the coherence of coalmining communities. Men described the sense of belonging they derived from participating in its various lodges, pubs and clubs, while women talked about the integrative potential and strength to be drawn from community networks. Community thus had a different meaning and was associated with different practices for men and women in coalmining regions, a finding reflected in other studies of other close-knit (and disadvantaged) population groups (Gatens and MacKinnon, 1999; Mumford and Power, 2003).

For example, Tony Bayliss, a former miner who was made redundant after the Strike, had long been active in the local miners' choir, which had been pivotal in the Strike's fundraising efforts in touring the country, and which continued long after the colliery to which it had been attached was closed. His wife, Kate, noted the multiple (legitimized) functions of this kind of community work:

'He knows most of the people in [village], they say, 'Oh there's Tony, he sings in the choir.' There's a lot of charity work with the choir, mind you it's a damn good excuse for the men to go out and enjoy, be under no illusions.'

By contrast, Rose Edwards, a woman who left the mining village where she had grown up after getting married, repeatedly referred back to the *informal* help provided by her old community, and contrasted this with her later experience living in a Swansea suburb where her neighbours remained an unknown quantity despite living there for several decades:

'The sense of community was wonderful . . . they all helped each other and you would borrow butter and eggs off your neighbour and she would borrow back off you. And they would help if someone had a new baby; if someone had a baby the neighbour would do the washing and feed your family for you until you were out of bed, you know. And if there was any bereavement they would come and you know, really good support, wonderful friendship.'

For women, this kind of support was traditionally provided within the informal framework of neighbourhood and familial ties. While communal gendered expectations provided women with an important resource, however, and offered validation, satisfaction and a source of strength, they also imposed restrictions upon their behaviour and limited social movement. This is comparable to the 'cultural capital' that Skeggs (1997) observed that her working-class women interviewees had amassed from participating in activities deemed 'respectable' by local social norms. Similarly, women in coalmining communities acquired status amid broader economic disadvantage through participating in gendered work, including labour promoting the social welfare of their communities.

Inter-connected structures and relationships thus formed the basis of 'community' in the coalfields, and provided the context for a multitude of (often invisible) labour activities. The purpose of community work for working class communities such as those studied here, in large part focused around mutuality (see Taylor, this volume). Historically, however, it has also transgressed such definitions, including work that demonstrated solidarity with other disadvantaged groups and took a broader humanitarian or ideological perspective[5].

Community work, representing collectivized interests, was manifested perhaps most visibly during the 1984/85 Miners' Strike, when coalfield populations formulated and sustained what came to constitute 'an alternative welfare state' (Sullivan, 1990). This was mobilized through women's support groups and picketing activities, in addition to in a host of less formalized ways. Significantly, it involved the active labour and support of a high proportion of local residents, whether or not they remained actively connected to the collieries (Parry, 2000). In large part, the artificially high level of community work necessary to sustain the Strike effort was possible because the demands of the situation permitted women to move into the public or structural face of community work, replicating their community labour there. The 'Strike generation', that is, individuals economically active around the time of the 1984/85 Strike, were particularly vocal in referencing the gendered patterning of community labour outlined above. This group represented a strong 'imagined community' (Anderson, 1983), and involved both men and women, whose shared experiences enabled them to mobilize habitus in an unusually coherent way (Parry, 2000).

It was somewhat inevitable that the momentum of community work declined after the Strike, but less predictable that it would be reconfigured in lasting ways. The alliances forged during the Strike were untypical of coalmining populations' routinised community work. Their meaningfulness, however, enabled the women most active in the Strike's activities to maintain an 'imagined community' long after the women's support groups had been dispersed. They have continued to get involved in a range of community work, maintaining a more diverse array of community solidarities than in the past. Some aspects of this involvement are explored below.

Community work in a reconfigured environment

The regional decline of coalmining and dismantling of many of its attendant institutions, has affected community labour activities at both conceptual levels described above. Traditional institutions' vitality has been impeded by the decline of the industry, and simultaneously the formation of women's supportive networks has been challenged by demands for them to juggle private and public sphere activities amid rising levels of male unemployment. These transformations are examined below in terms of three main themes which emerged from the research: change, stasis and reconfiguration. The coexistence of these highlights the inherent dynamism of community work and the multidimensionality of 'community time'. While interviewees attributed differential emotive weightings to structural and relational aspects of community work, a degree of fluidity characterized their ability to utilize different sorts of discourses. This emphasized the multiple meanings that individuals attach to their communal experiences, habitus serving as a flexible resource from which explanatory power is drawn in relation to dynamic circumstances.

a. The decline of community interaction

Change was the main theme to characterize interviewees' feelings about community, unsurprisingly in the context of recent accelerated socio-economic transformation. Men and women raised this point equally, although their perceptions of community change were manifested differently. Most prominently, interviewees reported a decline in their involvement in communal interactions, which they attributed to the disintegration of traditional institutions associated with coalmining, which had hitherto provided a forum for community activity. Women's heightened engagement in paid employment and the increased prevalence of commuting strategies in response to the elongation of local labour markets were also regarded as contributory factors, restricting individuals' time to engage in localist interactions. As Kate Bayliss observed, reflecting on changes over her lifetime:

'When I was a girl . . . I knew everyone, everyone knew everybody else's business . . . The community spirit is still there, but it's distant through lack of time . . . I think it's got a lot to do with the wives working personally, because the wives are not here to communicate . . . I mean a woman never went to work years ago, so she was the one that was the centre of that sort of community thing.'

Sheila Thomas, the wife of a former miner, explained how a shared sense of investment in local employment had bolstered community belonging, which was now suffering with the collapse of traditional industry in the area:

'I don't know, since the collieries have finished everybody goes out of the village to work, 'cause there's no jobs around here. So really, I think that has all broken down. You know, there's no togetherness.'

Thus interviewees' perceptions of reduced levels of communal interaction and involvement in informal community work invoked both elements of the gendered equation outlined above. They were also explicitly tied to transformed expectations of regional paid employment, highlighting the value of a TSOL framework in exploring the interdependencies between different forms of work for populations.

A second way that community was perceived to have changed was in terms of a reduced commitment to maintaining the cohesiveness of local social relations, sometimes linked to rising levels of apathy. This was particularly noted by those who had been active in the public spaces of the community on a long-standing basis, who reported finding it more difficult to enlist support for their causes. David Howells, a former miner and lodge secretary who moved into a paid position in local politics following his redundancy from the collieries, explained the situation in terms of a growing pressure to pursue individualised lifestyles, reflecting a more diverse labour market and a shift in people's priorities towards working for their families ahead (or instead) of working for their communities:

'It's changed because of Thatcherism. Because one thing that Thatcher taught everyone in the communities was to look after themselves and forget about everyone else. And because of the climate that people find themselves in with no work, then you are forced into a situation of looking after yourself. And not much time to look out for anyone else really.'

Slightly differently, an older group of interviewees contemplated younger generations' waning interest in community in terms of their failing to get involved in the invisible routine community work necessary to maintain and reproduce localist attachments. This group warned that the overall coherence of community solidarity would subsequently decline. Claire Davies, who had been involved in various community activities and informal voluntary work throughout her life, explained:

'I find it's [the community spirit] disappearing, and particularly with the younger generation. I mean you still have the [older] element where they have their coffee mornings and they go dancing together. But as they die off, nothing fills their place.'

This response was characterized by recognition that the problem was linked to the Valleys' reduced employment opportunities, which necessitated a proportion of the younger generation migrating out to find work (on a permanent or daily basis), reducing the density and accessibility of extended family networks among the remaining population. This issue reiterates the inseparability of paid and unpaid work for this former coalmining population; an appreciation of the one cannot be developed without the other. Reflecting this, the reportedly greater communal involvement of an older generation may be considered in terms of their greater locatedness in the region due to the availability of time provided by their retired status.

b. Communal stasis

A second conceptualization of community work drew upon continuity discourses, which sometimes overlapped with perceptions of decline. Most interviewees who described their community experiences thus had maintained a stable labour market positioning over the restructuring period. Their involvement in community labour activities had consequently undergone little transformation, and they were embedded in a set of relatively traditional industrial social relations. Notably, the perception that community activities had undergone little or no change was limited to the 'relational' aspects of community outlined above, a fairly predictable finding since institutional formats (being linked to the infrastructure of coal) were self-evidently transformed.

The main way in which communal activities were perceived to have remained static concerned the resources embodied in local interactions, which interviewees described as providing security and status. However, these networks continued to be perceived in gendered terms. Men emphasized the social positioning which participation in community activities imbued upon them, and valued these relations in terms of the information they provided, a feature which counterbalanced recent occupational transitions and a decline in established certainties. By contrast, women articulated the benefits of community networks in terms of providing emotional support. Peter Clark, who had moved from the Coal Board collieries to the private pits, and through a period of unemployment, before resolving his position by buying into the worker-owned Tower[6] colliery, described the stability his communal relationships had provided during this time of difficulty, being comparable in essence to the collegial relationships maintained within the collieries:

> 'The majority of people in this village I know, they know me, brought up with them, you know. They're sort of family or friends, I've always lived quite round about. So yes, there is a good sense of community spirit there, definitely.'

Gary Peters, a former miner who had set up his own business after being made redundant, pointed to the continuity of particular local employers in terms of maintaining communal relations, reemphasising the centrality of paid employment in the area's traditional TSOL:

> 'There's still quite a lot of people work in [local factory], so a lot of people are still working in a similar environment, possibly that holds it together a bit. Things like the rugby clubs and things like that hold it together a bit. So I'd say yes, there's still very much a sense of community.'

Older interviewees tended to locate stability in more cultural community formats, linked partly to their more protracted relationships with the labour market, but also reflecting the persistence of local communal institutions tied less explicitly to coalmining's fortunes. Fred Hale, a former trade union official who retired at the height of the pit closures, described a number of different types of community work in which he maintained an involvement after leaving his paid position:

> 'I mean I'm still with the union, I'm still quite active with the union [among other things, providing advice to former miners on industrial injury claims]. But yes, there's quite a lot going on. I mean the old age pensioners are very good, they organize quite a lot of things. And there's the choirs, you know.'

Morris's (1990) research on redundant steelworkers in Port Talbot observed the importance of communal networks for men, providing them with access to employment opportunities in both formal and informal labour markets. Similar conclusions can be applied to the former Welsh coalfields, where communal networks were to some degree maintained as a pragmatic survival tactic (Parry, 2003).

By contrast, female interviewees tended to place a greater emphasis upon communal networks in terms of the persistence of mutual support and reciprocity between friends and neighbours. These were regarded as providing significant material and emotional benefits, which contributed to interviewees' sense of solidarity, and which contrasted with more heterogeneous or urban environments, a finding comparable to Goodsell's analysis of the Mormon village (2000). Betty Morgan, who was married to a former opencast miner and who was active in local politics, explained:

'And I still think that, perhaps most of all, you have got neighbours who have known each other a long time. And who are prepared to look out for each other. I think you see this in the winter when you've got concern within the community for the elderly.'

Beth Jenkins explained how this communal trust had played a large part in giving her the confidence to go out to work after her husband was made redundant, since both then and now, she felt that her neighbours would '*look out*' for their children, and this recognition gave her peace of mind in negotiating the labour market:

'If I needed help any time, or if the children were in, you know, if they needed anything and I wasn't around, they could go and knock on a door anywhere in this village and they'd get a good response.'

This also concurs with Morris's (1990) research, conducted in a similarly gendered environment. She argued that communal networks provided women with important coping resources during times of restructuring, promoting flows of material aid and support (resources provided by employment in favourable economic conditions).

c. Reconfiguring community work

The research, which involved ethnography as well as qualitative interviews, uncovered activity in a number of new types of community organization, which constituted a radical departure from the community work that had previously gone on in the Valleys. In particular, where the coalfields' traditional institutions, such as miners' lodges and working men's clubs, had been maintained through a wage contribution, the material bases of new forms of community organization were not directly linked to paid employment in the same way, and a more imaginative approach to their funding has consequently been necessary. These organizations took a variety of forms, many of which were constructed and developed by the Valleys' populations, and which drew on a mixture of traditional and new resources. Most strikingly, individuals who participated in them tended to adopt, or be in the process of adopting, a 'strategic' approach to their paid employment (Parry, 2003), reconfiguring their occupational aspirations, often at the expense of short-term material gain. Additionally, more women than men were involved in these new forms of community work. In other words, this type of community work had a particular (and gendered) relationship to paid work within the local social organization of labour during this period of restructuring, and provided a critical social role which should be considered in the context of changed conditions.

Participation in these organizations tended to follow an integrative pattern, in that individuals' initial involvement often began on an informal or unconscious basis (which women often 'naturalized' in terms of activity that would further the interests of their families). The rewards of involvement might then prompt movement into more formalized and permanent organizations. Prior involvement in the women's support groups during the 1984/85 Miners' Strike, and connections made with Labour politics through husbands' enthusiasm and involvement in local lodges, were strong starting points for women's involvement. These new community organizations generated considerable enthusiasm and success among participants, providing a counter to structural losses, promoting the development of organizational skills and self-confidence, and reinvigorating communal values amongst a younger generation. The ways in which these new community activities manifested themselves were distinctive in terms of three main functions, although these too sometimes overlapped: leisure, education, and economic development.

The first of these, new communal organizations associated with leisure, were particularly appealing to women, being frequently associated with enacting improvements in their children's quality of life. For example, a number of women described getting involved in informal pressure groups to push for local play areas, and as they gained organizational and lobbying skills and extended their social networks, they moved on to help set up more formalized community organizations with a broader range of functions. Notably, the implicit linkage women made to traditional gendered expectations about work in getting involved in these organizations facilitated their involvement and generated little communal hostility, working as they were within a framework of local cultural norms whilst experimenting with the boundaries within which they operated. Lister (1997) has noted the significance of care-giving work, in acting as an impetus to women's involvement in collective activity. Likewise, women's involvement in these new leisure-focused organizations highlighted an important relationship between informal care work and community work within the local social organization of labour, which could be used to effect mobility. That the work associated with leisured community organizations tended to be *ad hoc*, requiring little specialist knowledge or experience, also appealed to women who had frequently experienced marginalization in the coalfields' more traditional political institutions (Parry, 2000).

Crucially, involvement and success in these organizations had a similar effect on participants as their contribution in the women's support groups during the 1984/85 Strike (Leonard, 1991; Measham and Allen, 1994; Seddon, 1996), increasing their self-confidence and fostering their enthusiasm for such activity. These qualities fostered a broader participation in community work, encouraging activists to spread the word about their experiences and experiment with a range of institutional forms. For example, Jill David, who was a community councillor, on the management committee of the local community centre, and an active Labour Party member, had her interest in local issues fuelled by a campaign to save the local school. When this was successful, her confidence grew, and she went on to take a more active role in securing funding for a sports centre. Her involvement in local issues thus grew incrementally and then exponentially.

A second form of work associated with new communal organizations took an educative dimension, being focused in large part around the DOVE workshop (Dulais (Valley) Opportunity for Voluntary Enterprise). This spin-off organization emanated from women's activities during the 1984/85 Miners Strike. Originally a grass-roots community action group, over the years it adapted and diversified, developing into the venue for the Community University of the Valleys, which offered a variety of vocational and artistic classes, provided childcare for those retraining, and housed one of the UK's few remaining miners' libraries. One of its more important elements has been a focus on sociopolitical education, often with a localist emphasis. While individuals taking these courses did not necessarily expect them to provide a route into local employment, they offered a context where the region's history was kept alive and valued, and fostered an ongoing interest in learning. Notably, DOVE has expanded to such an extent that it now plays an important role in local economic development, providing training for a workforce that was previously undertaken in the collieries and through NCLC (National Central Labour College) classes. Its policy of two-way curriculum development has been fundamental in ensuring its responsiveness to community needs, and its physical location within, and being mainly staffed by members of, the community has been vital in making education accessible.

Participation in DOVE illustrates the complex patterning of community work in the way that labour was organized in the Valleys. A number of the women involved in setting up the original co-operative went on to find paid employment within its later, more formalized, structure, for example, as administrators or childcare assistants. Others taught in classes on a voluntary or paid basis (sometimes a mixture of the two), or provided informal voluntary support through activities such as sitting on its management committee. Others again, who participated in the classes on a leisure or educative basis, went on to utilize the skills they acquired in various paid and unpaid forms of work, for example, in setting up their own businesses selling arts and crafts products, or in producing these goods for free for their friends and family. DOVE thus provides an illustration of the substantive local relationships between different forms of work. For example, this new type of community organization has provided a context which fosters movement from learning work into paid employment, and its classes offered an environment where community networks could be maintained, in which knowledge was transmitted, and new alliances forged within an increasingly mobile community. In turn, participation in these classes sometimes led to opportunities to get involved in other types of community or local voluntary work.

A third form of new community organization provided a distinctive context for community work that was associated with promoting local economic growth. These entailed an institutionalised form of community organization developed to create paid employment through support given to local enterprises. Formalized organizations (in this sense being comparable to the 'structural' aspects of community work performed by traditional coalmining populations) displayed a public hierarchy of paid and elected members, backed up by a network of individuals who worked for them on an informal and unpaid basis. In line with men's longer-term relationships with formal political structures in the area, and reflecting the importance of social networks in facilitating access to community work, male interviewees were more likely to become involved in these kinds of organizations. They also tended to raise most unease among those interviewed. Paradoxically their localized funding structures offered communities fewer powers of self-determination and autonomy than the global and national sources used in the leisure and educative organizations, and they called upon participants to conform to a very different set of expectations from the taken-for-granted routines associated with traditional local institutions.

New forms of community work were also observed in a variety of less formalized contexts. For example, an annual festival was established over the course of the research, which involved community work on a variety of levels, including fundraising, performance, running stalls and organising sporting events. A well-attended coffee morning was visited during the fieldwork period, which provided the impetus for a host of *ad hoc* fund-raising activities. Interviewees' accounts were peppered with descriptions of the various clubs and social activities in which they took part, and many of these utilized premises vacated by institutions associated with coalmining. Much of this involvement constituted productive activity, which might otherwise be considered as 'work', such as sports coaching or taking up formal positions, including acting as treasurer or secretary to new community organizations. Thus while the communities of the South Wales Valleys have experienced considerable transformation, much of which has been detrimental to their continued vibrancy, this has not left a vacuum. A plurality of formal and informal organizations have taken on the mantle of traditional structures in fostering and re-creating communal relationships. That this activity has ranged from and across formalized contexts to more impermanent and informal ones, provides evidence of the value of utilizing a TSOL framework to analyse how the Valleys' explicitly gendered community work has been reconfigured and fits together, having moved away from its more clearly defined 'structural' and 'relational' spheres of interaction.

Involvement in these new community-focused organizations had a considerable impact upon individuals, facilitating the development of more 'strategic' life perspectives (Parry, 2003) made possible through the knowledge and confidence accumulated in these contexts. The assets which individuals developed in this process, have positioned them more advantageously in terms of negotiating the demands of a transformed labour market. However, this kind of personal strategism rarely implied that individuals were steering more individualised trajectories, as suggested by theorists such as Beck (1992). Rather participation in new community organizations fostered a reinvigorated enthusiasm for communal participation and broadened the circumstances within which this was possible. That men tended to find engagement with new communal organizations more problematic, can be linked to their historical relationship with formalized institutional structures, which are re-imagined more slowly.

Extended attention has been devoted to new community organizations here, providing evidence of what Francis, in his prologue to Cope *et al.*'s (1996) review of community organizations in the coalfield, described as 'a collectivist revival'. Francis raised the point that recent success stories in the Valleys were notable for their collectivist outlook: for example, Tower Colliery, the Community University of the Valleys and the DOVE workshop. Work within and for the community crosses the formal/informal divide within any given population, encompassing a whole series of relationships connecting these two spheres. Part of the difficulty in conceptualizing community work is its diversity, in that it includes both formal and informal forms of voluntary work, care work, leisure activities, paid employment and informal work, which may take place in distinctive spheres, or simultaneously within the same institution. Indeed, there was evidence that some individuals utilized these very interconnections to effect movement across social space and to accumulate assets.

Conclusion

The ways in which community work has been reconfigured in the Welsh Valleys moves beyond a simple reproduction of community relations (arguably the main type of community work performed in traditional coalmining populations), and has utilized a range of new kinds of community organization to effect this. These have increasingly drawn upon voluntary and statutory sectors, as well as more informal formats. Despite their apparent diversity, they have shared a common humanitarian and communal self-help focus, echoing the social reformist philosophy fostered by coalmining's traditional institutions. These 'new' forms of community work represent a flexible response to restructuring, and have utilized global and national, in addition to local, forms of capital.

Labour market positioning remains influential in the ways that people get involved in community work (for example, via occupational networks), and there was evidence of this type of labour being employed as a strategy to effect mobility and build personal resources. However, involvement in community work was increasingly patterned by a multiplicity of work commitments. For women in particular, involvement often originated in the women's support groups forged during the 1984/85 Strike. Temporal considerations are also central in documenting community work, which for coalmining populations has varied from a raised level during the Strike to a less intense but more differentiated array of activities since then. This process of change is likely to continue as the old solidarities associated with employment in the collieries become less predictable. Communities, by virtue of their geography and historical patterns of colliery closures, will also be at different stages of responding to labour market restructuring, and this is reflected in the forms of community work in which they engage.

As ever, community work is not only expressed in institutional formats, although the latter are less challenging to document within traditional analytical frameworks. Many interviewees' stories were characterized by a 'decline of community' discourse, a feeling that '*other*' people were not sufficiently integrated into '*the community*', or did not care enough to perform the day-to-day maintenance work they associated with earlier times, a phenomenon which was felt to be compromising community coherence. In essence, what was being expressed was the emotional or relational work so often taken on by women in coalmining communities, which has been articulated in less homogenized ways in a transformed labour market where women's place within the TSOL is substantially reconfigured (Parry, 2003).

The 'decline of community' thesis might be more accurately described as a decline of *particular* (traditional and homogenous) forms of community. The people living in the former coalfields continue to be held together by multiple bonds of interest, place and perception, which are maintained and realigned through their involvement in diverse forms of community work, reflecting their differing attachments and priorities. Thus stasis, in terms of particular communities, is able to coexist with decline, although the former perception was more often associated with people who had maintained their place within local social relations. This population is likely to be further reduced in the coming years, and the balance will also be informed by particular communities being further on in the transition away from coalmining (for whom the 1984/85 Strike is a less a critical reference point).

We should not expect to see class interests submerged in the form of relatively unified and homogeneous community work outside certain critical or exceptional points in time, such as the 1984/85 Strike. This is likely to be amplified by the diversification of former coalfield populations in the context of restructured local labour markets. This chapter has provided evidence, however, that community work continues to play an important role in the social organization of post-coalmining populations, and that the plurality of forms maintained, reproduced and reconfigured reflect the multitude of groupings and regroupings of the population's interests. In an important sense, community work now plays a *more* coherent part in the social solidarities of these populations than paid employment, reflecting their shared interests in a matrix of organizational forms.

Notes

1 For example, local councillors, once unpaid, are now awarded a nominal sum, although the people doing this work and the work they perform often remain unchanged.
2 Interviews were conducted in the anthracite, westerly region of the South Wales Valleys – these focused mainly on the Dulais and Neath Valleys, with some additional interviews in the Amman and Cynon Valleys to capture mining communities associated with open-cast mining and the Tower Colliery enterprise (see below).
3 For all those interviewed, a household member had been employed in coalmining around the time of the 1984/85 Strike.
4 Interviews were taped, with interviewees' consent, and verbatim transcripts produced which were analysed both manually and (for this paper) on QSR NVivo.

5 This included community support for and local men's participation as International Brigaders during the Spanish Civil War (Parry, 1996). Such traditions were echoed in campaigning for the Greenham Common women, gay and lesbian and black welfare groups during the 1984/85 Miners' Strike.

6 The former British Coal mine which provided a landmark for miners in being successfully purchased by its former employees under threat of closure, and which has subsequently been run as a worker-takeover enterprise. See Waddington *et al.* (1998) for a detailed account.

Part 5
International comparisons

Public and private:
Implications for care work

Pat Armstrong and Hugh Armstrong

Western feminists of all persuasions have long argued that households and
formal economies, communities and markets, interpenetrate each other. At the
same time, they have demonstrated how the development of capitalism has
resulted in a move towards the separation of the public and private into what
appear at least to be quite different spheres or spaces, with different logics, different constructions of time and different relations.

Notions of public and private have become useful analytical constructs,
helping us to make gender a central concern and assisting in the development
of an historical understanding of the forces that influence relations among
women as well as between women and men, employers and employees. The path
to the separation of public and private has been uneven and incomplete, variable from region to region, with race, and from class to class. The whole is
shaped by capitalism in numerous and often contradictory ways, as well as by
resistance. Feminists, however, have documented the general tendency toward
separation of private and public, especially during the development of the
welfare state, and they have analysed the implications of this separation for both
struggle and inequality.

As western feminists have been exploring how a public/private divide influences women's relations, they have also been refining their conceptual tools in
ways that emphasize differences and complexity. Early second wave feminists
mainly talked about public and private as a single divide, with women relegated
primarily to the private sphere of household. This relegation was understood as
a major factor in, as well as an indicator of, women's inequality. Few of the post-
modern feminists have revisited the public/private debate in light of the more
recent transformations in the welfare state or in relation to the increasing appreciation of complexity and differences. We revisit and revise these notions here.

In this chapter, we argue both that there are a number of private and publics
and that the distinctions among them are blurring in ways that are detrimental
to many women. Public and private is used in two senses. First, a distinction is
made between households and the spaces outside them, especially the formal
economy, but also the informal economy and what is often called the third or
voluntary sector. For ease of discussion and as a means of linking them to past

feminist debates, these will be called public and private spheres. Second, there is the distinction between the public and private sectors within the formal economy, with government funded and controlled operations separated from the private ones. And within the private sector outside the household, there are for-profit and not-for-profit concerns. Again to aid discussion, private and public sectors are used here to refer to the 'public' and 'private' contained within the formal economy.

During the period following the Second World War, in western nations at least, both kinds of private and public became more distinct from each other. And within the public sector outside the household, distinctions among state organizations, private, for-profit and not for-profit concerns also became clearer. The search for profit remained dominant throughout society but somewhat different logics applied to the public and private spheres. The distinction was far from simply negative for women. Especially within the state sector in the Canadian formal economy, women enjoyed some success in drawing the distinctions in ways that brought them more recognition, pay, security and control. With the emergence of the neo-liberal state, however, has come an increasing blurring of the distinctions between and within the different kinds of private and public. At the same time, some distinctions between and within them have been reinforced. Along with this increasing blurring and new distinctions have come increasing precariousness for women as a group, and for particular groups of women.

The uneven and contradictory developments in the separation of public and private are particularly obvious in Canadian health care. In health care, there are continuing and often explicit debates about the rights and responsibilities of the public and private in all senses of the terms. Equally obvious is the gendered nature of work and of social relations. With the movement from a welfare state to a managerial state and the increasing privatization of health care, the lines of separation between private and public that were emphasized during the postwar period have become increasingly blurred. In the process, the labour and relations of women, in connection both to men and to other women, are being transformed. The results are contradictory, although often negative, for women and equality.

This chapter explores such developments in relation to the women working in health care, including those who cook, feed, clean and do laundry within the Canadian health care system. As this system was developed during the postwar years, the combination of employment in a well-supported public sector and high rates of unionization created decent working conditions and some measure of security in employment for the women who do the overwhelming majority of the work. Women in this public sector even had some success in getting their labour recognized as skilled, rather than as merely work any woman could do by virtue of being a woman. These developments were particularly important in terms of equity among women, because such work is frequently done by immigrants and women from racialized groups.

Over the last two decades, however, for-profit managerial strategies have been applied to this sector. The monopolies over areas of practice among professionals are under attack, blurring the boundaries between different kinds of work. At the same time, much of the labour involved in cooking, feeding, cleaning, and laundry has been redefined, not as health care, but as hotel or ancillary services, justifying the contracting out of the work to for-profit firms. A new logic and new relations are the result. It is becoming increasingly difficult to tell public from private care in the formal economy. Meanwhile, more care is provided in the home by mainly female, and mainly unpaid, caregivers. This movement of care into the home blurs the distinction between private and public spheres and sectors. It also makes many of the skills involved invisible. Meanwhile, what constitutes public sector employment and formal economy care work becomes, on the one hand more narrowly defined and on the other, more difficult to distinguish in terms of what is private sector and what is public sector. In the process, the work of these women becomes more marginalized and precarious.

Sorting out privates and publics

Our understanding of what constitutes private and public is developing over time. Our experience of public and private is being reconstructed at the same time as the public and private are themselves being reconstructed. In order to look at the ways public and private are being reshaped in health care, it is first necessary to look at what we mean by these terms.

The notion of the private household is not only western and modern; it is also gendered and classed. The idea that a man's home is his castle implies that he is the master, that he can do what he likes there and that he is by definition the property owner. Second wave feminists have struggled from the 1960s on to make visible both the labour and the relations hidden in the household. They have argued that the home was 'a haven in a heartless world' for more men than women. They have noted that virtually all women bear the major responsibility for household labour and care, even though there are significant differences among women in terms of their ability to escape this work or even the household itself. Understood as embodying relations of power, some feminists have also understood households as not only gendered and classed but racialized as well. They have sought to have domestic tasks and care recognized as work and to challenge the inequalities, along with the brutality, that flow from in this kind of household privacy. They have emphasized the nature of household labour, labour without end, labour never done. This timeless work, with overlapping responsibilities, was understood as embedded in personal relations that made it difficult to separate labour from love. One of the reasons the amount of time women spend on care is so often underestimated is the difficulty in separating out the labour from the relationship. For women, caring about is caring for (Baines, Evans and Neysmith, 1998). Loving, for women, means providing the constant work of care and the very privacy of the home hides the labour along with the social relations.

Second wave feminists understood the state as reinforcing women's location in the home, along with the work and the relations of households. Yet they looked to the state to protect them from violence, grant them rights and support their labour through direct and indirect means, such as the enforcement of alimony orders, the enhancement of welfare payments and the provision of childcare. Feminists, along with many other groups, also fought for state provision of other services, some of which had been provided by women without pay in the household. 'The personal is political,' a common slogan in the 1960s among western feminists, was both a call to expose the links that make personal troubles public issues, and a demand for state, or what was usually called public, action.

At the same time, the feminists of this period sought to make some issues more private for women, less a matter of public regulation. In postwar Canada for example, access to abortion and birth control were prohibited by law, and divorce was extremely difficult for women to obtain. Women successfully demanded that the state leave these decisions to individual women themselves. These feminists also sought to protect the privacy rights of poor women. For example, they successfully demanded that welfare agents had no right to enter the home of lone mothers in search of signs there was a man around who could, or at least should, provide financial support. In other words, second wave feminists wanted both more state action and less state intervention in some formerly private areas. The demands were less contradictory than they appear, because in both cases women were demanding a clarification of the rights and responsibilities of states and individuals; they sought a clearer as well as a different divide between private and public. In the process, they were seeking a new balance of power within households and among households, individuals, employers and the state along with new conditions of work. They wanted some space and time of their own, along with a more equal sharing of responsibilities and power.

The consequences of their success were, however, sometimes contradictory. Feminist demands for less medical intervention in birth, for example, were used as a justification for dramatically shortening hospital stays. Women were sent home within hours of delivery, without the benefit of midwives or other paid professional support. This lack of choice and formal support often made birth more difficult for women without knowledgeable relatives at home or the means to pay for additional care.

The public in this sense was the state sector, although it often also encompassed many non-governmental organizations that carried out state functions under its direction and with its funding. In theory at least, it was responsible to citizens. This public sphere provided regulations and supports to for-profit and not-for-profit organizations, as well as to households and individuals. The expansion of regulations, financial assistance and services meant the public sector also provided employment directly and indirectly throughout the country, especially for women. Brought together in large public-sector workplaces, women were able to organize effectively in unions and professional organizations in the public sector. Indeed, the majority of unionized women are employed in the public sector. In 1999, three-quarters of the women employed at the federal, provincial and municipal level in the public sector, compared to 14 per cent in the private sector, were covered by union contracts (Perspectives on Labour and Income, 2000:45). According to a study published by the Canadian Council on Social Development, women's wage gains between 1984 and 1994 were mainly attributable to the jobs in health, education and social services (Scott and Lockhead, 1997).

Their struggles here have been aided by the state's inability to relocate where labour is cheaper, by the state's international commitments to human rights, by labour shortages, by a booming economy and by pressure on the state to act like a model employer. They were also supported by an ideology that saw public sector work as different and by practices not driven by the search for profit. The impact, however, was contradictory for women because such work was often defined as a labour of love rather than as work, limiting their power and financial rewards. Unionization helped women clarify who does what under what conditions, drawing firmer lines between gender and work as well as challenging power relations at work. It gave them the right to say no to everything from extra work, especially tasks traditionally associated with women, to sexual harassment. Their success in the public sector also reduced differences among women in terms of both wages and conditions of work.

Although never viewed as simply benign or benevolent by feminists and often viewed as a problem rather than a solution, the state nonetheless offered some possibility for women collectively to influence decisions and to monitor decisions that were made. Not driven by the search for profit, public sector organizations were better able than for-profit ones to respond to many of women's demands. Time was not money in the same way as it is in for-profit concerns, leaving more leeway for work organizations that accommodated both ends and means. Struggles by women led to significant legal protections and prohibitions against discrimination in employment. Some of this legislation, such as that concerning equal pay for work of equal value, applies only to the public sector in many Canadian jurisdictions and thus further adds to the advantages for women of working in the public sector. These developments simultaneously expanded what was included in the public sector and distinguished it more clearly from households and for-profit firms. In the process, relations and conditions of work in the public sector became to some extent distinguishable from those in other areas.

'Public' was also used in the feminist literature as a counter to 'private' households. It encompassed the public sector, for-profit and not-for profit organizations as well as the informal economy. This lumping allowed women to expose the differences between public and private spheres and to reveal the ways inequalities hidden in the household spill into the public and are in turn reinforced by relations there (see Glucksmann, 2000a). Relations in the public sector were more likely to be formal, to be based on rules and organizational principles that contrast with the more intimate and informal ones in the household.

Time spent at work in the public sector was more clearly defined and limited than time spent at work in the home. Work was also more physically separated from what is defined as non-work, and most often paid. Even if employees have little control over their own time or effort at work in the public sphere, they can at least look forward to some time away from work that is under their control. In the private sphere, there is often little distinction for women between work and non-work time or space, and their control over their labour may be more apparent than real.

The notion of private is not restricted to households, however. Within the formal economy, private most often refers to for-profit concerns. Their profits come from paying less and selling more, or from eliminating the competition. Labour is not only commodified, in the sense of being paid, as it is in the state sector. It is also commodified in the sense that owners and managers are constantly searching to pay less for labour in order to realize a profit. This often means making employees work longer and harder or more quickly by reorganizing the work and by introducing technologies to do the work or control it. The logic is thus based on the drive to increase profits, and the relations are ones of ownership and control, secrecy and the virtual absence of democracy. The search for profit in the face of competition is understood to lead necessarily to efficiency, effectiveness and quality, as each owner seeks to have their products bought because they are the best and the cheapest to produce. In other words, the logic of the private sector is different from the logic in the public sector of the formal economy, just as the logic is different between the public and private spheres.

A profit-based system bases choice, as well as power, on ability to pay. Because most women have fewer financial resources than most men, and distribution of these resources is racialized as well as gendered, inequality between women and men and among women is greater the greater the strength of the for-profit sector. Because most women were segregated into jobs defined as unskilled, most had few means of resisting employers' pressures. Many feminists, among others, sought to limit the search for profit by removing some services entirely from the market, by pushing for restrictions on corporate powers through regulations, and by unionizing. They enjoyed some success in these struggles, although their efforts to unionize in the private sector largely failed. Paradoxically, their successes in this public sector were a factor in the current demand to eliminate regulations, free the market and privatize services.

A hundred years ago, profits throughout the world mainly came from producing goods, extracting resources and financing both. As profits began to decline in these sectors in the mid-20th century, owners looked more and more to the provision of services. And eventually they started to look at those services provided by the state as a new source for profit generation, as well as a source of both opposition to for-profit methods and a drain on for-profit earnings. In North America, for-profit health companies in the United States described Canada's public health care system as an 'unopened oyster', waiting to have its riches exploited (quoted in Nelson, 1995).

The fiscal crisis in the state, marked by growing deficits and debts, became the justification for an attack on the services provided by the state, as it did in the United Kingdom and the United States. The solution offered by neo-liberals was an elimination of differences between the public and private sectors of the formal economy, with a call for a marketization of the state. What could not be handed over to for-profit organizations could be done in partnership with them, or on the basis of their techniques. State activity in general became more narrowly defined, with the state increasingly policing families to take over the services it no longer provides, either by paying for these services through fees or by providing the unpaid labour. The state is back in the bedrooms of the nation, a place former Canadian Prime Minister Pierre Trudeau moved it from three decades ago.

These distinctions between publics and privates are not simply semantic exercises. Rather their importance lies in their capacity to help us see current developments more clearly and to use this understanding to develop strategies for equity. The blurring of these distinctions in practice further limits women's capacity to shape their lives, and to reduce inequalities among women as well as between women and men.

Women and public care

Health care is women's work. Wherever care is provided, whether paid or unpaid, it is overwhelmingly women who provide it. Women comfort, feed, bathe, toilet, record, clean for, shop for, do laundry for, manage and supervise those needing care, often combining these tasks with more clinical interventions. Forms of this work have traditionally been performed by women in the home, although a significant proportion of what is currently done in health care has not historically been provided in the household. Women have struggled hard to have the work of care recognized as both valuable and skilled, wherever it is provided. Nevertheless, much of the work and many of the skills remain invisible both in terms of the acquired nature of women's capacities and in terms of their contributions to health (Grant *et al.*, 2004). The success of these struggles is linked to the public and private provision of care.

Until the end of the Second World War, institutional care in Canada was primarily provided in charitable or religious institutions. Although private in the sense of being outside the state, these organizations were operated on a non-profit basis and focused primarily on responding to their constituency's needs. They were not, however, always transparent and democratic in terms of governance, nor were they necessarily good for women. Municipalities also provided some institutional care, as did federal and provincial governments. Asylums, for example, were provincially run while veterans' institutions and sanatoria were operated by the federal government. These state organizations at least held out the possibility of some democratic input.

The care provided in these institutions was quite unsophisticated by today's standards. Technology did not play a major role. The acceptance of germ theory by the beginning of the 20th century meant both that institutions had become safer places for care and that more emphasis was put on the care environment. At the same time, anaesthesia made surgery easier to endure. Both developments were highly gendered. The doctors, almost all of whom were men, claimed control over anaesthesia and were successful in acquiring state backing for this monopoly. Nurses, almost all of whom were women, cleaned up and provided care. As the primary daily providers of paid care, nurses included in their tasks the full range of women's traditional care work as well as some of the new approaches based on the advances in medical science (Armstrong and Armstrong, 2003).

Following in the Nightingale tradition, nurses in Canada struggled hard to emphasize the importance of the environment in health care while demanding that the skilled nature of nursing work be recognized. And like Nightingale, they defined a specific area of work for nurses, albeit one that was understood as primarily determined by doctors' orders. For a number of reasons, they had limited power. First, they were women with few resources or legal rights. Second, there was a high turnover because they were usually forced to leave when they married. Third, they were employed either in private homes, where their position as paid employees for private families and their isolation limited the possibilities for organized resistance, or in charitable and religious institutions where work was defined as a labour of love. Fourth, their numbers were limited. In 1901, there were only 208 student and graduate nurses, compared to 5,000 doctors. By 1931, there were three times as many nurses as doctors but by then medical dominance had long been established (Coburn, 1987: Table 2). And fifth, the nurses themselves disagreed on whether they should stress their 'natural' caring skills or the scientific nature of their tasks. Although for nurses 'caring was curing', the medical profession defined caring as secondary to the main job of curing (McPherson, 1994:85).

Nevertheless, Canadian nurses did finally manage by 1922 to have nursing registered as an occupation that required training. This registration was backed by the state, even though there was considerable variation across the country in terms of both the definition of a registered nurse and in the application of registration requirements (Coburn, 1987:454–455). The line between doctors and nurses was clearly drawn, although nursing remained broadly defined and difficult to distinguish from other work in health care. It was still understood mainly as a preparation for motherhood, blurring the lines between public and private spheres even though nurses struggled to have nursing separated from other women's work.

The Second World War marked a significant turning point in health care. Technology developed just before and during the war made hospitals both more effective and more necessary. The new, expensive equipment made sense only in a large, shared workplace where skilled workers were available. The mobilization of nurses for the war effort, combined with increased employment opportunities for others who might have been hired to replace them, altered the power relations in health care provided by women outside the home. Nurses, along with other workers, benefited from new legislation supporting collective bargaining and from new state programs such as unemployment insurance. During the war, they even had state-funded day care and stayed in the job after marriage. The war experience encouraged the Canadian population, and women in particular, to think differently about their role and that of the state. They sought more state intervention in market relations, more state services and supports and more redistribution of resources to reduce inequality. In response to these demands, the federal government began to invest heavily in hospitals. Then it followed the province of Saskatchewan in providing first hospital insurance and then medical insurance for everyone without charges at the point of service. Universal insurance for hospitals and doctors in turn encouraged yet more expansion in these services. Care was expanded in the public sector, located outside the household but not commodified in the sense that it was not offered for sale and thus not distributed on the basis of ability to pay. Much of it was delivered by non-profit, non-governmental organizations, but the larger of these became subject to regulations that made them difficult to distinguish from direct government services.

These developments had a number of important consequences for women in nursing. First, health care services became more accessible as user fees disappeared and services expanded, reducing inequalities among women. Second, more care was provided in the public sector, reducing the pressure on women to provide care at home and thus reducing inequalities in the unpaid care women provided. The impact was however contradictory, as feminists began to point out. Doctors were in charge, and their view of medical care was dominant. More and more aspects of women's life were medicalized. Care in the public sector outside the home, while separating care from other domestic work in terms of time, skill recognition and space, also often meant a loss of control over that care.

Third, employment for women in the public sector of the formal economy expanded enormously. Care work was increasingly commodified, as more women provided care in return for a wage. More worked together in large institutions and stayed in these jobs after marriage and children. This in turn helped women in their demands for better conditions of employment. So did the registration of nurses, because it limited the supply of labour. Their location in the non-profit sector also contributed, because no resources went to profits and the logic driving the organizations was more about care than costs. Through their new union status as well as through their older registration strategies, nurses sought not only better pay and hours but also a clearer distinction between nursing and what were increasingly defined as non-nursing tasks. Health care organizations, run primarily by doctors not pressured by a search for profit and allowed considerable scope by governments, responded to their demands.

The consequences were not simply beneficial; they were also contradictory. Nursing work became more narrowly defined in increasingly clinical terms. The result was less holistic care provided by Registered Nurses (RNs). This development was not welcomed by those who saw nursing as based on an approach to care that was fundamentally different from, if complementary to, that of doctors. As the work of RNs became more narrowly defined and these nurses more expensive, more of the work was delegated to nursing assistants, general aides, clerks, cleaners, laundry and dietary workers. This delegation divided both the care and women workers, often pitting them against each other in terms of scope of practice and control. Many of those with delegated tasks came to the work as new immigrants. Consequently, the new divisions were linked to racialization and immigration status as well as to class[1].

The women who took up these former nursing tasks also began organizing into unions to improve their wages, benefits, work relations and job security. The women doing laundry, dietary, cleaning and clerical work described themselves as health care workers. The significance of this identification became evident in an Ontario hospital when the women were prepared to take illegal strike action over what they saw as changes that would mean a deterioration in patient care. Indeed, they put concern over patient care above concern over their own wages. Their commitment to care as part of a public service took precedence (White, 1990).

Like the nurses before them, these workers had to struggle hard to have their work recognized as skilled rather than simply something any woman could do, and to have the job understood as critical to care, rather than simply as work identical to that done in hotels and homes. It was harder for them to gain recognition because they did not have the association with science that nurses claimed and because their jobs were not only equated with unpaid domestic work, but also with low paid, precarious employment in the for-profit sector. The predominance of immigrant women and women from racialized groups compounded their difficulties. The particular prejudices against these women, combined with language and cultural barriers among the women themselves, made organizing difficult. Pay equity legislation helped in some jurisdictions. In the process of conducting the required job evaluations and comparisons between male and female dominated jobs, women were able to make at least some of the skills visible so they could be appropriately valued. Often described as ancillary or support workers, they were nonetheless central to the health care teams.

The women who did this support work enjoyed considerable success in their efforts to gain material resources and recognition, especially in comparison to women who did similarly labeled jobs in the for-profit sector. Unionization was undoubtedly a major factor in their success. But so was their location in a public sector, where service, rather than profits, was defined as the central goal and where employers had obligations to meet human rights, as well as other legislated requirements. Health care was understood as a public good, a separate space that required practices different from those in the for-profit sector. This location had an impact not only on employers but also on employees, and, as a result, on their unions. Unionization was easier in the public sector and so was an emphasis on rights, on training against racism and sexual harassment, on services such as day care and on benefits such as adequately paid maternity leave.

None of this is to suggest that things were perfect and perfectly harmonious in women's public health care work. Sharp differences among recognized skills and in conditions remain within what is a very hierarchically organized service. Those involved in clinical or diagnostic services have had more success than ancillary workers in gaining pay, benefits and power. Some of the latter still work for minimum wages and with minimum protections; a significant proportion do not have pensions or extended health benefits[2]. This is particularly the case for those who work for small, non-profit organizations delivering public services. Registered Nurses define themselves more often as professionals than as workers, and have consequently been slow or have failed to join the labour centrals in several provinces precisely because they have not seen themselves as unionists. Many of the immigrants who find health care work have not had their credentials accepted, and persons of colour and immigrants remain clustered at the bottom of the pyramid. Several unions are involved in the sector, and even in specific workplaces, often representing workers employed in the same kind of job and often struggling against each other. Hospital workers have fared better than those employed in other health services, and more of these other workers are still without union protection (Armstrong and Laxer, forthcoming). Such divisions among women limit their strength and leave them more vulnerable to the neo-liberal strategies now being introduced. Overall, however, women employed in the public sector have fared better than women in the for-profit sector and have narrowed the pay and benefits gap with their male counterparts more than have their sisters in the for-profit sector. In other words, public sector remuneration and recognition have been more equal not only between women and men but also among women.

In sum, the development of public hospital and doctor care made access to care and to decent employment more equitable for women. It also meant households, and the women in them, had fewer responsibilities for care. This too reduced inequalities among women. In the process, clearer lines were drawn between public and private care. In the formal economy, the bulk of care work was defined as a public service, located in what was termed the broader public sector where profit was not part of the logic constructing the work. Clearer lines were also established between public and private responsibilities, with the public sphere taking on important aspects of care work. With the commodification of care work and its location in the public sphere, it was easier to distinguish care time and non-care time as well as identify what was involved in care work. And there was less state intrusion into the households and into women's personal lives.

Women and private care

The benefits of public payment for hospital and doctor care are obvious to Canadians. Public care has demonstrated its effectiveness and in the process reinforced support. Health care continues to be the country's best-loved social program. Canadians even cite it as the most significant element distinguishing the country from the United States. Such support means there have been few obvious attacks on public care by politicians or those who seek to gain directly from for-profit care. Instead, there has been what has been called privatization by stealth. By promising to continue paying for most hospital and physician services, governments seek to assure Canadians they will continue to enjoy equitable access to care. But they simultaneously promote the privatization of delivery throughout the system, in the name of saving it for all Canadians and of following in the best practices initiated in both the United Kingdom and the United States.

Over a decade ago, the Canadian federal state joined other western states setting about *Reinventing Government* along market lines. 'Smarter and more affordable government' meant, among other things, a blurring of the lines between public and private (Osborne and Gaebler, 1993). Governments began devolving responsibilities to for-profit and voluntary sectors and applying for-profit management techniques to the public institutions that remain. In what is increasingly called a modernization project, every attempt is made to reduce or eliminate the differences between private and public sectors in the formal economy. The latest, and most obvious example, are the public/private partnerships in health care. Indeed, the differences in the relations and conditions of work in the public and for-profit sectors were identified by neo-liberals as a primary problem with government. Public service is viewed as an anachronism and relations there understood as a critical factor in government debt. The new strategies are designed to bring market logics and market relations to bear throughout the formal economy, either directly through privatization or indirectly through making the state function like a business. It is assumed rather than demonstrated that markets, and for-profits methods, mean efficiency and effectiveness defined as costs saving combined with the best possible quality. Consumer choice in the public sector has become part of the discourse, replacing shared responsibilities and collective or citizenship rights. The purpose and result is the reduction of differences not only between private and public sectors and spheres but also among countries. At the same time, differences among classes and other groups increase.

Equally important, governments also began devolving responsibilities to voluntary agencies, individuals and families. Hospital and physician services, the two aspects of public care protected by federal government legislation, are being redefined to include only the most acute interventions. The number of providers per patient has been significantly reduced for the services that remain, making patients more and more unhappy with access to care. Public care has been more narrowly prescribed, leaving more room for the for-profit sector and leaving patients demanding expansion of the private sector. Voluntary agencies have to act like for-profit concerns as a condition for eligibility for government funding. More of the long-term care is provided by for-profit concerns.

As a result, family and friends have to enter the public spaces to take up the work previously done by paid providers. Patients are sent home quicker and sicker; fewer are admitted to institutional long-term care. In consequence, more paid care is provided in the home. But eligibility for this care is means-based rather than universal, and it fails to make up for the reductions in care provided in institutions. As a result, homes become the location for public care blurring the lines between public and private spaces. More of what was previously provided as public care is provided as unpaid care in the home or by for-profit providers paid by individuals. Welfare payments have been reduced at the same time and eligibility requirements increased, leaving fewer people with adequate support for care and renewing old patterns of public surveillance of private relations.

All these developments are profoundly gendered in terms of both the assumptions on which they are based and in their consequences. Within public health care institutions, the work of the mainly female labour force is being transformed to mimic for-profit practices. Restructuring along market lines has meant an enormous job loss. Between 1994 and 1996, 12 per cent of the nursing staff lost their jobs (Wager and Rondeau, 2000:iv). More of those employed by the public sector have part-time, part-year or temporary employment. By the beginning of this century, only 52 per cent of those working in health care had full-time employment (Canadian Institute for Health Information, 2002:xi). Few have a sense of security in their employment, unlike the civil servant in the past. A growing number are employed by temporary service agencies that contract out their work to the public services. So nurses employed by for-profit firms work side by side with nurses employed in the public sector, further blurring the lines between public and private.

Restructuring has also meant the work itself has changed. With only patients who have acute, often multiple, problems entering or staying in hospitals, fewer nurses are looking after more demanding patients and are increasingly doing so under technocratic methods of control. This intensification of labour was in part based on a measurement of nursing work that focused on visible tasks and ignored the complexity of the work, as well as the individual skills of the nurses. What was missing from these measurements was much of traditional women's work, such as social support, and thus the time involved in care. In spite of this speed-up, nurses still *feel* responsible for providing care in ways that reflect their gender, their choice of profession, and their professional obligations. But they are also *held* responsible by a management now trained in business rather than, or in addition to, nursing or medicine. It is a management that assumes that, because nurses are women, they will not abandon their patients even in the face of care deficits. And for the most part this assumption has proved correct.

The RNs' response to these developments has contradictory consequences. Seeking to achieve greater control through credentials, the RNs have received a sympathetic response to their request that nurses be required to have university degrees rather than college training. They have also been successful in demonstrating how critical RNs are to care and in using union action to extract promises to hire more nurses, although the promises have yet to be realized. In addition, they have supported the deregulation of some medical acts previously restricted to physicians, as well as the expansion of a Nurse Practitioner programme and a primary care model which would, in theory at least, extend the nurses' right to participate in a range of services and decisions. None of these responses has been successful, however, in changing the conditions under which nurses work in the hospital or in halting the move to new relations of control. Moreover, their demands have frequently been based on their claim to a science that follows a medical model more than a care model. In the process, they are more often distancing themselves from any association with traditional female skills rather than demanding a different evaluation of those skills. And their focus on separate strategies for RNs weakens the power women as a group could have in care. Thus, the work of RNs has become more narrowly defined in relation to that of most other women working in care, and more narrowly defined as professional work. At the same time it has become more broadly defined in relation to that of doctors, even as more and more women become doctors.

Just as the RNs have sought the right to perform tasks previously restricted to doctors, so too have nursing assistants with fewer years of formal training fought to do work previously monopolized by RNs. The deregulation of professions in this manner does mean RNs and nursing assistants get to do more work that is recognized as skilled. The move has been supported by both employers and governments because it also means a deskilling, in the sense that those with less formal training and lower pay get to do more of the work. There is a cascading effect, with nursing aides doing nursing assistants' work and 'generic workers' doing nursing aide work with little if any formal training or recognized skills. These contradictory developments often put the different groups of women in conflict with each other, frequently within the same union.

One consequence of these strategies is a nursing shortage. Women have been leaving the country and the profession, or failing to take up nursing as a career. This shortage reflects at least in part nurses' success in emphasizing their deteriorating conditions and relations under for-profit techniques. It also reflects their success in demonstrating their critical contribution to clinical care and in separating this work from association with traditional women's work. The women who do the cooking, feeding, cleaning, laundry and clerical work have been less successful. This became particularly evident in a recent Royal Commission report on health care. *Building on Values: The Future of Health Care in Canada* (Romanow Report) distinguishes between direct health care services and ancillary services. It argues that, based on the evidence, direct care provided by nurses or other diagnostic and clinical care providers should remain within the public sector. It then goes on to suggest that there would be no problem contracting out the ancillary work to for-profit concerns, although no evidence is offered to support the case for this transfer (Canada, 2002:6–9).

This ancillary work is the work most traditionally associated with women. It is the work most often assumed to come naturally to women as women. It is the work most frequently done by immigrant and racialized groups of women, the ones with the least power. And it is the easiest to dismiss as unskilled and to equate with both hotel services and work in the home, blurring the lines among the different demands of the work in different sectors. It is also the work most likely to be undertaken by international corporations. Yet there are important reasons not to equate health and hotel work, reasons that reflect the specific nature of health care outlined above.

First, the demands are different in these different kinds of workplaces. Although the research on ancillary workers in either sector is limited, there are clear indications that the jobs in the two sectors cannot be equated. For example, health care laundry that has not been appropriately handled can become life-threatening for patients (Orr *et al.*, 2002). Health care laundry can be equally dangerous to those cleaning it, with hepatitis A or B providing only one example (Borg and Portelli, 1999: Wa, 1995). In addition, health care necessarily involves a team that includes those who do surgery and those who make sure the surgery is clean; those who determine whether patients eat and those who help them eat; those who determine what records should be kept and those who keep them. Team members are interdependent in ways that mean distinctions between ancillary and direct care are blurred. All those who work in health care require health specific knowledge, and most describe themselves as health care providers, whatever their job in care. The British House of Commons Health Select Committee warned in 1999 that '[t]he often spurious division of staff into clinical or non-clinical groups can create an institutional apartheid which might be detrimental to staff morale and to patients' (quoted in Sachdev, 2001:33).

Second, the hazards are different in both kinds of work. That health care cleaners have three times the injury rate of other cleaners is just one indicator of such hazards (Cohen, 2001). And obviously, the risks of infection are greater and different in health care. Third, the consequences of mistakes or poor quality are significantly greater and different in health care. The wrong data recorded, for example, could cause life-threatening mistakes. Records must be meticulously kept in ways that require considerable specialized knowledge about health issues, and poor records can create a health hazard. Finally, hotel services work to different standards, and there is little evidence that quality is immediately evident to the customer, as the Romanow Report suggests. The work organization in hotel services results in standards of cleanliness that are not only low but may be dangerous to the health of even healthy customers. Research in the United States revealed a host of dangerous bacteria, even in the most expensive and seemingly clean hotels (referenced in Cohen, 2001:11). Applying such methods of work organization through contracted services could well mean inadequate or even risky quality in health care.

In spite of the specificity of health care work, those jobs defined as ancillary are being contracted out to for-profit firms that operate in hotels and airports as well as in hospitals and long-term care facilities. The more narrow definition of care work has helped this development. So has the association with women's work. But women's success in gaining some power and control within health care has also been a factor, as governments and employers seek to cut costs and increase control by carving out significant aspects public care to open it up for profit.

Women lose significantly in this redefinition of public and private. When women clean, cook, feed, do laundry and clerical work in the for-profit sector, the work is low paid and often precarious in other ways as well. The 'hotel services' sector is characterized by low pay and job insecurity. Almost three-quarters lack union coverage, compared to health care where the majority are in unions. Unions not only mean more pay and benefits, they also mean more employment security and the right to say no to unreasonable demands. This is particularly important to women who face racism or sexual harassment. Employees in food and accommodation services are among those with the lowest job quality, and the quality is often low as well for those in part-time, temporary and irregular shift employment (Hughes, Lowe and Schellenberg, 2003:22). Women who do this work in health care are much more likely than women in other industries to have full-time permanent work and to have pensions (Armstrong and Laxer, forthcoming). Although jobs in the public sector can be precarious for the women doing such work, when the services are contracted out the private sector the degree of precariousness is likely to increase (McMullen and Schellenberg, 2003).

Research in several western countries suggests that contracting out services makes work more precarious. Case studies in the United Kingdom and Northern Ireland 'found that exposure to tendering led to the, often dramatic, erosion of terms and conditions of employment . . . Estimates state that some 40 per cent of the NHS ancillary jobs were lost.' (Sachdev, 2001:5). Moreover, the impact on women is more extensive, resulting in a widening of the gender gap. According to the Equal Opportunities Commission of Northern Ireland, most work contracted out was female-dominated (1996). The rate of female job loss was more than double that of men. While both women and men experienced wage reductions, the proportionate reduction was larger for women. Some benefits disappeared, along with some entitlements. Employers with the contracts were less likely than public sector employers to have policies that are critical for women, such as strategies to prevent sexual harassment. In the Canadian province of British Colombia, contracting out has eliminated wage gains under pay equity and reduced wages for the primarily female cleaners by 44 per cent (Cohen and Cohen, 2004:16)

Contracting out not only has an impact on those working in the firms with the contracts. It also has an impact on those who remain in the public sector. In order to maintain its position, the public sector that remains is increasingly pressured to act like the private contractors. British research shows the way the same practices applied by the for-profit firms were introduced in the public sector. Manual staff, including cleaners and caterers among others, 'in particular, have borne the brunt of the changes that have been made in working methods, pay and conditions' (Walsh and Davis, 1993:12).

Not surprisingly, the contracting out strategy seems to have had an impact on the environment for care. This contracting out began more than a decade ago. Although contracting out was supposed to improve quality while reducing costs, a 'national listening exercise' by the Labour UK Government indicated 'the need for basic care to be reviewed'. One response has been the introduction of ward housekeepers whose job it is to make 'sure wards are clean, patients are fed properly and that the surroundings are well maintained and welcoming'[3]. Another has been the introduction of strategies to assess and improve food and cleaning services in care. Both have been required by the failure of strategies that introduced for-profit methods in ancillary services. In Canada as well, there are clear indications that contracting out does not improve quality of care and may even undermine it (Cohen, 2001).

Meanwhile, unpaid care work in the home has been increasing enormously with the shift to day surgery, shorter patient stays and deinstutionalization. A recent study found that, between 1996 and 1999, 'the system changes more than doubled the mean number of personal care services per surgical patient' at home (Tousignant *et al.*, 2004:222). Women in particular have been 'conscripted' into home care, with women providing almost 80 per cent of the personal service work (Decima, 2002:3)[4]. While these unpaid careworkers come from all classes, more of the unpaid workers come from the lowest income categories, both because women give up paid work in order to care and because those with low income cannot afford to pay for substitutes. (Decima, 2002:3). The work that is most often transferred to them and the work that is most likely to remain invisible is that Romanow defines as ancillary. Even the women who do the work seldom define it as care, leading to an underestimation of the hours women spend doing this work. Women are also increasingly required to take on complex care technologies, however, as catheters, intravenous tubes and oxygen masks are sent home with the patients.

Some paid care is provided in the home. While previously nurses, therapists and social workers decided on the kinds and amounts of care time required, new Ontario government guidelines set 'a maximum of 4 nursing visits per day and 80 hours of homemaking per month for the first month and 60 hours of homemaking per month thereafter' (Canadian Homecare Association, quoted in Ontario Health Coalition, 1999:2). They also say that, in order to be eligible for publicly funded services, individuals must have exhausted the caregiving and support capacities of their friends, relatives and other community services (Ontario Health Coalition, 1999:6). This means that '[i]ndividuals who have a capable caregiver are not eligible for home support services. This includes caregivers who work outside the home.' (Ontario, 1999:2). It is clear that these capable caregivers are women.

In the process, private lives and private households get invaded by strangers who assess needs and determine eligibility, while others pop in to provide the nanosecond of care. Nurses take minutes to teach unpaid care workers tasks that the nurses spent entire courses learning in university. As a result, the skills of the paid providers and the autonony of the individuals providing unpaid care are undermined because it is increasingly assumed that any women can, and should, do this work. So is the solidarity among women undermined. The few women who can afford to pay for their own care or supplement the limited care paid for by the state do have choices and can dictate terms to the paid providers. But many more women have to beg for care and put up with whatever the services offered. As a result, differences among women increase and new frictions emerge. The private is no longer private, with contradictory and often negative consequences for women.

Conclusions

Using these notions of private and public helps us to see more clearly the developments shaping women's opportunities and their work. Some feminists once argued that the separation into private and public spheres was detrimental to women, excluding them from public spaces and public power. Others pointed to the ways public and private spheres interpenetrated, serving to mutually reinforce women's subordination. Here we have argued that there are a number of privates and publics and that we have to understand their varied development in order to understand what is happening to women as a group and to particular groups of women.

Using the case of health care, we have argued that many women benefited not only from the expansion of the public sector in the formal economy but also from clearer lines being drawn between the two kinds of public and private considered here. Women's care work was commodified while the services they delivered were not, thus improving access to care and giving women paid work. Contradictions remained, and success in demanding clarification for some has meant setbacks for others. With privatization of the public sector, it has become increasingly difficult to distinguish public sector employment from private, for-profit work and to separate the household from the formal economy. Services have become commodified just as some care work has become decommodified. The benefits and costs are both unevenly distributed and contradictory.

Registered Nurses have recently been able to carve out a role for themselves that simultaneously draws a clearer line between their work and that of other women who work in care while blurring the line between their job and that of doctors. At the same time, for-profit managerial practices applied to the public sector in which they work have meant a deterioration in their conditions and relations of work. Equally important, the clearer lines drawn between direct and ancillary care have been the basis for defining some women's work in care as hotel services and for contracting out the work to the private for-profit sector. The result has been more precarious employment for women who do this work. This redefinition of such women's work as unskilled assists in the transfer of

186 © The Editorial Board of the Sociological Review 2005

work previously done for pay in the public sector into the home to be done without pay by women or with pay by a few women who invade the private household. In the process, the lines between public services and private households and among women's various kinds of domestic work are blurred. More work for women and more inequality among women are the results.

Notes

1 In 2001, 16% of those in assisting occupations, compared to 11% of nurses and 12% of all occupations, are visible minorities (Armstrong, Laxer and Armstrong, 2004: Chart 3b).
2 In 2001,only 39% of female ancillary workers had pensions, compared to 64% of the women working in direct health care occupations (Armstrong, Laxer and Armstrong, 2004: Chart 8a).
3 NHSEstates http://patientexperience.nhsstates.gov.uk/ward_housekeeping/wh_content.home . . . 28/o2/2003.
4 This term was employed by the National Forum on Health, [Values report] *Canada Health Action: Building on the Legacy*, Vol. II, *Synthesis Reports and Issues Papers*, Ottawa: Minister of Public Works and Government Services, 1997, p. xx.

Care, work and feeling

Clare Ungerson

Introduction

Recent writing on paid and unpaid work has suggested that the dichotomy between them is breaking down, particularly in the field of domiciliary care. Increasingly, forms of unpaid work, named as 'informal care' are having cash attached to them through state subsidy. For example, in Italy in 2003, 1.1 million disabled people were receiving such a payment including 797,000 elderly care users; in France, in 1999, 796000 elderly people were receiving an allowance they were expected to spend on the direct employment of care workers; and in Germany, in 2002, 1.2 million care users received cash benefits under the long-term care insurance scheme, which they could use as they wished but with the expectation they would use it to employ their own caring labour. I have named this process as the 'commodification' of care (Ungerson, 1997). The effect has been that hybrid forms of 'work' and 'care' are developing, whereby the cash nexus enters the care relationship within the domestic domain, and the nexus of affect enters and permeates the work relationship (Ungerson, 1999). Within Europe and the United States these systems have taken various forms, as their various names – 'independent living', 'consumer directed care', 'direct payments', 'dependence subsidy', 'personal budget schemes', 'companion payments' – indicate. But all of them have the same basic intent – to allow the users of social care support to receive cash instead of services and spend that money on the direct employment of carers who deliver care to them in their own homes. In effect, frail elderly and disabled people are being given the actual means to enter the labour market and contract caring labour for themselves. The specific form of commodification that these systems demonstrate is named by Ungerson as 'routed wages' (Ungerson, 1997).

This chapter builds on work that the present author has been concerned with over a long period. A central question of my work, and that of many others, has always been the ambiguity contained within the use of the word, in the English language, of 'care'. The founding collection of papers on 'care' in the British literature was entitled *A Labour of Love* (Finch and Groves, 1983) and a number of the papers in that collection referred to the difficulty of distinguishing between 'care' as feeling and 'care' as work. The basic distinction between 'caring about' someone, which was defined within feeling terms, and 'caring for' someone, which was defined as task orientated activity and hence most closely defined as 'work', was made by both Graham and by the present author (Graham, 1983; Ungerson, 1983) and that basic distinction, crude as it is, remains in use in the literature on 'care'. More recently a significant North American literature has developed a perspective on care that treats care as work (Harrington Meyer, 2000). At the same time, a US literature on emotion at work, and in the care relationship, has been strongly developed by Arlie Hochschild (2003). Within the British context, two related literatures, coming from the care tradition on the one hand, and the work tradition on the other have begun to coalesce. Thus Twigg's work on bathing in the care relationship considers the way in which paid care workers negotiate the intimacies that derive from touch (Twigg, 2000) and Glucksmann has developed the concept of the 'total social organization of labour' to describe the way in which a range of activities, both paid and unpaid and including the activities of care, can be construed as labour (Glucksmann, 1995; 2000a). At the same time policy changes have also brought together 'work' and 'care'. The introduction of schemes which commodify and attach an income to care activities, which in the past have been unpaid, has introduced new hybrids of paid work and unpaid care activity, such that, materially as well as theoretically, the boundaries between paid and unpaid care-work are shifting and blurring in many developed welfare states – particularly in relation to the care of frail elderly and other disabled people. The chapter that follows draws on the ideas contained within all these literatures to explore the way in which systems of care commodification are introducing (or reintroducing) new types of work relationship between 'employers' – all of whom are frail and elderly – and their directly employed 'employees'.

Drawing on the long-standing ambiguity in the meaning of the word 'care', the particular dimension of these new types of employment relationships that will be examined in this chapter will be that of feeling. It is not really surprising that there are likely to be strongly loaded emotional attachments and detachments that develop as a result of the commodification of care in general and 'routed wages' in particular: these care relationships usually involve regular delivery of personal care involving touch which in its turn has the potential to promote intimacy. Furthermore, there are some funding systems that positively encourage the 'employment' of close relatives and co-residents such that the individuals involved have shared biographies in the past and now into the present. As I have argued before, the form of these relationships is a hybrid of 'work' on the one hand, based on contract, and 'care' on the other, based on affect. This chapter will also suggest that different methods of funding and organizing these systems are likely to lead to different types and levels of emotional attachment, which, in their turn, drive further consequences for the care relationship as a whole.

The analysis that follows is based on a study undertaken by myself and Sue Yeandle and four research teams working in four other EU nations[1]. The study was funded under the British Economic and Social Research Council (ESRC)

'Future of Work Programme'; a number of articles describing the study in more detail and providing preliminary findings have already been published (Ungerson, 2003; Ungerson, 2004). The five countries under scrutiny were Austria, France, Italy, the Netherlands, and the UK. The data collected in this project were largely exploratory. We were concerned to investigate the employer/employee relationship in depth and to develop an understanding of how and whether the presence of the cash nexus alters the care relationship, such that it emerges as a hybrid of work and care. In addition the cross-national framework allowed us to look at the expected differential impact of the five funding regimes, and to explore the impact on differently organized labour markets. The methods adopted were appropriate to these aims and contexts. In each of the five countries the research teams interviewed ten elderly care users who were in receipt of monies through a 'cash for care' scheme. In three of the countries – Austria, the Netherlands and the UK – the sample was found through the agency or agencies involved in either allocating the monies or acting as a support for care users. In France the sample was found through an agency providing care workers, and in Italy through local Church organizations who directed the researchers to frail elderly care users. In no sense, then, can the samples be said to be representative but the qualitative data generated provided considerable insight into the meaning of cash for care schemes for the elderly care users themselves. Once contacted and interviewed, the elderly care users were invited to provide the names and contact addresses of their caregivers and the majority of interviews with caregiver/workers were conducted within these caring dyads. It became clear, however, during the studies in Italy and Austria, that there were interesting migratory and global features of the care labour market, and in both these studies some purposive sampling, using snowballing methods, was used to find additional migrant careworkers. In each of the five countries approximately twenty caregiver/workers were interviewed using qualitative interview methods. The research teams had collaborated in devising the interview schedules for both elderly care users and caregiver/workers, and the interviewers, who all spoke excellent English, had actively participated in these meetings, thus ensuring that each of the research teams fully understood the aims and objectives of the study.

The 'cross' of 'routed wages'

The arrangements of these 'cash for care' systems vary: some of them are highly regulated, and designed to ensure, for example, that 'employees' are properly covered for their social rights, receive holiday entitlement and holiday pay, and work regular and contracted hours. Other schemes allow a complete free-for-all: care users who receive these payments are not monitored to see how and on whom they spend the money. Indeed, if they wish they can put the money under the proverbial mattress. The use of illegal and/or undocumented labour is not explicitly forbidden or sanctioned. Thus there is a major difference between these schemes along the axis of regulation/non-regulation. But cross-cutting this regulation/non-regulation axis is a further distinction: namely, whether care users can use the cash to 'pay' their relatives. The regulated British scheme of 'direct payments' for example has until 2004 expressly forbidden the payment of relatives, while the even more highly regulated 'personal budget' scheme of the Netherlands allows care users to pay their relatives (who actually receive their wages from the Social Insurance Bank). In the unregulated schemes, the payment of relatives may actually be part of the prevailing culture of the scheme. The model I investigate is based on two cross-cutting axes: one axis consists of regulation/non-regulation; the other consists of 'care' and 'work' producing a model that may be named the 'cross' of 'routed wages'.

In this diagram of commodified care schemes, the vertical axis describes the policy context, and the way in which schemes are or are not regulated in their implementation. The regulation of care can take two forms: first, regulation can ensure that care, construed as work, falls within the generic regulations governing work as a whole: earnings from care are taxed, social rights are derived from employment in care, hours of work are regulated. Second, the nature of the care that is delivered can be subject to regulation specific to caring activities: certain standards can be imposed (generally through care qualifications), credentials are visible and checkable, and authorization – in the form of, for example, police checks – is imposed. Non-regulation is less easily categorized: it represents a rather large 'black box' in which many different kinds of care relationship and 'contract' can occur but where none of these arrangements are publicly accountable. In a non-regulated setting, the cash payment is contingent on demonstration of need on the part of the care user rather than on any demonstration of an aspect of the ensuing commodified care relationship. Its impact on the type of person who comes forward to care may vary from members of the care user's household, recruited through affect, to informally employed workers operating in a 'grey' labour market.

The horizontal axis describes the type of care relationship involved in commodified care. In those schemes which allow relatives to be paid, the relationship, and the work of care, may most resemble that of informal care – a relationship based on kinship and affect rather than contract, and providing holistic care. In those schemes which most strongly promote the activity of care as paid work, the activities of care may most resemble conventionally paid work – subject to contract, and with the right (and legitimacy) of the employer to hire and fire, and the right (and legitimacy) of the employee to exit employment.

Developing the model: arrangements of carers, commodified care and time

Before turning to the analysis of the data to illuminate the nature of the care relationship that follows, it is important both to define terms a little more closely, and to elaborate the model further. The model can be used to identify different

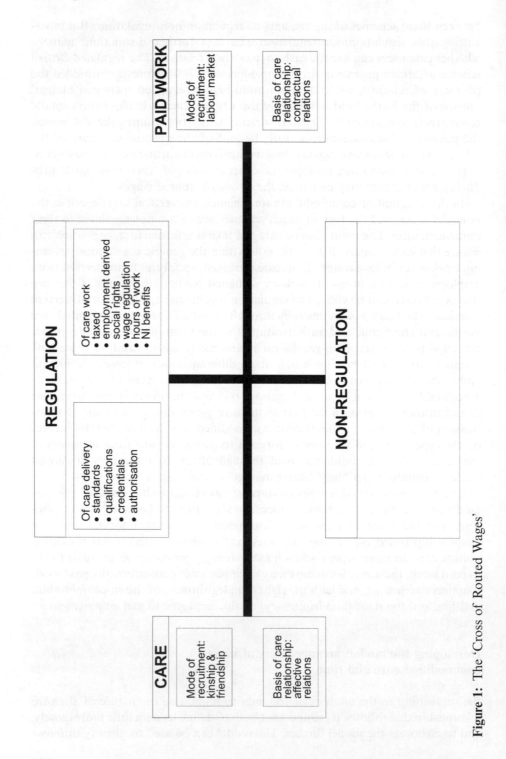

Figure 1: The 'Cross of Routed Wages'

types of arrangements for commodified domiciliary care and different types of caregiver/worker. Figure 2 identifies different types of *carer*, along the two axes of regulation/non-regulation, and care/work. In this figure, various types of carer are schematically located in various parts of the 'cross'. In the left-hand lower quadrant are the 'classic' informal carers – wholly unregulated, and recruited through affective relations. In contrast, in the upper right hand quadrant are the care workers and professionals recruited through the labour market, and subject to contractual relations. Some carers straddle quadrants – for example, a group named as 'remunerated' carers, who are paid a wage to care for their relatives, are subject to a mix of affective and contractual relations. They could also be further up the 'regulation' axis and move into the upper quadrants depending on how far their income is subject to taxation, their hours contracted, and their social rights guaranteed. Similarly, 'agency' workers could consist of workers who are heavily regulated through, for example, the British Care Standards Act (2000), which imposes minimum training and quality assurance procedures on domiciliary care agencies, but they could also be workers who are self-employed and possibly beyond the frameworks of employment law. Hence this group could be both relatively heavily regulated, and be situated in the lower right hand quadrant to indicate relative lack of regulation. As should be clear, this figure is schematic: the policy and labour market contexts will impact on the precise position of particular groups of carers, and since both policy shifts and labour markets change, there are moments when groups of carers will move around this 'map'.

Figure 3 uses the same axes to identify *different ways of organizing 'commodified' care* that is specifically the type named by the present author as 'routed wages' (1997a). In this model, different types of routed wage systems are located along the axes. This figure is also descriptive as well as schematic: it uses data from the empirical studies described later in this chapter to locate particular forms of organization of commodified care. In addition, Figure 3 introduces a new element in the model: that of time spent in the delivery of care.

The spectrum of 'care'/'work' contains within it implicit distinctions between time: typically, at the 'care' end, the time of the carer is flexibly available, normally for very long periods. Hence, in the left hand upper quadrant, *despite* the commodification of the care relationship and the payment, in some sense, of the caregiver, care remains very like that of 'classic' informal care: one carer, solely responsible, and providing care in a holistic way and, commonly, for 24/7 time. At the 'work' end, time is often very carefully organized and subject to contractual arrangements. Care giving is likely to be distributed in very short bursts to multiple clients. As we shall see, however, in the unregulated quadrant at the 'work' end of the spectrum, flexible time over very long periods and including 24/7 work, may well be a feature of the ability to employ very cheap labour that is constrained within the 'grey' labour market.

These different types of arrangement already exist. For example, the Dutch system, which is highly regulated by quasi government agencies – in this case, the Social Insurance Bank – falls into the upper left quadrant (A, Figure 3) – it

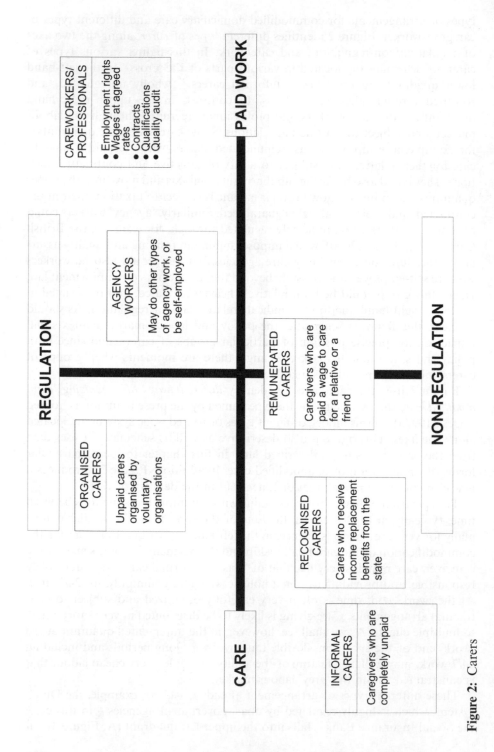

CAREWORKERS/ PROFESSIONALS
- Employment rights
- Wages at agreed rates
- Contracts
- Qualifications
- Quality audit

PAID WORK

REGULATION

NON-REGULATION

AGENCY WORKERS

May do other types of agency work, or be self-employed

REMUNERATED CARERS

Caregivers who are paid a wage to care for a relative or a friend

ORGANISED CARERS

Unpaid carers organised by voluntary organisations

RECOGNISED CARERS

Carers who receive income replacement benefits from the state

CARE

INFORMAL CARERS

Caregivers who are completely unpaid

Figure 2: Carers

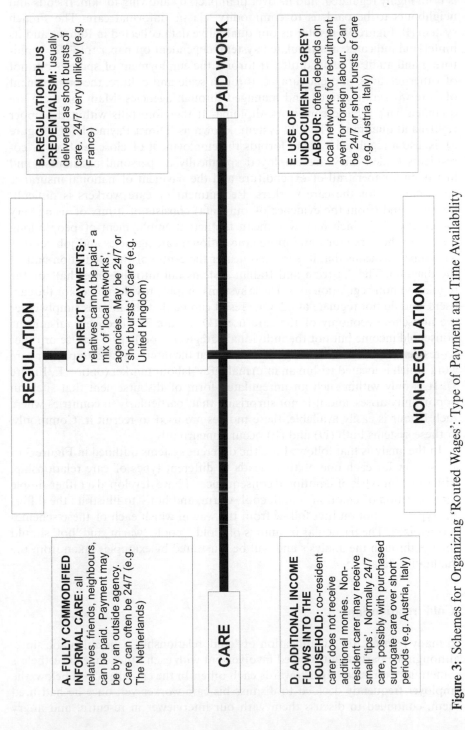

B. REGULATION PLUS CREDENTIALISM: usually delivered as short bursts of care. 24/7 very unlikely (e.g. France)

E. USE OF UNDOCUMENTED 'GREY' LABOUR: often depends on local networks for recruitment, even for foreign labour. Can be 24/7 or short bursts of care (e.g. Austria, Italy)

PAID WORK

REGULATION

C. DIRECT PAYMENTS: relatives cannot be paid - a mix of 'local networks', agencies. May be 24/7 or 'short bursts' of care (e.g. United Kingdom)

NON-REGULATION

A. FULLY COMMODIFIED INFORMAL CARE: all relatives, friends, neighbours, can be paid. Payment may be by an outside agency. Care can often be 24/7 (e.g. The Netherlands)

D. ADDITIONAL INCOME FLOWS INTO THE HOUSEHOLD: co-resident carer does not receive additional monies. Non-resident carer may receive small 'tips'. Normally 24/7 care, possibly with purchased surrogate care over short periods (e.g. Austria, Italy)

CARE

Figure 3: Schemes for Organizing 'Routed Wages': Type of Payment and Time Availability

is both highly regulated, and its overall impact, by allowing for kin, friends and neighbours to be paid, is to commodify 'classic' informal care. The French system (B, Figure 3), insofar as our qualitative data collected in Rennes and its hinterland indicates, is a regulated system, dependent on paper trails for monitoring and audit of expenditure. It forbids the employment of spouses but not of other relatives, and encourages, through scale and culture, the employment of care workers recruited and managed through agencies. Many of them are qualified with a basic care work diploma. It therefore falls within the upper right hand quadrant. The UK system, known as 'Direct Payments' (C, Figure 3), is also a regulated system, forbids the employment of close relatives or co-residents (unless they are employed specifically as personal assistants), and insists on a paper trail of expenditure and the payment of national insurance contributions for the care workers. Recruitment of care workers is difficult, however, and (from the evidence of our data) consists of a mix of using very local networks, which may well mean the actual employment of people long known to the care users, and more conventional care agencies and job centres. This mixture means that it is located nearer the centre of the regulation half of the diagram. The Austrian and Italian systems fall into the lower half of the regulation/non-regulation axis. These systems simply provide monies for the care users, and do not regulate at all. One result can be that the monies simply enter the household economy of the care user (D, Figure 3), effectively raising the household income but not the individual caregiver's (perhaps a spouse or other co-resident) income. Another possibility is that the money is used to pay for care work which is located within an informal 'grey' labour market (option E, Figure 3). It is only within such an unregulated form of disbursement that such an opportunity arises, and it is not surprising that, particularly in countries where such labour is easily available, these monies are used to recruit it. Commonly, in these systems both (D) and (E) occur concurrently.

In the analysis that follows I use the different systems outlined in Figure 3 to assess how far each one of them leads to different types of care relationship, with different types of emotional consequences. I have developed a rather simple categorization of emotion – cold, cool, warm, and hot – to illustrate the different types of emotion that follow from the way in which each of these schemes is organized. The particular meanings of 'cold', 'cool', 'warm' and 'hot' should emerge through the analysis and will be illustrated by examples taken from the qualitative data.

'Cold' relationships

In many respects, the identification of 'cold' relationships is problematic since, although the participants denied involvement with each other, they nevertheless sometimes expressed anger towards each other. In the case described below, the employer frequently decided to dismiss his care worker yet, once he had fired them, continued to discuss them with our interviewer in resentful and angry terms. Thus some of these relationships, which were very rare in our small qualitative samples, came close to the 'hot' relationships described later in this chapter. Nevertheless, I have characterized them as 'cold' because, despite continued anger, they were relationships that were easily brought to an end with no feelings of guilt on either side. Unlike the 'hot' relationships described later, which were characterized by long-term volatility based on strong feelings, these 'cold' relationships were essentially short-term.

In our surveys there was probably only one relationship that could be described as 'cold' in the extreme, and it is therefore somewhat risky to try to generalize from this single case. There were some characteristics of this employment relationship, however, that may well be generalizable and hence it is important to discuss it analytically. The first generalizable point is that the care workers in this relationship were recruited through the British Direct Payments scheme, which encourages care users to find their caring labour within the conventional labour market using a variety of methods, including advertisement, use of job centres, word of mouth. Only recruitment of relatives was, at the time of the study, formally forbidden. This recruitment process is therefore likely to mean, unless word of mouth is used, that strangers are employed by strangers – in other words, there is no initial basis for feeling within the relationship and no past shared biography. Moreover, it is assumed that a contractual relationship between employer and employee is enough to guarantee quality of care, since the employer has the power to hire, and, of course, to fire. An employer may choose to hire only those with care qualifications, and subject them to a referencing process, or they may choose not to do so and/or, given a shortage of qualified care workers, find it impossible to find such labour. In this particular case, the employer generally found his labour through adverts in local shops and selected them by personal interview. Given his personality he was, at the time of the interviews, experiencing considerable staff turnover and hence he was frequently confronted with an urgent need to replace staff that he had either dismissed or had left. The result was that he faced severe problems of labour shortage and was unable to choose among a range of candidates.

All his care workers (five were interviewed in the study) were unqualified. A number of them were very young women who, through lack of educational qualification, had encountered their own problems in the labour market. Hence the care workers he found were in no sense professional: from the evidence of our interviews with them they found it very difficult to maintain professional distance combined with warmth, and appeared not to have displayed, in their own and his accounts, generalizable and learnt caring behaviour. They behaved, within the care relationship, authentically as themselves responding, or not responding, to their employer's personality. The relationships that ensued were close to breaking point at all times, and the workers were at a loss as to how to relate to their employer:

> I went in at 10 o'clock. I sat there and he didn't speak to me. It were like he'd sent me to Coventry. I sat there for about two hours until it was 12 o'clock. I didn't go to

the shop; didn't do nothing; he didn't speak to me for two total hours! So when I left, I just left. I come back in the evening and he made me stay until 7.30 at night and just sit there. He had the telly on; he were just watching telly and he just made me sit there and that were it. He didn't speak to me for a whole day. That were it. (*Care worker paid through UK Direct Payments Scheme who had been to a doctor's appointment which she had previously warned her employer would make her late*).

As has already been suggested, this set of care relationships with this particular employer, was very unusual. There is no suggestion that the British Direct Payments Scheme (classified in box C, Figure 3) with its embedded assumption that employers know best how to process and conduct the employment relationship on a contractual basis, is *likely* to lead to such cold stand-offs. But in schemes which rely on and encourage a culture of empowerment of care users within an employment relationship, there may be a risk that those inexperienced and untrained in the more conventional mores of the employer/employee relationship played out in more conventional paid work settings, will encounter difficulties of this kind. Hierarchical work relationships, based in theory on pure contractual relations, could break down in a mixture of coldness and resentment.

'Cool' relationships

'Cool' relationships were rather more common than the rarely found 'cold' relationship in this study of commodified care relationships. 'Cool' relationships were characterized by acceptance and respect on both sides of the relationship. In these employer/employee interactions, both sides understood and agreed upon the boundaries of the relationship, understood its task and service orientation, and tended to regard the relationship as, inevitably, empty of strong feeling. In other words, to use the long-standing distinction of the informal care literature, they understood the relationship to be concerned with 'caring *for*' rather than 'caring *about*'. Most of these types of relationship were organized by outside agencies which managed the recruitment and matching process of care user to care worker. Where relationships failed for any reason, the replacement of the care worker was the responsibility of the agency. Hence neither care user or care worker had a vested interest in ensuring that the selection process had been successful – both entry and exit to these relationships was relatively easy and managed by others.

'As people came along they were asking me would I like to do this job and sometimes you go there on trial and see if either the client likes you or you like the client and work it out from there. So often we get introduced by the co-ordinator to the family, it's all sort of very you know, you play it by ear as well'. (*Care worker registered with agency working for multiple clients in the UK, some of whom use Direct Payments to pay the agency*)

In addition, it was very likely that care workers had multiple clients, and that their visits to them were carefully time-managed by the outside agency. Interactions between care user and care worker were professionalized, task-orientated and generalized.

> Well, you become quite close to them because they trust you and you trust them. I would say you *almost* become like friends really. You are very important to them and they are to you of course . . . some you become closer to than others, but on the whole I think you don't want to let them down. That's very important. (My italics) *(Care worker recruited through agency in the UK)*

Similarly, care users who used agencies as a recruitment method reported their own sense of coolness and task orientation. A French care user who used an agency said 'You can always say that you are not happy' and later, when asked what the nature of the relationship was with his wife's care worker, he said:

> We have a certain consideration, esteem, I cannot say affection . . . she is very kind, very competent.

These types of relationship occurred predominantly within the French system of care allowances (classified B in Figure 3), where the culture of the national scheme encourages care users to engage their caring labour through agencies. Although this costs slightly more than careworkers recruited directly by care users, there has been a recent rapid growth in the numbers of care workers registered with agencies and large numbers of these workers have a basic care qualification. Even so, the French government continues to be concerned that care is being delivered by unqualified workers and some municipalities have introduced their own training schemes for care workers directly employed by frail and disabled people (Martin and LeBihan, 2006). One can expect, therefore, that these types of 'cool' and instrumentally organized care relationships will expand in this type of funding regime that is committed to professionalized delivery of care services.

'Warm' relationships

'Warm' relationships occurred frequently in the five country samples included in this study. Many care users reported enjoying the company of their caregivers or workers and vice versa and appreciated the two-way flow of support that often arises in good care relationships. Such warmth often arose out of care relationships that had continued over a long period and the warmth itself meant that these relationships were not at risk of breaking down, at least in the short-term. Often the good feelings that people had for each other appeared to be a matter of serendipity and it is difficult therefore to relate the likelihood of warmth developing with a particular funding regime. However, it was noticeable that the two systems that allowed for and, indeed in the Austrian case of the charity CARITAS, positively encouraged the contract based employment of relatives, provided a good basis for warm relations to develop in some instances. These care arrangements are identified as 'fully commodified informal care' in Box A (Figure 3), and, as the name indicates, these were almost always pre-existing informal care arrangements which now had full pay for the caregivers embedded within them. This meant that they were long-term relationships, and often long-term shared biographies, particularly where a spouse was paid to care – as frequently happens in the Dutch 'personal budget' scheme. The general feature of this form of commodified care work is that the workers are recruited through affect rather than through the labour market (to the left of the horizontal axis outlined in Figure 1) and the affect is likely to be the basis for the continuation of the relationship. These relationships, unlike the 'cool' task orientated relationships, are likely to be one-to-one thus allowing for the development of communication and further shared biography should the two members of the caring dyad wish it. In the best of these warm, fully commodified informal care relationships, there appeared to be a strong respect on both sides, meaning that the relationship was both equitable and equable.

> We understand each other very well. Previously we scarcely knew each other . . . It's quite different now. She is sweet, grateful and easy to look after. If I really want to go somewhere she says: 'of course, my dear, just go'. She doesn't cling to me either. She tries to relieve me of everything and make things as easy as possible for me'. (*Austrian daughter caring for her mother, paid by Caritas*).

Another Austrian care user whose daughter and a friend of the daughter cared for her on a fortnight on/fortnight off basis said of her daughter:

> She's a good friend. That's very obvious to me when I see her scampering around with a feather duster and a pinny and a cap on.

It has to be said that not all the outcomes of these systems were quite so satisfactory. Just as one finds in studies of unpaid informal carers, so there were fully paid caregivers who found it very difficult to establish their right to their own time and space. As another Austrian care worker paid to look after her mother said: 'I'll be 39 this year but I have to be home by 3 a.m.'

Nevertheless it is clear that such systems that allow for the payment of relatives, may, if they work well, provide for non-professionalized high quality care where both sides feel they are engaged in a satisfactory and satisfying care relationship based on equality and respect.

'Hot' relationships

As has already been indicated, in certain respects the 'cold' relationships we encountered, outlined above, were angry and passionate as well as cold, although the participants denied this. 'Hot' relationships, however, are distinct from 'cold' relationships in that they are essentially long-term relations which have survived despite tension. That these volatile relationships had lasted so long demonstrated that they were not easy to exit.

The reasons as to why exit was difficult varied across the dimensions of choice and constraint. Some care users found recruitment difficult and hence stuck with the careworkers they were familiar with, however occasionally unsatisfactory. Many of the careworkers, particularly the undocumented migrant workers, would have preferred a higher status and better paid job in care such as nursing, but they felt that they were unlikely to enter an alternative occupation and that they were better off with a familiar employer. A Peruvian woman working in Milan said:

> Even if I don't like it, what can I do? It is a stressful job, not easy work. Here the only work that one can do is to care for old people. What I did in my own country [nurse training] is not recognized here.

Yet others, despite difficulties, still chose to maintain the relationship because there were some satisfactions that both parties derived from it and/or because they would feel particularly guilty (sometimes a guilt manipulated by the care user and his or her family) if they left the post:

> The son and the daughter-in-law tell me 'We cannot change over to another person. You must stay here as long as mother survives'. I have committed myself . . . I got ill, but I live here so I stay and work as usual.

All these ingredients for tension were compounded by the fact that many of these types of relationship occurred where the careworker was highly dependent on the employer for housing and hence residence, in a situation where the residence rights of the care worker were unclear. In other words, these 'hot' relationships tended to occur where the care worker was undocumented due to illegal immigration, and where she had resolved her and, occasionally, her children's housing problems by becoming a co-resident with her employer. This was a feature of the unregulated Italian funding regime (classified E in Figure 3), where there is a well-established culture of employment of undocumented migrant workers, particularly in the major cities (our interviews were conducted in Milan). These relationships were essentially unequal and potentially exploitative, and the workers, although often employed in the very long term (up to twenty-six years in one instance) by the same employer, were often unhappy, particularly where they had difficulties maintaining their own time and space (Ungerson and Yeandle, 2005). But it was also the case that in some instances, the length of the relationship and the intimacy that had built up over the years between elderly 'employers' and their care worker had also provided the basis for a relationship strongly based on affect. It became impossible to maintain the boundary between a contractual and a personal relationship and this led to further difficulties:

> At a certain point we didn't understand each other . . . this all happened because she became jealous of my little grandchild. One time I said that I could not come to her house for a week because I had to take care of my grandson, and she got very angry – perhaps she felt herself a little neglected, as if she had been 'put aside' . . . so

we quarrelled and I decided to go . . . but I'm sure we shall manage to make peace
before long. *(Migrant care worker in Italy, 26 years continuous employment with same
employer).*

Such relationships are unprofessionalized and unregulated in exactly the
same way as non-commodified informal care relationships are, and rely on the
ability of the employer to judge quality of care and act when they find that care
unsatisfactory. But both sides in these relationships are vulnerable to forms of
exploitation and even abuse particularly since the relationships are acted out
behind closed doors within the domestic domain. Given the core vulnerability
of frail old age on the one hand, and illegal immigration on the other, combined
with spatial proximity, very low wages, and twenty-four hour availability, it is
not surprising that these relationships are full of feelings, not all of them healthy
or likely to underwrite reasonable quality care.

Conclusion

The argument of this chapter has been that the way in which schemes to fund
the direct employment of care workers are organized and regulated does indeed
impact on the nature of the care relationship that is likely to develop. As I have
argued, the extremes of feeling – 'coldness' or 'heat' – are likely to arise in those
relationships where there is hierarchy, inequality and overdependency on the
part of employer and worker – and these qualities are more likely to occur in
situations which allow for, and encourage, unprofessionalized care work. I have
also suggested, however, that in schemes that encourage the employment of
relatives, which is also essentially unprofessionalized, there is a possibility that
these relationships will be equable, equitable and 'warm'. In these cases, a shared
past biography and recruitment through affect can smooth the edges of a purely
contractual relationship, while the contract and payment, can, in themselves, act
as cohesive agents, allowing these relationships to develop into warm inter-
dependency within loosened time constraints.

All this, however, has to be said within serious caveats. These findings are
very tentative, based, as they are, on small qualitative samples, and using a very
simple typology of emotion located within care relationships. Moreover, there
is clearly more to the development of feeling within care relationships than
the exogenous features of the funding regime of the scheme which underwrites
them. That said, it is essential that policy makers recognize the implications of
the cash for care schemes they put in place for the quality of the care provided,
and the emotional context of those care activities.

It has been the purpose of this chapter to lay out the territory over which
further research can – and should – be undertaken. Such schemes to fund the
direct employment by care users of their care workers are rapidly expanding,
and it is important that an understanding of the impact of macro policy change
on the micro care relationship and its quality is also developed at the same speed.

Such further research on commodified care relationships will contribute to a new sociology of work and build upon the knowledge that we have already of particular aspects of these new types of working conditions and 'employment'. There are certain aspects of these new types of employment that are *re*introducing a traditional hierarchical type of employment, particularly where workers are very easily exploited. Hence any future research in this area should take account of historical work on the relationship between masters and mistresses and their domestic servants and develop tools with which to contrast commodified domesticized relationships of the 21[s] century with those of previous eras. Moreover, it is evident that the globalization of care work can be encouraged by the establishment of some funding systems, particularly those where there is little or no regulation of the labour process. There is a growing literature on the use of migrant labour from the South to produce domestic and care work in the West (Ehrenreich and Hochschild, 2003; Anderson, 2000) which has made a major contribution to our understanding of the macro and global changes which are driving new forms of work relationship and the way in which they impact on the care relationship. In this chapter I have taken this literature a tentative step further, and suggested that policy instruments play an important role in determining the nature of these new forms of employment, who the participants are, and how they feel about each other as they 'work' together in the domestic domain.

Notes

1 The research teams were: Austria: August Oesterle and Elisabeth Hammer; France: Claude Martin & Blanche Le Bihan; Italy: Crisitano Gori, Barbara da Roit & Michela Barbot; Netherlands: Marja Pijl, Clarie Ramakers and Fransje Baarveld; UK: Sue Yeandle & Bernadette Stiell.

Welfare State regimes and the social organization of labour: Childcare arrangements and the work/family balance dilemma

Margarita León

Introduction

Access to paid employment has increasingly become a central aspect of social integration and a main route to accessing welfare and social rights in the post-industrial world. Recently, the 'full employment strategy' has been placed at the forefront of social and employment policies in Europe at both country and EU level. The participation of women in paid employment is a crucial part of the strategy (female employment being the major source of employment growth in Europe over the last few years). This social and economic concern for increasing labour force participation has also been articulated politically in terms of discussions about gender equality and women's right to engage in paid labour. Issues of work and family balance have been a salient policy discourse regarding female employment and gender equality, including different forms of employment flexibility, the balance between paid employment and unpaid domestic work and the social organization of care[1]

In this chapter, these current formulations of access to paid employment and their implications for work and family arrangements will be critically assessed. It starts from the basic premise that any shift in the policy logic that aims to give more salience to the employment issue should begin from a cautious consideration of the balance between paid and unpaid work, and the extent to which it is influenced by welfare divisions between the state, the market, the family and the informal sector. The recalibration between paid and unpaid work introduces important changes in the logic of welfare rights as well as in the way we think about the world of labour.

The first section describes the shifts in the literature on welfare systems and policy definitions regarding female employment. It points out that, by acknowledging and supporting the entrance of women in the labour market, the interaction between paid and unpaid work has been made more explicit. Targets to increase the level of female participation in the labour market have, to a certain extent, helped to overcome the once generally ignored contribution of the unpaid work of women in the domestic sphere to the welfare mix and the social organization of labour. It is noted, however, that beyond the agreement on the centrality of access to paid employment and the need to balance work and family, fundamental issues regarding the (re)organization of work are still outstanding. The chapter will then look at the ways in which different European welfare state regimes are currently addressing issues of employment growth, reconciliation between paid employment and unpaid caring tasks, and the extent to which diverse welfare state architectures impact differently on the social organization of labour (including the balance between different forms of paid and unpaid work). Developments in childcare in Spain and the UK will be used to illustrate, on the one hand, the different ways in which welfare regimes are adapting and responding to the shifting forms of work, and on the other hand, individuals' and families' strategies to combine work with care in response to existing forms of provision. Although public provision of services for children is generally included within the education system in most countries, there is a tendency to analyse this provision from the perspective of parents' patterns of employment. This explains why the development of provision for childcare is being increasingly framed in the context of policies addressing work/life balance (Daly, 2002).

Social care, in particular childcare, represents an interesting case for understanding and explaining the social organization of labour. The economy of care is truly a mixed one that does not easily permit a clear distinction between the market, the state and the family in terms of provision, nor is it easy to classify different care tasks in terms of work and non-work. In this terrain, the distinction between work and non-work, and between paid and unpaid labour, is an especially complex one for social policy which adopts different shapes and shadows in different welfare state regimes.

Social rights revised: from dependency to autonomy

The single most fundamental critique that feminist scholars have made against mainstream analyses of welfare states concerns the exclusive attention analysts have given to the market-state nexus, with no real acknowledgement of the relevance of the family in shaping the inputs and outcomes of welfare programmes. Mainstream indicators of welfare rights have traditionally relied on the assumption that participation in the labour market on a standard and full-time basis was the norm for all individuals. The concept of decommodification (Esping-Andersen, 1990) defined as the degree to which social rights are guaranteed independently of pure market forces, is probably the best-known example. Early feminist research in the welfare state and social policy studies claimed that the social reality of women in the domestic sphere was not considered, and also that, by focusing exclusively on the citizen-worker, the connection between female unpaid work and male paid work was neglected (Clarke & Cochrane,

1993; Meyer, 1994). It has been argued that a gender approach to welfare state analysis would look at the capacity of welfare states to weaken women's economic dependence on the family through employment.

As has been the case for the sociology of work, the background of the problem has been a narrow definition of the concept of work, where work has been equated with paid employment, leaving aside not only unpaid domestic and care work mainly done by women, but other forms of unpaid labour in the public domain. As a consequence, the complexity of arrangements of social labour is not fully acknowledged. As Taylor (2004:37) points out 'focusing only on the period of time spent in paid employment can produce a very limited understanding of someone's working life'. Applied to the welfare state, the trouble is not only that important forms of work (mostly work in the sphere of care done by women) are invisible, but also, that restricted definitions of work have an impact on entitlements to social rights, especially in countries where access to welfare benefits is fundamentally determined by participation in formal paid employment.

Several authors (Orloff, 1993; Ostner, 1997; Sainsbury, 1999) have attempted to modify or add to concepts – such as independence from the labour market – that have been fundamental to mainstream theories, so as to render visible women's working trajectories and to consider the impact of their working trajectories on accessing social benefits. Contributions have emphasized the need to assess analytically (1) access to paid work as a welfare indicator, to analyse the extent to which welfare states either promote or discourage women's engagement in paid employment; and, in relation to this, (2) women's independence from family obligations, that is, whether welfare states provide or facilitate autonomy from family dependency.

In terms of welfare state typologies, other authors have made efforts to redefine welfare state regimes according to criteria that differ from those used in mainstream theories. Lewis (1992) introduced variations in attachment to the male breadwinner ideology as a way to examine how different welfare regimes were reflecting upon different gendered logics of division of labour. Her model intends to reveal the interaction of public and private spheres of life in the organization of welfare, which also implies the recognition of women's unpaid role as welfare providers. The different constellations of Lewis's 'breadwinner model' illustrate how different welfare state regimes operate within an ideal-type of organization of labour that is deeply gendered.

Mainstream scholars have largely accepted these feminist critiques and, to a certain extent, the two bodies of literature have merged together quite consistently. What used to be two discrete spheres of investigation are now fairly complementary. Gender is at present recognized as a fundamental variable in shaping welfare states, and welfare states are likewise treated as a determinant not only of social class, but also of gender relations. Welfare state scholars such as Pierson (2000) and Korpi (2000) have recently recognized that the literature on gender and the welfare state generated a fundamental break with traditional research by institutionalizing a profound re-conceptualization of the area.

© The Editorial Board of the Sociological Review 2005

Reviewing his much quoted concept of de-commodification, Esping-Andersen has agreed that the notion of de-commodification is not operable for women unless welfare states contribute towards their commodification. The author has also recognized the importance of considering 'defamilialization' along with 'decommodification' since, despite decades of absence from welfare analysis, the household economy might be the most important 'social foundation' of post-industrial economies (Esping-Andersen, 1999: 6).

This recognition of the different forms of attachment of men and women to the welfare state – in so far as genders tend to represent different 'work' spheres – and their different positioning in terms of paid and unpaid employment, has understandably occurred at a time when social change in post-industrial societies has already challenged fixed gender divisions. Female employment has clearly been activated by the emergence of the service sector, as the cause of much of the growth in employment rates in European countries. It is in fact a mutually reinforcing process. The service sector economy both provides for and facilitates the entrance of women into employment, and increased female employment in turn usually creates an increased demand in the sector. Some-what paradoxically, there is a potential tension between women's lack of par-ticipation in the formal economy and the development of the welfare state (Crouch, 1999). Activities that were previously understood as belonging to the sphere of unpaid domestic work are transformed into either privately or pub-licly paid employment in the service sector. Therefore, the issue of women's access to employment and social rights is now much more visible and measur-able than before. On the other hand, the 'gender dimension' of welfare states plays an important part in the so-called welfare state crisis and needs to be addressed in order to solve some of the problems that contemporary welfare systems face today. In general, there is a considerable consensus about the need for reform on key aspects of welfare provision. With the increasing prevalence of family breakdown, the growing variety of personal arrangements, and the disappearance of the 'standard male industrial worker', familialistic types of benefits are neither adequate nor appropriate for today's patterns of family or-ganization. These benefits do not only discriminate against women, but are also largely inefficient and, in light of fiscal pressures, quite costly. Many of the 'new risks' of contemporary western societies, such as the example of lone mothers, are a consequence of patterns of individual and family trajectories that do not follow the prescribed picture of welfare states. Also, the sustainability of today's pensions systems relies heavily on the participation of women in the labour market. Increasingly, then, welfare states are being evaluated according to their capacity to bring individuals into employment; access to work has become one of the indicators through which social policy is being assessed. Accordingly, welfare states are moving to find ways to 'defamilialize' social rights, which implies, among other things, looking at the success of policies dealing with work/family dilemmas.

Beyond the agreement, however, on the centrality of access to paid employ-ment and the need to find a work/family balance, there are important issues to consider, such as the sharing and distribution of public and private responsibilities, and the effect that this distribution has on gender relations. The social organization of work needs to address the specific allocation between the state, the market and the family in terms of distribution of resources, provisions and incentives and their impact on personal arrangements with regards to combining 'productive' and 'unproductive' times. Indubitably, changes in paid employment impact on other forms of labour. Higher percentages of labour force participation imply some kind of adjustment between different forms of work, especially if those moving into paid employment were previously working without pay in the private, domestic or care sector. The question is whether these developments lead to a re-organization of work (for example, to a commodification of previously unpaid care work or a more equal distribution of unpaid work between men and women within the household) or an increase in labour supply (for instance, trans-national migration in the case of care).

Recent policy developments with regard to the reconciliation of work and family seem to have an effect on the chances of women to be in paid employment, but little on men's involvement in unpaid care work. Research on the division of time between women and men within the family suggests that the main responsibility for care continues to fall on women even when they are in fulltime employment (see for instance Windebank, 2001:270). Women's engagement in paid employment often implies a 'double burden' for them, more than a reorganization of different spheres of work. The debate between women's engagement in paid employment and the state's involvement in social care has often neglected, perhaps because intervention is harder, the division of domestic labour and caring tasks between men and women within the household, and yet this can hardly be dissociated from concerns about reconciliation of working and family life.

Furthermore, female participation in paid work is leading towards alternative forms of informal/formal arrangements for care that needs to be evaluated. Although the availability of public provision for social care has an impact on the demand for other forms of care provision, there will always be 'tasks' falling outside the domain of state or market intervention. Whether we consider these as forms of work or not is a relevant aspect for the social organization of labour and for gender and other forms of social inequalities[2].

Finally, access to employment is a weak indicator to measure transfers from unpaid to paid work and it would need to be studied together with the conditions of such employment, such as class and gender patterns of segregation in the occupational structure, working time arrangements, or earning differentials. Women might be able to move from unpaid to paid work or to combine both, and yet the structures of hierarchies and value systems that determine access to and contents of different types of jobs might remain extensively gendered. The division between private and public goes well beyond the divide between paid and unpaid work and things can change very little if the debate on the organization of work does not include issues of the definitions and categories added to specific forms of work. Although the shift from the 'male breadwinner model' to an 'adult worker model', where both partners are in paid employment, should be seen as improving women's position, the actual outcome might be more or less promising depending on the conditions attached to this adult worker model (Lewis, 2001). In this respect, the division between paid work and care stands as a crucial issue. As Gallie (2002:119) points out with reference to targets at EU level on full employment and social exclusion, employment in itself does not resolve the problems of social inclusion. Many jobs do not provide people with the opportunities for self-development to participate in society. This is particularly the case for forms of work organization that increase the vulnerability of low-skilled groups.

Welfare State regimes: Social care and models of work

The way in which social care is organized in a society is the result of a combination of many factors that range from the institutional set (the provision of welfare services), to the social and economic environment (social perceptions and attitudes towards care work) and individual characteristics (educational background, household composition and the like). These factors lead to a particular allocation of social care needs between the market, the state, the family and other informal sectors, which is strongly rooted in the historical development of countries though with commonalities for the welfare regimes in which welfare states cluster.

At the European level, recent policy developments have attempted to achieve a higher degree of standardization between the nation-states. As has already been said, the European Union has produced a great number of regulations and recommendations in the area of employment and social policy on issues relating to reconciling work and family, and more generally on gender equality. To a certain extent, there has been a process of homogenization of the conditions and framework in which policymaking at the national level operates in terms of targets and direction of the reforms. Still, the specific characteristics and institutional arrangements, that is, the attributes of the welfare and gender regime, have an impact on the development of policies addressing the work/family balance. The relationship between the different work spheres is hence mediated by a complexity of specific welfare regimes in which these relations develop.

The conservative/corporatist model (see Table 1) encourages a partial reconciliation between work and family. The state assumes a certain degree of responsibility for the family and facilitates caring duties through subsidies and tax deductions. There is a tradition of low public childcare provision and in turn, tax privileges favouring single-earner families. Female participation rates are middle/low and (short hours) part-time employment is common, since women often enter the labour market as secondary earners. Women tend to leave the labour market for periods of childbearing and child raising.

Corporatist countries, such as Germany, are in general experiencing serious difficulties in adjusting to the 'full employment strategy' and orienting their

Table 1: *Four Welfare Regimes and Conciliation Models*

Welfare Regime	Conservative	Social-Democrat	Liberal	Mixed
Location	Continental Europe	Nordic countries	Anglo-Saxon countries	Southern Europe
Entitlement to Social Rights	Principle of Maintenance	Principle of Need	Citizenship	Principle of Maintenance
Women in paid employment	Middle/low	High	Middle/high	Low
Women working part-time	Middle	High	High	Low
Continuity in employment during child raising	High discontinuity	High continuity	High discontinuity	High continuity
State involvement in childcare	Partial state involvement	Strong State Involvement	Weak State Involvement	Partial State Involvement

Source: Elaboration from León (2002b)

labour markets towards consumption-based service employment. The male breadwinner-based social insurance system has discouraged the entrance of new groups (mainly women and young people) into the labour market (Scharpf and Schmidt, 2000) and yet, to make their welfare systems sustainable, they need to reduce the dependency ratio by including more people into the labour market. Pressures for reform to make welfare states more employment oriented have led to conflicts over mothers-at-home benefits against day care provision in the field of childcare (Taylor-Gooby, 2004). The expansion of childcare provision as one crucial way to facilitate female employment is a key element in recent reforms in corporatist countries such as Germany and France. In this regime-type the shift from the 'male breadwinner model' to the 'dual-earner model' will eventually change the labour market structure (in the sense that there will be an expansion of jobs at the lower-end of the service sector), as well as modifying the contours of divisions between paid and unpaid and public and private forms of work.

Countries of the social democrat welfare tradition such as Denmark or Sweden present high female employment rates and high continuity rates. In general, women do not leave paid employment for childbearing but are allowed to take long maternity leaves. The reconciliation between work and family is considered a social and political issue. This is partly the reason why the social-democrat regime has always placed a great emphasis on collective forms of provision for social care in general. Nordic countries are well beyond EU average on public provision for childcare. Childbearing does not interfere with engagement in paid employment, but it does have an impact on the organization of working time and patterns of gender segregation in the labour market. Part-time employment and the public sector provide an appropriate scenario for women who want to be in paid employment and have children but face a high degree of gender segregation in the labour market. The employment strategy of the European Union does therefore not represent a problem to the Nordic welfare states in terms of participation rates. The main question confronting this regime-type is whether the high levels of universal provision can be maintained in the light of increasing international competition from countries with higher degrees of social inequality and lower expenditure levels (Taylor-Gooby, 2004).

The liberal model such as the United Kingdom represents the 'choice' formula between paid work and unpaid care work. As Table 1 shows, reproduction often implies 'high' discontinuity in the sense of interruption periods from paid employment to take care of small children. At the same time there is 'high' combination between employment and childbearing because women are allowed to stay in the labour market even if long leaves are unpaid. Hence, employment rates are high but women tend to temporarily leave the labour market for childrearing. Low unemployment rates together with high levels of part-time jobs allow for an easy fluctuation between paid and unpaid employment. Ideologically, the sphere of the family is considered private and the state has no tradition in regulating the relations between public and private spheres except for extreme cases of need. Thus, childcare provision has been managed primarily through the market, and families are responsible for juggling different forms of formal and informal childcare arrangements to meet labour market needs. Over the last few years, partly to achieve EU targets but perhaps more predominantly to tackle poverty and social exclusion problems, countries of a liberal tradition have aimed at extending public childcare provision and regulating the private sector. Payments for care are partly subsidized through the tax credit system, but as we will see when looking at childcare in the UK, personal strategies outside the reach of the state are still the main form of provision for childcare, albeit with different forms of state supervision.

Welfare states in Southern Europe are derived from the Conservative continental regime-model although with common features that have made worth a fourth distinctive category within the welfare state literature. Apart from Portugal, countries of Southern Europe possess the lowest female employment rates in Europe. Although female employment rates are lower than the EU average, however, the speed of growth of participation has been higher than the EU average. Reforms have been enforced to deregulate the labour market to assist the incorporation of women and reduce high levels of unemployment. Flexible working-time arrangements, which in many countries have become crucial for women's access to employment, are scarcely developed in these countries. Other measures to facilitate the combination of family obligations with paid employment are being introduced in the labour law, following recommendations from the European Commission (EC, 2000; EC, 2002). As has been extensively explored in the literature, informal arrangements of family care are a predominant feature of the 'southern model' (see Table 1). Recent developments of welfare reforms and the changing labour market situation are, however, forcing state interventions in the field of social care. There is an increasing marketization process of a particular kind that is transforming (or combining) unpaid family support with paid formal and/or informal work within the household, done mainly by migrant women. We will see these developments in greater detail in the following section when contrasting the British and Spanish welfare systems in relation to childcare arrangements.

Crossing nebulous boundaries:
Childcare arrangements in the UK and Spain

The UK and Spain each has a different welfare state form, yet they could both be labelled as 'strong male breadwinner models', following Lewis' (1992) categorization. The countries also have dissimilar labour markets, with different patterns of female labour participation. In the UK, the labour market provides opportunities for short hours of part-time work to fit with childcare responsibilities. A large proportion of women work part-time in the British labour market. In Spain, by contrast, part-time employment for both men and women is among the lowest in the EU. Flexibility takes the form of short-term contracts, which increased rapidly after the 1990s labour market reforms. This deregulatory change managed to move a high proportion of women from inactivity and unemployment into employment but at a high price. This form of *vulnerable* flexibility cannot be considered, as part-time employment can, as a strategy to reconcile paid employment with child-raising given the short-term employment prospects and low social rights coverage of these contracts.

Although the features of the British labour market, unlike the Spanish one, do facilitate the engagement in paid work of women with small children, motherhood has a strong impact on women's professional life, given the low levels of institutional support for childcare. Both countries have a tradition of low support for working parents, but the response to this lack of support has been different. Both countries have different types of symmetries between public/private or formal/informal spheres, and their relation to childcare.

Compared to the UK, the system of childcare arrangements in Spain is relatively simple. Childcare provision is fundamentally developed through the national education system, although highly decentralized for children under three years of age. Care for children from birth to three, and pre-school education for children aged three to six, have been developed as two different branches of public policy. Before the 1990 reform of the education system, childcare for children under three fell within the domain of the social services. With the intention to increase and standardize levels of provision for children under three, reforms are moving towards an inclusion of this public provision under the education system instead of social services. The first step has been a change in terminology to stress the educational aspect as opposed to the 'care' aspect[3]. Although schooling rates are still low, levels have been increasing steadily[4]. Public provision is growing, especially in some regions, but 57 per cent of the total provision is still private (MEC, 2003). Parents have to bear the cost of childcare for these first years, though low-income families can apply for subsidized public provision. In 2000, the centre-right government introduced a 100 Euro (69 GBP) monthly 'premium' to be paid to female employees who have a child under three years of age, the measure is intended to cover some of the childcare costs.

Pre-school education (3–6) by contrast is mainly publicly provided (69 per cent of the total provision) with private centres subsidized. The public administration – whether central or regional – assumes the costs of this provision. It is located within the primary and secondary schools and engagement is usually full-time. Schooling rates are 100 per cent for four and five years old and 88 per cent for children aged three, although there are strong regional differences (MEC, 2003). Finally, although new legislation has been into force to improve several aspects of maternity leave, it has failed to provide real paternity leave. Parents do not have equal rights (or obligations) to take employment leave. Thus, the care of small children is primarily linked to mothers (León 2002a)[5].

Given these recent developments within the education system, Spain conforms to EU targets regarding childcare provision[6]. Other forms of support are, however, still needed for care of children under three and for childcare outside school hours and school terms. Research on Southern European welfare states has reported that the family provides for the main form of informal care support in the welfare mix of these countries, supplanting a tradition of weak state involvement (Tobío, 1998; Trifiletti, 1999; Valiente, 2003). Informal support, however, is increasingly fragmenting into a variety of forms of provision, both paid and unpaid. Given increasing female participation in the labour market (and women's expectations toward paid employment), changing gender roles and family structures, and recent global migratory flows, personal strategies for social care are increasingly moving toward a marketization process, although still within the limits of the households. One increasingly common solution to cover the needs for childcare, and perhaps eventually elderly care as well, is the employment of migrant women as domestic minders6. Its classification however seems rather complex. This form of care arrangement falls somewhere in between informal and formal paid work, into a vague area of paid work that can be economically visible (through a proper employment contract) or invisible if it stays within the limits of the grey economy[7]. This type of arrangement places care not just as a gender conflict but as a class conflict as well, in the sense that women of different socio-economic positions face very different opportunities and constraints. This sort of 'grey marketization' (Hammer and

Osterle, 2003), which is pervasive in other continental and south European countries such as Italy and Austria, does not imply a totally new form of caring arrangement but a way of renovating patterns of traditional societies, 'replacing' the social group who performed these tasks under similar working conditions. The implications regarding renewed social and economic inequalities are strong. The associated unequal distribution of income, working conditions and life chances might be implicitly legitimate.

Whether informal childcare is organized through the extended family as a form of private (unpaid) solidarity or whether it adopts the form of unregulated paid work within the household, there still are outstanding issues regarding the conditions of the care offered. As Daly (2002: 262) points out 'the matter is not exhausted by whether the work is paid or not'. From the perspective of the social organization of labour we would need to move beyond fixed categories of paid and non-paid work to identify the conditions of care work organized as employment (in terms of pay, security, and social rights) and the impact that the different arrangements has on the well-being of both the care receiver and the care provider and the relationship among them.

Childcare in Britain has traditionally been located in the private market sector or within the community on an unpaid or informally paid basis. Although public provision for children under compulsory school age is lower compared with Spain, the forms of provision in the UK are wide-ranging.

Childcare provision for children under compulsory age in the private sector can take place in the market or within the household. Day nurseries are mainly run by private companies, although there are also nurseries run by local social services departments and workplace nurseries-offering full-time or part-time sessions. Childminders and nannies are private options for families. The former offers childcare sessions within a home based setting, they need to be qualified and registered with the non-ministerial government department (OFSTED) whose aim is to control the quality and standards of childcare (Eurostat, 2004:94). The latter works either by living in within the family or coming to the home on a daily basis. Nannies can be qualified nurses or unqualified workers and do not need to be registered.

Given the fact that women have been in paid employment for several decades and that most British women with small children work part-time, childcare provision in the UK does take into account, even if in an informal or private way, the problem of flexibility when it comes to combining work and childcare. There are a variety of childcare options for part-time provision to meet families' needs (such as playgroups, nursery schools and toddlers groups). There are also options for after-school hours and holiday periods, something which in Spain might happen informally; for example, parents co-ordinate themselves to pick up children, or grandparents take the children to the park after the school, but this has not been formalized and 'named' as in Britain, for instance, 'Before' and 'After' School Club and 'Holiday Clubs'[8].

Moreover, given perhaps a tradition of voluntary and community work, the informal sector seems to be more *formalized* than in Spain. There seems to be a more collective organization of informal solutions to childcare. Much of the childcare provision can be run by volunteers and be provided in public premises, such as parks or community centres. 'Parent and Toddler Groups' for instance, are informal groups which may be offered within a community centre or a school for children up to five years. They may be staffed by qualified childcare workers or volunteers, with the participation of the parents. The previously mentioned 'After School' and 'Holiday Clubs' can also be run by voluntary organizations. As Ungerson (2000) has explained, voluntary work in the provision of social care is at the crossroads of public and private employment, and paid and unpaid work.

Nonetheless, present research shows that most dual-earner families with small children, even if one of them works part-time, need additional help from other members of the family. Although southern Europe seems to have taken all the credit for it, the *extended* family (mainly grandmothers) are actively involved in different forms of childcare arrangements in the UK. Skinner (2003: 51), for instance, talking about co-ordination points[9] between childcare, paid work and the family in a small sample of English families, argues that even when formal childcare is used, there is still a large reliance on informal care to transport children to and from different settings and as back-up support in case of a change in routine. Parents use a mixture of strategies, some of them paid, some of them unpaid, formal or informal, that all combine together to conform a network of support, which goes along temporal, spatial and time dimensions. In a similar vein, the study of Wheelock and Jones (2002:443)[10] also shows that families arrange complex 'jigsaws' of childcare relying heavily on informal provision to complement the formal one. This 'complementary care', as the authors call it, is overwhelmingly provided by the maternal grandmothers. Similar to the previous study, their results show that the demand for informal care reflected the mismatch between parents' working hours and school hours. Furthermore, claims for the recognition of the role that grandparents play in looking after their grandchildren are being formulated in terms of their own work/life balance (The *Guardian* 28/02/2005). In contrast to the Spanish case where the majority of women over 55 are outside the labour market (and thus have more time availability), many grandparents with childcare responsibilities are still in paid work, which gives a different, and often neglected, dimension of the reciprocities and fluctuations between different forms of work.

The *National Childcare Strategy* set up by the Labour Government in 1998 stresses the need for greater availability, more affordable and better quality childcare, as part of the New Deal on welfare to work investment. Although the strategy has been an important step in acknowledging gaps in the provision of childcare, it has been criticised for widening the breach between paid and unpaid childcare. As Rake (2001:226) points out, the focus on paid employment of the New Deal programmes is increasing the opportunity costs of care work, sustaining the long-standing under valuation of unpaid caring work and the pre-established association of care work with female work. The way in which the Working Family Tax Credit has been formulated, for instance, excludes payment to family members who care for the children (Wheelock and Jones, 2002; Rake 2001). The absence of paid parental leave is also inhibiting the ability of fathers to participate in unpaid caring work.

Therefore, although the UK and Spain are confronting different dilemmas in relation to paid employment and childcare, they are both currently trying to move away from the underlying foundational principles of their welfare systems in relation to the public and private divide. Both countries are attempting to increase levels of institutional support to childcare as a way to deal with the *employability* issue of women and problems of poverty and social exclusion. It has been pointed out, however, that by concentrating in some policy spheres and not in others, gender roles in relation to care and work continue to be reinforced. In addition, the interactions and transfers between the formal and informal spheres in the provision of care do not only occur but are in a continuous process of redefinition.

Concluding Remarks

The once prevailing gender dichotomy between paid employment and unpaid domestic work around which social rights were granted in different welfare state regimes is now recognized as being too oversimplified a picture of people's working and life trajectories. Changes in labour markets have forced a revision of 'familialistic' welfare states and the male-breadwinner model to facilitate the entrance of women into paid employment. Needing women in the labour market, recent reforms in many countries have aimed at 'defamilializing' social provision by breaking the relationship between the independent male breadwinner worker and economically dependent female housewife.

It has been argued, however, that while much attention has been given to women entering the world of paid work, the relationship between participation in the labour market and caring responsibilities remains problematic on a number of accounts. The issue is not simply access to paid employment; looking at the conditions under which participation in the labour market takes place is also essential. If we take the example of women who will be in paid employment as a result of more jobs in the childcare sector, that is, women employed as carers in the public sphere, issues of inequalities between genders and also between women will still be outstanding if these jobs are located at the bottom of the occupational scale. Moreover, policies addressing female employment and childcare availability have often not dealt comprehensively with men's engagement in unpaid work or with challenging gendered roles relating to care. Higher percentages of labour participation for women seem to be causing both an increasing 'double burden' in their working arrangements and, a more complex combination of work in the different spheres of the social organization of labour.

Looking at welfare state regimes helps to understand the degree to which the relationship between different work spheres is mediated by the complexity of the specific welfare mix in which these relations develop. Women's engagement in paid work is crucially influenced by the way in which the welfare state conceptualizes care work as either paid or unpaid, and public or private. Furthermore, current trends to increasing female participation rates in European labour markets are forcing toward a re-conceptualization of the content of and conditions under which care is given in a particular society.

Childcare has been used as an illustration of the way in which a particular welfare domain cannot be easily traced in separated and isolated categories of paid and unpaid work. Care work is an area where the nature of work is contestable. As Glucksmann (2000a) has argued, 'contemporary' changes raise questions about the shifting place of labour activity in different modes of provision and the formation of new boundaries and interactions across them. It has been argued that the mixed welfare economy of social care does not allow for a neat division between the market, the state and the family, the three axes comprising the welfare state. Boundaries often get blurred in different ways depending on each specific welfare system (as shown in Table 1). The commodification of unpaid care work has implied different degrees of intersection between the spheres of the market, the state, and the family depending on various paths for policy reform. The acknowledgement of this complexity in the provision of childcare is necessary in order to grasp the full reality of all those involved in care and to understand the full picture of family and/or individual strategies to deal with work and family balances.

Notes

1 The Lisbon European Council of March 2000 recognized the necessity to facilitate the reconciliation of working life and family by investing in childcare provision; The Employment Guidelines from 2000 onwards argue in favour of promoting policies that would facilitate the combination of working and caring times through measures such as affordable, accessible and high-quality caring services for dependants and arrangements for parental leave; The Community Action programme on equal opportunities for men and women (1996–2000) also had as one of its priorities the reconciliation of work and family life for men and women, focusing on the quality of care services, flexible work and the sharing of domestic and caring responsibilities for men and women.

2 Using qualitative data from the SOCCARE project to analyse childcare and work strategies in four European countries, Larsen (2004) points out that formal care services in all countries are insufficient to cover all the families' childcare needs and therefore, families everywhere use some kind of informal support in their work and care strategies, the outcome being a mix of different care providers (Larsen, 2004: 673).

3 Previously called 'Guarderias' (day nurseries), they are now called 'Escuelas Infantiles' (Infant schools).

4 For the period 2000–2001, schooling rates (full time) were 1.7% of infants up to one year; 7.5% for one year olds and 17.4% for two year olds (MEC, 2003).

5 Mothers have the option of transferring a maximum of ten of the sixteen weeks of leave to the father. This has not encouraged fathers to take leave or induced mothers to give up their right because it is not an independent right of the worker.

6 The 2002 Barcelona European Council agree to target childcare provision by 2010 to at least 90% of children between age three and the mandatory school age and at least 33 per cent of children under three years of age (European Commission, 2003).

7 For the year 2002, 86 per cent of foreign women registered in the social security system were employed in the service sector. Half of the work permits given in 1999 to the service sector corresponded to the category 'households that employ domestic personnel' (CES, 2003). Moreover, the figures underestimate the real level. This is an occupational sector with significant presence in the grey economy. According to the 2001 census the number of foreign women actually working is about 30% higher than the number of foreign women registered with social security that same year (CES, 2003: 110).

8 These clubs provide care for children from 3 to 14 years on school premises or in a community or day care centre outside school hours and during school holidays.

9 Skinner (2003) has carried out a qualitative study of 40 English mothers living in two different areas, exploring their coordination strategies to combine childcare with paid work. By 'coordination points' she means those times in the day when children need to be taken to and from different childcare/educational settings.

10 Their study on the contribution of informal childcare to the employment of parents consisted of interviews and focus groups with informal carers and parents in a conurbation of the north east of England.

Bibliography

Abiala, K. (1999) 'Customer orientation and sales situations: variations in interactive service work', *Acta Sociologica*, 42 (3): 207–222.

Adam, B. (1990) *Time and Social Theory*, Cambridge: Polity Press.

Adam, B. (1995) *Timewatch*, Cambridge: Polity Press.

Adkins, L. (1995) *Gendered Work. Sexuality, family and the labour market*, Buckingham: Open University Press.

Adkins, L. and Lury, C. (1999) 'The labour of identity: performing identities, performing economies'. *Economy and Society*, 28 (4): 598–614.

Akyeampong, E. (2000) 'Unionisation – An Update', Perspectives on Labour and Income, 12 (3): 39–59.

Aldridge, T., Tooke, J., Lee, R., Leyshon, A., Thrift, N. and Williams, C. C. (2001) 'Recasting work: the example of Local Exchange Trading Schemes (LETS)', *Work, Employment and Society*, 15 (3): 565–579.

Allen, I. (2001) *Stress among ward sisters and charge nurses*, London: Policy Study Institute.

Anderson, Benedict (1983) *Imagined Communities: Reflections on the origin and spread of nationalism*, London: Verso.

Anderson, Bridget (2000) *Doing the Dirty Work: the Global Politics of Domestic Labour*, London: Zed Books.

Anderson, M. (1971) *Family Structure in Nineteenth Century Lancashire*, Cambridge, England: Cambridge University Press.

Armstrong, P. and Armstrong, H. (2004) 'Thinking It Through: Women, Work and Caring in the New Millennium', in K. R. Grant, C. Amaratunga, P. Armstrong, M. Boscoe, A. Pederson and K. Wilson (eds), *Caring For/Caring About: Women, Home Care and Unpaid Caregiving*, Aurora, Canada: Garamond.

Armstrong, P. and Armstrong, H. (2003) *Wasting Away: The Undermining of Canadian Health Care*, 2nd Ed., Toronto: Oxford University Press.

Armstrong, P., Laxer, K. and Armstrong, H. (2004) 'Conceptualizing Health Care Work', paper presented at Gender and Work; Knowledge Production in Practice Conference, York University, Toronto.

Armstrong, P. and Laxer, K. (2005) 'Mapping Precariousness in the Canadian Health Industry: Privatization, Ancillary Work and Women's health', in L. F. Vosko (ed.). *Precarious Employment: Understanding Labour Market Insecurity.* Montreal and Kingston, McGill-Queen's University Press.

Audit Commission (2001) *Hidden talents; education, training and development for healthcare staff in NHS Trusts*, London: Audit Commission, March.

Austrin, T. and West, J. (2004) 'New deals in gambling: global markets and local regimes of regulation', in L. Beukema and J. Carillo (eds) *Globalism/Localism at Work*, Amsterdam: Elsevier.

Baines, C. T., Evans, P. M. and Neysmith, S. M. (eds) (1998) *Women's Caring*, Toronto: Oxford University Press.

Bales, K. (1996) 'Measuring the propensity to volunteer', *Social Policy and Administration*, 30 (3): 206–226.

Ball, J. and Pike, G. (2004) *Stepping Stones: Results from the RCN membership survey 2003*, London, Royal College of Nursing, www.rcn.org.uk.

Ball, S. (2003) *Class Strategies and the Education Market: The middle classes and social advantage*, London: Routledge Falmer.

Barnes, H., Parry, J. and Lakey, J. (2002) *Forging a New Future – the experiences and expectations of people leaving paid work after 50*, Bristol: Policy Press.

Barry, K. (1995) *The Prostitution of Sexuality*, New York: New York University Press.

BBC News (1 February 1999) 'Doctors dissatisfied with the NHS' http://news.bbc.co.uk/1/hi/health/background_briefings/nhs_pay_99/269574.stm.

BBC News (23 April 2003/ Business) 'Why flexible hours can work' http://news.bbc.co.uk/1/hi/business/2966629.stm.

Beck, U. (1992) *Risk Society: Towards a New Modernity*, London: Sage.

Beck, U. (2000) *Brave New World of Work*, Cambridge/Oxford: Polity Press in Association with Blackwell.

Beechey, V. (1987) *Unequal Work*, London: Verso.

Beechey, V. and Perkins, T. (1987) *A matter of hours: women, part-time work and the labour market*, Cambridge: Polity Press.

Bell, S. and Coleman, S. (eds) (1999) *The Anthropology of Friendship*, Oxford and New York: Berg.

Benner, C. (2002) *Work in the New Economy; flexible labour markets in Silicon Valley*, Oxford: Blackwell.

Benson, S. P. (1988) *Counter Cultures: Saleswomen, Managers, and Customers in American Department Stores, 1890–1940*, Urbana and Chicago: University of Illinois Press.

Bernstein, B. (1975) *Class, Codes and Control*, Vol. 3, London: Routledge and Kegan Paul.

Beynon, H., Grimshaw, D., Rubery, J. and Ward, K. (2002) *Managing Employment Change: the new realities of work*, Oxford: Oxford University Press.

Billis, D. (1989) *A Theory of the Voluntary Sector: Implications for Policy and Practice*, London: Centre for Voluntary Organizations, Working Paper No. 5, LSE.

Bindel, J. (2003) 'Sex workers are different', *The Guardian*, 7 July.

Bindman, J. and Doezema, J. (1977) *Redefining Prostitution as Sex Work on the International Agenda*, London: Anti-Slavery International.

Blackburn, R. M. and Marsh, C. (1991) 'Education and social class: revisiting the 1944 Education Act with fixed marginals', *British Journal of Sociology*, 42 (4): 507–536.

Blackburn, R. M. and Prandy, K. (1997) 'The reproduction of social inequality', *Sociology*, 31 (3): 491–509.

Blackstone, T., Cornford, J., Hewitt, P. and Miliband, D. (1992) *Next Left: An Agenda for the 1990s*, London: IPPR.

Blanden, J. and Gregg, P. (2004) *Family Income and Educational Attainment: A Review of Approaches and Evidence*. Centre for the Economics of Education: London School of Economics.

Bolton, S. C. and Boyd, C. (2003) 'Trolley dolly or skilled emotion manager? Moving on from Hochschild's managed heart'. *Work, Employment and Society*, 17 (2): 289–308.

Bond, S., Hyman, J., Summers, J. and Wise, S. (2002) *Family-friendly working? Putting policy into practice*, Joseph Rowntree Foundation Report, York: York Publishing Series for the Policy Press.

Borg, M. A. and Portelli, A. (1999) 'Hospital Laundry Workers – An At-Risk Group for Hepatitis A?', *Occupational Medicine*, 49 (7): 448–450.

Boris, E. and Prügl, E. (eds) (1996) *Homeworkers in Global Perspective: Invisible no more*, New York: Routledge.

Bottero, W. and Prandy, K. (2001) 'Women's occupations and the social order in nineteenth century Britain', *Sociological Research Online*, 6 (2).

Bottero, W. and Prandy, K. (2003) 'Social interaction distance and stratification', *British Journal of Sociology*, 54 (2): 177–197.

Bottero, W. (2004) 'Class identities and the identity of class', *Sociology*, 38 (5): 985–1004.

Bourdieu, P. (1984) [1979] *Distinction: A social critique of the judgement of taste*, London: Routledge and Kegan Paul.

Bourdieu, P. (1985) 'Social space and the genesis of groups', *Theory and Society*, 14 (6): 723–744.

Bourdieu, P. (trans. Richard Nice) (1990) *The Logic of Practice*, Stamford: Stamford University Press.

Bourdieu, P. (trans. Richard Nice) (1993) *Sociology in Question*, London: Sage.

Bradley, H. (1996) *Fractured Identities*, Cambridge: Polity Press.

Bradley, H., Erickson, M., Stephenson, C. and Williams, S. (2000) *Myths at Work*, Malden, MA: Policy Press.

Brannen, J. and Moss, P. (1991) *Managing Mothers*, London: Unwin Hyman.

Brannen, J. (2002) *The Work Family Lives of Women: Autonomy or illusion?*, paper presented at Gender Institute Seminar, LSE.

Brewis, J. and Linstead, S. (2000) *Sex, Work and Sex Work: Eroticising Organization*, London: Routledge.

Britton, N. J. (1999) 'Recruiting and Retaining Black Volunteers: A Study of a Black Voluntary Organization', *Voluntary Action*, 1 (3): 9–23.

Broadbridge, A., Swanson, V. and Taylor, C. (2000) 'Retail change: effects on employees' job demands and home life', *International Review of Retail, Distribution and Consumer Research*, 10 (4): 417–432.

Brubaker, R. (1985) 'Rethinking classical theory: the sociological vision of Pierre Bourdieu', *Theory and Society*, 14 (6): 745–775.

Buchan, J. (2002) 'Global nursing shortages', *British Medical Journal*, 321 (30 March): 750–751.

Buchan, J. and Seccombe, I. (2003) *More nurses working differently? A review of the UK nursing labour market 2002 to 2003*, London: Royal College of Nursing, www.rcn.org.uk.

Burchell, B., Day, D., Hudson, M., Ladipo, D., Mankelow, R., Nolan, J., Reed, H., Wichert, I. and Wilkinson, F. (1999) *Job insecurity and work intensification: flexibility and the changing boundaries of work*, Joseph Rowntree Foundation Report, York: York Publishing Series for the Policy Press.

Burger, A. and Dekker, P. (2001) *The Non-profit Sector in the Netherlands*, Working Document 70, The Hague: Social and Cultural Planning Office. www.scp.nl.

Burgess, A. (1997) *Fatherhood Reclaimed: the making of the modern father*, London: Vermilion.

Callaghan, G. and Thompson, P. (2002) ' "We recruit attitude": the selection and shaping of routine call centre labour', *Journal of Management Studies*, 39 (2): 233–254.

Callon, M. (ed.) (1998) *The Laws of the Markets*, Blackwell: Oxford.

Canada, Commission on the Future of Health Care in Canada (2002) *Building on Values: The Future of Health Care in Canada* [Romanow Report], Ottawa: Commission on the Future of Health Care in Canada.

Canadian Home Care Association (1999) cited in the *Ontario Health Coalition Fact Sheet #8*, Toronto, January.

Cavendish, R. (1982) *Women on the Line*, London: Routledge and Kegan Paul.

Chapkis, W. (1997) *Live Sex Acts: Women Performing Erotic Labour*, London: Cassell.

Charles, N., James, E. and Ransome, P. (2002) 'Gender dimensions of job insecurity' in P. Stewart (ed.) *Organizational Change and the Future of Work: The Experience of Work and Organizational Change*, ESRC Future of Work Programme Working Paper Series.

Charles, N. and James, E. (2003) 'Gender and work orientations in conditions of job insecurity', *British Journal of Sociology*, 54 (2): June: 239–257.

Clarke, J. and Cochrane, A. (eds) (1993) *Comparing Welfare States. Britain in International Context*, London: Sage.

Coburn, J, (1987) ' "I See and Am Silent": A Short History of Nursing in Ontario, 1850–1930', in D. Coburn, C. D'Arcy and G. M. Torrance (eds), *Health and Canadian Society*, 2nd edn. Markham: Fitzhenry and Whiteside.

Cockburn, C. and Ormrod, S. (1993) *Gender and Technology in the Making*, London: Sage.

Cohen, M. G. and Cohen, M. (2004) *A Return to Wage Discrimination. Pay Equity Losses Through the Privatization of Health Care*, Vancouver: Canadian Centre for Policy Alternatives.

Cohen, T. F. (1993) 'What do fathers provide? reconsidering the economic and nurturant dimensions of men as parents' in J. C. Hood (ed.) *Men, Work and Family*, Newbury Park CA: Sage.

Cooke, L. and Chitty, A. (2004) *Why do doctors leave the profession?* Health Policy and Research Unit, London, BMA, April.

Cooper, C. L. and Williams, S. (1994) *Creating Healthy Working Organizations*, John Wiley and Sons: Chichester.

Cope, P., Hill, P., Jones, S. and Turner, J. (eds) (1996) *Chasing the Dragon: Creative community responses to the crises in the South Wales coalfield*, A European Community (ERGO 2) Coalfields Community Campaign VIAE report: Gwent Tec and Mid Glam Tec.

Cowan, R. S. (1983) *More Work for Mother: The Ironies of Household Technology from the Open Hearth to the Microwave*, New York: Basic Books.

Crompton, R. (1996) 'The fragmentation of class analysis', *British Journal of Sociology*, 47 (1): 56–67.

Crompton, R. (1997) *Women and Work in Modern Britain*, Oxford: Oxford University Press.

Crompton, R. (1998) *Class and Stratification*, 2nd Edition, Cambridge: Polity Press.

Crompton, R. (1999) 'The decline of the male breadwinner: explorations and interpretations', in R. Crompton (ed.) *Restructuring gender relations and employment: the decline of the male breadwinner*, Oxford: Oxford University Press.

Crompton, R. (2002) 'Employment, flexible working and the family' *British Journal of Sociology* 53 (4): 537–558.

Crompton, R. and Sanderson, K. (1990) 'Credentials and careers', in G. Payne and A. Abbott (eds) *The Social Mobility of Women: Beyond Male Mobility Models*, Basingstoke: Falmer Press.

Crompton, R. and Scott, J. (2000) 'Introduction: the state of class analysis' in R. Crompton, F. Devine, M. Savage and J. Scott (eds) *Renewing Class Analysis*, Oxford: Blackwell.

Crouch, C. (1999) *Social Change in Western Europe*, Oxford: Oxford University Press.

Crow, G. and Allan, G. (1994) *Community Life: An Introduction to Local Social Relations*, Hemel Hempstead: Harvester Wheatsheaf.

Crow, G. P. and Allan, G. (1995) 'Community types, community typologies and community time', *Time and Society*, 4 (2): 147–166.

Crow, C. (1996) 'Community time as community's fourth dimension', *Annotations: Mixed Belongings and Unspecified Destinations*, London: Institute of International Visual Arts.

Crozier, G. (2000) *Parents and Schools: partners or protagonists*, Stoke on Trent: Trentham Books.

Coyle, A. (1995) *Women and organizational change*, EOC Research Discussion Series no. 14, Manchester: Equal Opportunities Commission.

Cunningham, H. (1975) *The Volunteer Force: A Social and Political History 1859–1906*, London: Croom Helm.

Daly, M. (2002) 'Care as a good for social policy', *Journal of Social Policy*, 31 (2): 251–270.

Daly, M. and Lewis, J. (2000) 'The concept of social care and the analysis of contemporary welfare states', *British Journal of Sociology*, 51 (2): 281–298.

Davidoff, L. (1995) *Worlds Between: Historical Perspectives on Gender and Class*, Basingstoke: Macmillan Education.

Davies, C. (1995) *Gender and the Professional Predicament of Nursing*, Buckingham: Open University Press.

Davis Smith, J. (1992) 'What we know about volunteering: information from the surveys' in J. Davis Smith, C. Rochester and R. Hedley (eds) (1995) *An Introduction to the Voluntary Sector*, London: Routledge.

Davis Smith, J. (1998) *The 1997 National Survey of Volunteering*, London: Institute for Volunteering Research.

Davis Smith, J., Rochester, C. and Hedley, R. (eds) (1995) *An Introduction to the Voluntary Sector*, London: Routledge.

Day, S. (1996) 'The law and the market: rhetorics of exclusion and inclusion among London prostitutes, in O. Harris (ed.) *Inside and Outside the Law: Anthropological Studies of Authority and Ambiguity*, London: Routledge.

Dean, D. and Jones, C. (2003) 'If women actors were working . . .', *Media, Culture and Society*, 25: 527–541.

Decima Research Inc. (2002) *National Profile of Family Caregivers in Canada 2002*, Ottawa: Health Canada.

Dennis N., Henriques, F. and Slaughter, C. (1956) *Coal is our Life: An analysis of a Yorkshire Mining Community*, London: Tavistock.

Department for Education and Employment (DfEE) (1998a) *Excellence in Cities*, London: HMSO.

Department of Health (2000) *The NHS Plan: a plan for investment a plan for reform*, Cm4818-1, July, London: The Stationery Office.

Department of Health (2001) *Improving working lives standard*, London: Department of Health.

Department of Health (2002a) 'Statistics for General Medical Practitioners in England: 1991–2001', *Bulletin*, 2002/03 February.

Department of Health (2002b) 'Hospital, public health medicine and community health services medical and dental staff in England: 1999–2001', *Bulletin*, 2002/04 February.

Dermott, E. (2003) 'The intimate father: defining paternal involvement', Sociological Research Online, 8 (4) http://www.socresonline.org.uk/8/4/dermott.html.

Deven, F., Inglis, S., Moss, P. and Petreis, P. (1998) *State of the art review on the reconciliation of work and family life for men and women and the quality of care services*, DfEE Research Report no. 44 London: Department for Education and Employment.

Devine, F. (1998) 'Class analysis and the stability of class relations', *Sociology*, 32 (1): 23–42.

Devine, F. and Savage, M. (2000) 'Conclusion: Renewing class analysis', in R. Crompton, F. Devine, M. Savage and J. Scott (eds) *Renewing Class Analysis*, Oxford: Blackwell.

Dex, S. and Smith, C. (2002) *The Nature and Pattern of Family Friendly Employment Policies in Britain*, Joseph Rowntree Trust, York: The Policy Press.

Dex, S. and McCulloch, A. (1995) *Flexible Employment in Britain: a Statistical Analysis*, EOC Research Discussion Series no.15, Manchester: Equal Opportunities Commission.

Dicken, P. (2003) *Global Shift: Reshaping the Global Economic Map in the 21ˢᵗ Century*, 4ᵗʰ ed., London: Sage.

Dienhart, A. (1998) *Reshaping Fatherhood, The Social Construction of Shared Parenting*, Thousand Oaks, CA: Sage.

Du Gay (1996) *Consumption and Identity at Work*, London: Sage.

Du Gay, P. (ed.) (1997) *Production of Culture/Cultures of Production*, London: Sage.

Du Gay, P. and Pryke, M. (eds) (2002) *Cultural Economy: Cultural Analysis and Commercial Life*, London: Sage.

Edler, D. and Scarlet Alliance (1999) *Occupational Health and Safety in the Australian Sex Industry: a Guide to Best Practice*, Australian Federation of Aids Organizations. Edwards, A. and Warin, J. (1999) 'Parental involvement in raising the achievement of primary school pupils: why bother?', *Oxford Review of Education*, 25 (3): 325–341.

Edwards, C. and Robinson, O. (2002) 'A "new" business case for flexible working?: The case of part-time qualified nurses in the UK National Health Service', paper presented to the Women and Equality Unit Gender Research Forum, November.

Ehrenreich, B. and Hochschild, A. R. (2003) *Global Woman: Nannies, Maids and Sex Workers in the New Economy*, London and New York: Granta Books.

Entwistle, J. (2002) 'The aesthetic economy: the production of value in the field of fashion modelling', *Journal of Consumer Culture*, 2 (3): 317–39.

Equal Opportunities Commission of Northern Ireland (1996) *Report on the Formal Investigation into Competitive Tendering in Health and Education Services in Northern Ireland*, Belfast: Equal Opportunities Commission of Northern Ireland.

Erikson, R. and Goldthorpe, J. (1992) *The Constant Flux: The Study of Social Mobility in Industrial Societies*, Oxford: Clarendon Press.

Esping-Andersen, G. (1999) *Social Foundations of Postindustrial Economies*, Oxford: Oxford University Press.

Esping-Andersen, G., Gallie, D., Hemerijck, A. and Myles, J. (eds) (2002) *Why we need a New Welfare State*, Oxford: Oxford University Press.

European Commission (2000) *Employment in Europe 2000*, Brussels: Directorate-General for Employment and Social Affairs, http://europa.eu.int.

European Commission (2002) *Employment in Europe 2002. Recent Trends and Prospects'*, Brussels: Directorate-General for Employment and Social Affairs, http://europa.eu.int.

European Commission (2003) 'Council Decision of 22 July 2003 on guidelines for the employment policies of the member states', *Official Journal of the European Union*, L97: 13–21.

Eurostat (2004) *Development of a Methodology for the Collection of Harmonised Statistics on Childcare*, Final report July 2004, European Commission.

Evans, T. (1988) *A Gender Agenda*, Sydney: Allen and Unwin.

Fagan, C. and O'Reilly, J. (1998) 'Conceptualising part-time work' in C. Fagan and J. O'Reilly (eds) *Part-time prospects: an international comparison of part-time work in Europe, North America and the Pacific Rim*, London, Routledge.

Family Policy Studies Centre (1995) *Families in Britain*, Family Report no. 3, London: Family Policy Studies Centre.

Felstead, A. and Jewson, N. (1999) (eds) *Global Trends in Flexible Labour*, Basingstoke: Macmillan Business.

Felstead, A. and Jewson, N. (2000) *In Work, At Home. Towards an Understanding of Homeworking*, London: Routledge.

Felstead, A., Jewson, N. and Walters, S. (2005) *Changing Places of Work*, London: Palgrave.

Ferri, E. and Smith, K. (1996) *Parenting in the 1990s*, Report for the Family Policy Studies Centre and the Joseph Rowntree Foundation, London: Family Policy Studies Centre.

Finch, J. and Groves, D. (eds) (1983) *A Labour of Love: Women, Work and Caring*, London: Routledge and Kegan Paul.

Fine, B., Heasman, M. and Wright, J. (1996) *Consumption in the Age of Affluence. The World of Food*, London: Routledge.

Finlayson, G. (1994) *Citizen, State and Social Welfare in Britain 1830–1990*, Oxford: Clarendon Press.

Fitzsimons, A. (2002) *Gender as a Verb: Gender Segregation at Work*, Aldershot: Ashgate.

Forbes, I. (2002) 'The political meanings of the equal opportunities project', in E. Breitenbach, A. Brown, F. Mackay and J. Webb (eds) *The Changing Politics of Gender Equality in Britain*, Basingstoke: Palgrave.

Francis, H. (1990) 'The Valleys' in R. Jenkins and A. Edwards (eds) *One Step Forward? South and West Wales Towards the Year 2000*, Llandysul: Gomer Press in association with SSRI Swansea.

Gallie, D. (2002) 'The quality of working life in welfare strategy' in G. Esping-Andersen, D. Gallie, A. Hemerijck and J. Myles (eds) *Why We Need a New Welfare State*, Oxford: Oxford University Press.

Gaskin, K. (1998) *What Young People Want from Volunteering*, London: Institute of Volunteering Research.

Gatens, M. and MacKinnon, A. (eds) (1999) *Gender and Institutions: Welfare, Work and Citizenship*, Cambridge: Cambridge University Press.

Gay, P. (1999) 'Getting into work: volunteering for employability', *Voluntary Action*, 1 (2): 55–66.

Gershuny, J. (2000) *Changing Times. Work and Leisure in Postindustrial Society*, Oxford and New York: Oxford University Press.

Gherardi, S. (1995) *Gender, Symbolism and Organizational Cultures*, London: Sage.

Giddens, A. (1992) *The Transformation of Intimacy*, Cambridge: Polity Press.

Glenn, E. (1992) 'From Servitude to Service Work: Historical continuities in the racial division of paid reproductive labour', *Signs*, 18 (1): 1–43.

Glennerster, H. (2003) *Understanding the Finance of Welfare*, Bristol: Policy Press.

Glucksmann, M. (1990) *Women Assemble: Women Workers and the 'New Industries' in Inter-war Britain*, London: Routledge.

Glucksmann, M. (1995) 'Why "Work"? Gender and the "total social organization of labour"', *Gender, Work and Organization*, 2 (2): April: 63–75.

Glucksmann, M. (1998) '"What a Difference a Day Makes": a theoretical and historical exploration of temporality and gender', *Sociology*, 32 (2): 239–258.

Glucksmann, M. (2000a) *Cottons and Casuals: the Gendered Organization of Labour in Time and Space*. Durham: sociologypress.

Glucksmann, M. (2000b) 'Retailing: production and consumption's missing relation', *Economic Sociology*, European Electronic Newsletter, 1 (3): 12–16 http://econsoc.mpifg.de.

Glucksmann, M. (2004a) 'Call connections: varieties of call centre and the organization of labour', *Work, Employment and Society* 18 (4): 795–811.

Glucksmann, M. (2004b) 'Call encounters: shopping and retailing by telephone.' Mimeo.

Gold, M. and Fraser, J. (2002) 'Managing self-management: successful transitions to portfolio careers', *Work, Employment and Society*, 16 (4): 579–597.

Goldberg, I. and Paice, E. (2000) 'Job sharing in medical training: an evaluation of a 3-year project', *Hospital Medicine*, 61 (2): 125–128.

Goldthorpe, J. and Erikson, R. (1992) *The Constant Flux*, Oxford: Clarendon Press.

Goldthorpe, J. H. (with C. Llewellyn and C. Payne) (1980) *Social Mobility and Class Structure in Modern Britain*, Oxford: Oxford University Press.

Goldthorpe, J., Lockwood, D., Bechhofer, F. and Platt, J. (1969) *The Affluent Worker in the Class Structure*, Cambridge: Cambridge University Press.

Goldthorpe, J. and Marshall, G. (1992) 'The promising future of class analysis', *Sociology*, 26 (3): 381–400.

Goodsell, T. (2000) 'Maintaining solidarity: a look back at the Mormon village', *Rural Sociology*, 65 (3): 357–375.

Goodwin, J. (1999) *Men's Work and Male Lives: Men and work in Britain*, Aldershot: Ashgate.

Graham, H. (1983) 'Caring: a labour of love' in J. Finch and D. Groves (eds) *A Labour of Love: Women, Work and Caring*, London: Routledge and Kegan Paul.

Granovetter, M. (1973) 'The Strength of Weak Ties', *American Journal of Sociology*, 78: 1360–1380.

Granovetter, M. (1974) *Getting a Job – A Study of Contacts and Careers*, Cambridge, Mass.: Harvard University Press.

Granovetter, M. (1985) 'Economic action and social structure: the problem of embeddedness', *The American Journal of Sociology*, 91 (3): 481–510.

Granovetter, M. (1992) 'Economic institutions as social constructions: a framework for analysis', *Acta Sociologica*, 35: 3–11.

Granovetter, M. and Swedberg, R. (eds) (1992) *The Sociology of Economic Life*, Boulder, Oxford: Westview Press.

Green, F. (2001) 'It's been a hard day's night: the concentration and intensification of work in late twentieth-century Britain', *British Journal of Industrial Relations*, 39: 53–80.

Gregson, N. and Lowe, M. (1995) *Servicing the Middle Classes: Class, Gender and Waged Domestic Labour in Contemporary Britain*, London: Routledge.

Griffiths, H. (1979) 'Community action and voluntary organizations', *Journal of Voluntary Action Research*, 8: 36–53.

Grint, K. (1991) *The Sociology of Work: An Introduction*, Cambridge: Polity Press.

Griswold, R. L. (1993) *Fatherhood in America*, New York: Basic Books.

Guardian (3 May 2003) 'Childcare grows into £2.15bn business.'

Guardian (17 April 2002) 'Rural repair', *Guardian Society*.

Guardian (17 July 2002) 'Cutting edge', *Guardian Society*.

Guardian (17 August 2004) 'Britain's Family Revolution'.

Hadley, R. and Hatch, S. (1981) *Social Welfare and the Future of the State: Centralised Social Services and Participatory Alternatives*, London: Allen and Unwin.

Hakim, C. (1991) 'Grateful slaves and self-made women: fact and fantasy in women's work orientations', *European Sociological Review*, 7 (2): 101–121.

Hakim, C. (1996) *Key Issues in Women's Work*, London: The Athlone Press.

Halford, S. (2004) 'Towards a sociology of organizational space', *Sociological Research Online*, 9 (1): http://www.socresonline.org.uk/9/1/halford.html.

Halford, S., Savage, M. and Witz, A. (1997) *Gender, Careers and Organizations: Current Developments in Banking, Nursing and Local Government*, London: Macmillan.

Hall, C. (1979) 'The early formation of Victorian domestic ideology' in S. Burman (ed.) *Fit Work for Women*, London: Croom Helm.

Hall, C. (1992) *White, Male and Middle Class*, Cambridge, Polity.

Hammer, E. and Osterle, A. (2003) 'Welfare state policy and informal long-term care giving in Austria: old gender divisions and new stratification processes among women', *Journal of Social Policy*, 32 (1): 37–54.

Handy, C. (1988) *Understanding Voluntary Organizations*, Harmondsworth: Pelican.

Harkness, S. (2002) *Low Pay, Times of Work and Gender*, EOC Working Paper Series no. 3, Manchester: Equal Opportunities Commission.

Harrison, B. (1971) *Drink and the Victorians: The Temperance Question in England 1815–1872*, Pittsburgh: University of Pittsburgh Press.

Harvey, M. (1999) 'Economies of time: a framework for analysing the restructuring of employment relations', in A. Felstead and N. Jewson (eds) *Global Trends in Flexible Labour*, Basingstoke: Macmillan.

Harvey, M. (2002) 'Instituting economic processes in society', paper to workshop on Polanyian Perspectives on Instituted Economic Processes, Development and Transformation, ESRC Centre for Research on Innovation and Competition, University of Manchester.

Harvey, M., McMeekin, A., Randles, S., Southerton, D., Tether, B. and Warde, A. (2001) *Between Demand and Consumption: A Framework for Research*, CRIC Discussion Paper No 40, ESRC Centre for Research on Innovation and Competition: University of Manchester/UMIST.

Harvey, M., Quilley, S. and Beynon, H. (2002) *Exploring the Tomato: Transformations of Nature, Society and Economy*, Cheltenham: Edward Elgar.

Harvey, M. and Randles, S. (2002) 'Markets, the organization of exchanges and 'instituted economic process', *Revue d'Economie Industrielle*, 101 (4): 11–30.

Hatch, S. (1983) *Volunteers: Patterns, Meanings and Motives*, Berkhampstead: The Volunteer Centre.

Hatter, W., Vinter, L. and Williams, R. (2002) *Dads on Dads; Needs and Expectations at Home and at Work*, EOC Research Discussion Series, Manchester: Equal Opportuntities Commission.

Hausbeck, K. and Brents, B. (2000) 'Inside Nevada's brothel industry', in R. Weitzer (ed.) *Sex for Sale: Prostitution, Pornography and the Sex Industry*, New York and London: Routledge.

Health Policy and Economic Research Unit (2003) *BMA Cohort Study of 1995 Medical Graduates, Eighth Report*, London: British Medical Association.

Health Policy and Economic Research Unit (2003) *BMA Cohort Study of 1995 Medical Graduates, Eighth Report*, London: British Medical Association.

Health Policy and Economic Research Unit (2004) *BMA Cohort Study of 1995 Medical Graduates, Ninth Report*, London: British Medical Association.

Hedley, R. and Davis Smith, J. (eds) (1992) *Volunteering and Society: Principles and Practices*, London: Bedford Square Press.

Higginbotham, E. and Romero, M. (eds) (1997) *Women and Work: Exploring Race, Ethnicity and Class*, London: Sage.

Hill, L. and McCarthy, P. (2000) 'Hume, Smith and Ferguson: Friendship in Commercial Society' in P. King and H. Devere (eds) *The Challenge to Friendship in Modernity*, London, Portland, Oregon: Frank Cass.

Hirsch, D. with Millar, J. (2004) 'Labour's welfare reform: progress to date', *Foundations* 44, York: Joseph Rowntree Foundation.

Hochschild, A. (1983) *The Managed Heart: Commercialization of Human Feeling*, Berkeley: University of California Press.

Hochschild, A. with Machung, A. (1989) *The Second Shift*, London: Piatkus.

Hochschild, A. (2001) *The Time Bind: When Work Becomes Home and Home Becomes Work*, New York: Owl Books (second edition).

Hochschild, A. R. (2003) *The Commercialization of Intimate Life: Notes from Home and Work*, Berkeley, Los Angeles and London: University of California Press.

Hogarth, T., Hasluck, C. and Pierre, G. with Winterbotham, M. and Vivian, D. (2000) *Work-Life Balance 2000: Baseline Study of Work-Life Balance Practises in Great Britain*, London: Department for Education and Employment.

Hoigard, C. and Finstad, L. (1992) *Backstreets: Prostitution, Money and Love*, Cambridge: Polity Press.

Home Office (2000) *Setting the Boundaries: Reforming the Law on Sexual Offences*, London: Home Office Communication Directorate.

Home Office (2004) *Paying the Price: a Consultation Paper on Prostitution*, London: Home Office Communication Directorate.

Horton Smith, D. (1981) 'Altruism, volunteers and volunteering', *Journal of Voluntary Action Research*, 10: 21–36.

Household Satellite Account, National Statistics www.statistics.gov.uk/hhsa.

Houston, D. (ed.) (2005) *Work-Life Balance in the 21st Century*, Palgrave: Macmillan.

Howlett, S. and Locke, M. (1999) 'Volunteering for Blair: the Third Way' *Voluntary Action*, 1 (2): 6776.

Hubbard, P. and Sanders, T. (2003) 'Making space for sex work: female street prostitution and the production of urban space', *International Journal of Urban and Regional Research*, 27 (1): 75–89.

Hughes, E. (1971) *The Sociological Eye: Selected Papers*, Chicago: Aldine Press.

Hughes, K., Lowe, G. S. and Schellenberg, G. (2003) *Men's and Women's Quality of Work in the New Canadian Economy*, Ottawa: Canadian Policy Research Networks.

Hughes, M., Wikely, F. and Nash, T. (1994) *Parents and Their Children's Schools*, Oxford: Blackwell.

Huws, U. and O'Reagan, S. (2001) *eWork in Europe: results from EMERGENCE 18-country Employer Survey*, IES Report no. 380, Brighton: Institute for Employment Studies.

Huws, U., Jagger, N. and Bates, P. (2001) *Where the Butterfly Alights: the Global location of eWork*. Insitute for Employment Studies Report 378.

Huws, U., Jagger, N. and O'Regan, S. (1999) *Teleworking and Globalisation*, Brighton: The Institute for Employment Studies.

Hutton, W. (1995) *The State We're In*, London: Verso.

IPI (Institute for Prostitution Issues) (1998) *Between the Lines*, September, Newsletter of the Mr A de Graaf Foundation, Amsterdam.

Jackson, S. and Scott, S. (eds) (1996) *Feminism and Sexuality: a Reader*, Edinburgh: Edinburgh University Press.

Jamieson, L. (1998) *Intimacy; Personal Relationships in Modern Societies*, Cambridge: Polity Press.

Jenkins, S. (2004) 'Restructuring flexibility: case studies of part-time female workers in six workplaces', *Gender, Work and Organization* 11 (3): 306–333.

Jordan, B., Redley, M. and James, S. (1994) *Putting the Family First: Identities, Decisions, Citizenship*, London: UCL Press.

Judd, D. (1995) 'Promoting tourism in US cities', *Tourism Management*, 16 (3): 175–187.

Kaul, H. (1991) 'Who cares? Gender inequality and care leave in the nordic countries', *Acta Sociologica*, 34 (2): 115–123.

Keat, R., Whiteley, N. and Abercrombie, N. (1994) *The Authority of the Consumer*, London: Routledge.

Kempadoo, K. and Doezema, J. (eds) (1998) *Global Sex Workers: Rights, Resistance and Redefinition*, London and New York: Routledge.

Kendall, J., Knapp, M. and Forder, J. (2003) 'Social care and the non-profit sector in the developed world', Mimeo, London: LSE Health and Social Care.

Kinnell, H. (2001) 'Murderous clients and indifferent justice: violence against sex workers in the UK', *Research for Sex Work*, 4: 22–24.

Knell, J. (2000) *Most Wanted*, London: Industrial Society.

Knight, B. (1993) *Voluntary Action*, London: Home Office.

Knights, D. and Willmott, H. (1999) *Management Lives: Power and identity in Work Organizations*, London: Sage.

Kodz, J., Harper, H. and Dench, S. (2002) *Work-life balance: beyond the rhetoric*, IES Report no. 384, Brighton: Institute for Employment Studies.

Kondo, D. K. (1990) *Crafting Selves: Power, Gender and Discourses of Identity in a Japanese Workplace*. University of Chicago Press, Chicago and London.

Korczynski, M. (2003) 'Communities of coping: collective emotional labour in service work', *Organization*, 10 (1): 55–80.

Korpi, W. (2000) 'Faces of inequality: gender, class and patterns of inequalities in different types of Welfare States', *Social Politics*, 7 (2): 127–191.

Kozak, M. (1998) *Employment, family life and the quality of care services: a review of research in the UK (1994–1996)*, DfEE Research Report no. 54, London: Department for Education and Employment.

Kramer, R. (1990) *Voluntary Organizations in the Welfare State: On the Threshold of the 90s*, London: Centre for Voluntary Organizations, LSE.

Kumar, K. (1988) 'From work to employment and unemployment: the English experience', in R. Pahl (ed.) *On Work: Historical, Comparative and Theoretical Perspectives*, Oxford: Blackwell.

La Rossa, R. and La Rossa, M. M. (1981) *Transition to Parenthood: How Infants Change Families*, Beverley Hills, CA: Sage.

La Rossa, R. (1997) *The Modernization of Fatherhood: a Social and Political History*, Chicago: University of Chicago Press.

La Valle, I., Arthur, S., Millward, C., Scott, J. with Clayden, M. (2002) *Happy Families*, Joseph Rowntree Foundation, York: The Policy Press.

Lan, P. (2003) 'Among women: migrant domestics and their Taiwanese employers across generations' in B. Ehrenreich and A. R. Hochschild (eds) (2003) *Global Woman: Nannies, Maids and Sex Workers in the New Economy*, London: Granta.

Lane, N. (1998) 'Barriers to women's progression into nurse management in the National Health Service', *Women in Management Review*, 13 (5): 184–191.

Lareau, A. (1989) *Home Advantage*, London: The Falmer Press.

Larsen, T. P. (2004) 'Work and care strategies of European families: similarities or national differences?' *Social Policy and Administration*, 38 (6): 654–677.

Larson, M. (1977) *The Rise of Professionalism*, Berkeley: University of California Press.

Lash, S. and Urry, J. (1994) *Economies of Signs and Space*, London: Sage.

Leat, D. (1995) 'Funding matters' in J. Davis Smith, C. Rochester and R. Hedley (eds) (1995) *An Introduction to the Voluntary Sector*, London: Routledge.

Le Feuvre, N. (2004) 'Childcare policies and practices in France: women's employment patterns' paper presented to ESRC Seminar Employment and the Family, City University, London, 22–23 April.

León, M. (2002a) 'The individualisation of social rights: hidden familialistic practices in Spanish social policy', *South European Society and Politics*, 7 (3): 53–79.

León, M. (2002b) *Reconciling Work and Family. Impact on Gender Equality*, EUI Working Paper RSC 2002/41.

Leonard, A. (1991) 'Women in struggle: a case study in a Kent mining community', in N. Redclift and M. Sinclair (eds) *Working Women: International Perspectives on Labour and Gender Ideology*, London: Routledge.

Levitas, R. (1998) *The Inclusive Society? Social Exclusion and New Labour*, Basingstoke: Macmillan.

Lewis, C. (2000) *A Man's Place in the Home: Fathers and Families in the UK*, York: Joseph Rowntree Foundation.

Lewis, J. (1992) 'Gender and the development of welfare regimes', *Journal of European Social Policy*, 3: 175–197.

Lewis, J. (1999) 'Reviewing the relationship between the voluntary sector and the state in Britain in the 1990s', *Voluntas: International Journal of Voluntary and Non Profit Organizations*, 10 (3): 255–270.

Lewis, J. (2001) 'The decline of the male breadwinner model: implications for work and care', *Social Politics*, 8 (2): 152–169.

Lin, C. J. (1999) *Filipina Domestic Workers in Taiwan: Structural Constraints and Personal Resistance*, Taipei: Taiwan Grassroots Women's Center.

Lister, R. (1997) *Citizenship: Feminist Perspectives*, Basingstoke: Macmillan.

Lockwood, D. (1975) 'Sources of variation in working-class images of society', in M. Bulmer (ed.), *Working-Class Images of Society*, London: Routledge and Kegan Paul.

Longhurst, B. and Savage, M. (1996) 'Social class, consumption and the influence of Bourdieu: some critical issues' in S. Edgell, K. Hetherington and A. Warde (eds) *Consumption Matters*, Sociological Review Monograph Series A, Oxford: Blackwell.

Lopes, A. and Macrae, C. (2003) 'The oldest profession', *The Guardian* 25 July.

Lucey, H. and Reay, D. (2000) 'Social class and the psyche', *Soundings*, 15: 139–154.

Lummis, T. (1985) *Occupation and Society: The East Anglian fishermen 1880–1914*, Cambridge: Cambridge University Press.

Lupton, D. and Barclay, L. (1997) *Constructing Fatherhood: discourses and experiences*, London: Sage.

Lutz, H. (2002) '"At your service madam": The globalisation of domestic labour', *Feminist Review*, 70: 89–104.

MacDonald, C. and Sirianni, C. (eds) (1996) *Working in the Service Society*. Philadelphia: Temple University Press.

MacErlean, N. (2002) 'Sexual union', *The Observer*, 28 July.

McBride, T. (1976) *The Domestic Revolution*, London: Croom Helm.

McDowell, L. (1997) *Capital Culture. Gender at Work in the City*, Oxford: Blackwell.

McDowell, L. and Pringle, R. (1992) *Defining Women: Social Institutions and Gender Divisions* Cambridge: Polity Press in association with the Open University.

McGauran, A.-M. (2000) 'Vive La Différence: The gendering of occupational structures in a case study of Irish and French retailing', *Women's Studies International Forum*, 23 (5): 613–627.

McGrath, D. J. and Kuriloff, P. J. (1999) '"They're going to tear the doors off this place": upper-middle class parent school involvement and the educational opportunities of other people's children', *Educational Policy*, 13 (5): 603–629.

McIntosh, M. (1996) 'Feminist debates on prostitution', in L. Adkins and V. Merchant (eds) *Sexualizing the Social: Power and the Organization of Sexuality*, Basingstoke: Macmillan.

McKeganey, J. and Barnard, M. (1996) *Sex Work on the Streets*, Buckingham: Open University Press.

McKie, L., Gregory, S. and Bowlby, S. (eds) (1999) *Gender, Power and the Household*, Basingstoke: Paulgrave Macmillan.

McKie, L., Gregory, S. and Bowlby, S. (2002) 'Shadow times: the temporal and spatial frameworks and experiences of caring and working', *Sociology*, 36 (4): 897–924.

McManus, I. and Sproston, K. (2000) 'Women in hospital medicine in the United Kingdom: glass ceiling, preference, prejudice or cohort effect?', *Journal of Epidemiology and Community Health*, 54 (1): 10–16.

McMullen, K. and Schellenberg, G. (2003) *Job Quality in Non-Profit Organizations*, Ottawa: Canadian Policy Research Networks, 2003.

McNamara, O., Hustler, D., Stronach, I., Rodrigo, M., Beresford, E. and Botcherby, S. (2000) 'Room to manoeuvre: mobilising the 'active partner' in home-school relations', *British Educational Research Journal*, 26 (4): 473–490.

McPherson, K. (1994) 'Science and techniques: nurses work in a Canadian hospital, 1920–1939', in D. Dodd and D. Gorham (eds) *Caring and Curing*, Ottawa: University of Ottawa Press.

McRobbie, A. (1998) *British Fashion Design: Rag trade or Image Industry?*, London: Routledge.

Marchington, M., Rubery, J., Grimshaw, D. and Willmott, H. (2004) *Fragmenting Work. Blurring boundaries and disordering hierarchies*, Oxford: Oxford University Press.

Marshall, G. (1986) 'The workplace culture of a licensed restaurant', *Theory, Culture and Society*, 3 (1): 33–48.

Marshall, G. and Firth, D. (1999) 'Social mobility and personal satisfaction: evidence from ten Countries', *British Journal of Sociology*, 50 (1): 28–48.

Marshall, T. F. (1994) *The Assessment Of Local Voluntary Activity: Developing the Method*, London: Home Office.

Marsiglio, W. (1995) 'Fatherhood scholarship: an agenda and overview for the future' in W. Marsiglio (ed.) *Fatherhood: Contemporary Theory, Research and Social Policy*, Thousand Oaks, CA: Sage.

Martin, C. and LeBihan, B. (2006) 'Cash for care in the French welfare state: a skilful compromise?' in C. Ungerson and S. Yeandle (eds) *Commodified Care Work in Developed Welfare States*, London: Palgrave.

Massey, D. (1994) *Space, Place and Gender*, Cambridge: Polity Press.

Matthews, R. (1997) *Prostitution in London: an Audit*, London: Middlesex University.

Mayall, B. (2002) *Towards a Sociology for Childhood: Thinking from Children's Lives*, Buckingham: Open University Press.

Measham, F. and Allen, S. (1994) 'In defence of home and hearth? families, friendships and feminism in mining communities', *Journal of Gender Studies*, 3 (1): 31–45.

MEC (Ministry of Education and Culture) (2003) *Las Cifras de la educación en España*, http://www.mec.es/estadistica/CifEdu.html.

Melucci, A. (1996) *The Playing Self: Person and Meaning in the Planetary Society*, Cambridge: Cambridge University Press.

Mercer, K. (1995) 'Imagine all the people: constructing community culturally', in R. Hylton (curator) *Imagined Communities*, National Touring Exhibitions, London: 12–17.

Merttens, R. and Vass, J. (1993) *Partnership in Maths: Parents and Schools*, London: The Falmer Press.

Metcalfe, S. and Warde, A. (2002) *Market Relations and the Competitive Process*, Manchester: Manchester University Press.

Meyer, M. H. (ed.) (2000) *Care Work: Gender, Class and the Welfare State*, London and New York: Routledge.

Meyer, T. (1994) 'The German and British Welfare States as employers: patriarchal or emancipatory?' in D. Sainsbury (ed.) *Gendering Welfare States*, London: Sage Publications.

Midwinter, E. (1992) *Citizenship: From Ageism to Participation*, Research Paper No. 8, Fife: Carnegie UK Trust.

Mirchandani, K. (2004) 'Practices of global capital: gaps, cracks and ironies in transnational call centres in India' *Global Networks*, 4 (4): 355–373.

Momsen, J. H. (ed.) (1999) *Gender, Migration and Domestic Service*, London: Routledge.

Mooney, A. and Statham, J. with Simon, A. (2002) *The Pivot Generation: Informal Care and Work after 50*, Joseph Rowntree Foundation, York: The Policy Press.

Mooney, A. and Statham, J. (2003) *Childcare Services and Atypical Working Hours*, Joseph Rowntree Foundation/Policy Press.

Morris, L. (1990) 'The household and the labour market', in C. C. Harris (ed.) *Family, Economy and Community*, Cardiff: University of Wales Press.

Morris, L. and Scott, J. (1996) 'The attenuation of class analysis: Some comments on G. Marshall, S. Roberts and C. Burgoyne "Social Class and the Underclass in Britain in the USA"', *British Journal of Sociology*, 47 (1): 45–55.

Morris, R. J. (1983) 'Voluntary societies and British urban elites, 1780–1850: An analysis', *The Historical Journal*, 26 (1): 95–118.

Morgan-Thomas, R. (2003) 'The impact of closing Edinburgh's "non-harassment" zone', paper at *Prostitution in the 21st Century: Pulling apart the Myths and Exploring the Realities*, Mainliners and the UK Network of Sex Work Projects, Birmingham, 5 December.

Mountford, L. and Rosen, R. (2001) *NHS Walk-in centres in London: an initial assessment*, London: King's Fund.

Mumford, K. and Power, A. (2003) *East Enders: Family and community in East London*, Bristol: The Policy Press.

Munro, G. (2000) 'How do individuals relate to their local communities through work and family life? Some fieldwork evidence', The Arkleton Centre for Rural Development Research, University of Aberdeen, Arkleton Research Paper Number 3.

Myrdal, A. and Klein, V. (1956) *Women's Two Roles*, London: Routledge.

Nagle, J. (ed.) (1997) Whores and Other Feminists, New York and London: Routledge.

National Forum on Health (1997) [Values report] *Canada Health Action: Building on the Legacy*, Vol. II, Synthesis Reports and Issues Papers, Ottawa: Minister of Public Works and Government Services.

Neave, M. (1994) 'Prostitution laws in Australia: past history and current trends', in R. Perkins, G. Prestage, R. Sharp and R. Lovejoy (eds), *Sex Work and Sex Workers in Australia*, Sydney: University of New South Wales Press.

Nelson, J. (1995) 'Dr Rockefeller will see you now: the hidden players privatizing Canada's health care system,' *Canadian Forum* January/February: 7–12.

Noon, M. and Blyton, P. (1997) *The Realities of Work*, Basingstoke: Paulgrave Macmillan.

Nuffield Trust (1998*) Improving the health of the NHS workforce*, London: Nuffield Trust.

Nursing Times (2 January 2002) 'A&E nursing posts unfilled'.

Nursing Standard (28 January 2004) 'Unions urge ministers to combat UK nurse exodus', 18 (20): 5.

Nursing Standard (4 February 2004) 'Employee-friendly policies delayed by huge workload', 18 (21): 9.

Nursing Standard (21 July 2004) 'Students find it hard to secure jobs', 18 (45): 5.

O'Brien, M. and Shemilt, I. (2003) *Working fathers: fathers and caring*, EOC Research Discussion Series, Manchester: Equal Opportunities Commission.

O'Connell Davidson, J. (1998) *Prostitution, Power and Freedom*, Oxford: Polity.

O'Malley, M. (1992) 'Time, work and task orientation: a critique of American historiography', *Time and Society*, 1: 341–358.

Obaze, D. (1992) 'Black People and Volunteering', in R. Hedley and J. Davis Smith (eds) *Volunteering and Society: Principles and Practices*, London: Bedford Square Press.

Observer (12 September 2004) 'Benefit figures reveal stress on women workers'.

Office for National Statistics (2002) *General Household Survey 2002*, London: ONS.

Office For Standards In Education (OFSTED) (1994) *Reporting Pupils' Achievements*, London: HMSO.

Office For Standards In Education (OFSTED) (1995) *Guidance on the Inspection of Nursery and Primary Schools*, London: HMSO.

Ontario, Ministry of Long-Term Care (1998) *Central region: Suggestions for Priorization and Eligibility criteria for CCACs*, July: 6.

Orloff, A. (1993) 'Gender and the social rights of citizenship: state policies and gender relations in comparative research', *American Sociological Review*, 58 (3): 303–328.

Orr, K. E., Holliday, M. G., Jones, A. L., Robson, I. and Perry, J. D. (2002) 'Survival of Enterococci During the Hospital Laundry Process', *Journal of Hospital Infection*, 50 (2): 133–139.

Osborne, D. and Gaebler, T. (1993) *Reinventing Government: How the Entrepreneurial Spirit Is Transforming the Public Sector*, New York: Penguin.

Osnowitz, D. (2005) 'Managing time in domestic space: home-based contractors and household work', *Gender and Society*, 19 (1): 83–103.

Ostner, I. (1997) 'Lone Mothers in Germany Before and After Unification' in J. Lewis (ed.) *Lone Mothers in European Welfare Regimes: Shifting Policy Logics*, London: Jessica Kingsley Publishers.

Outshoorn, J. (1998) 'Sexuality and international commerce: the traffic in women and prostitution policy in the Netherlands', in T. Carver and V. Mottier (eds) *Politics of Sexuality*, London: Routledge.

Owen, D. (1964) *English Philanthropy 1660–1960*, London: Oxford University Press.

Page, R. (1996) *Altruism and the British Welfare State*, Aldershot: Avebury.

Pahl, R. E. (1984) *Divisions of Labour*, Oxford: Basil Blackwell.

Pahl, R. (ed.) (1988) *On Work: Historical, Comparative and Theoretical Approaches*, Oxford: Basil Blackwell.

Pahl, R. (2000) *On Friendship*, Polity Press: Cambridge.

Paradeise, C. (2003) 'French sociology of work and labor: from shop floor to labor markets to networked careers', *Organization Studies*, 24 (4): 633–653.

Parke, R. D. (1996). *Fatherhood*, Cambridge, MA: Harvard University Press.

Parry, J. (1996) *A History of the Labour Movement in Neath*, Neath: Peter Hain.

Parry, J. (2000) *Class and identity processes: Restructuring in the (former) coalmining communities of the South Wales Valleys*, PhD thesis, University of Southampton.

Parry, J. (2003) 'The changing meaning of work: restructuring in the former coalmining communities of the South Wales Valleys', *Work, Employment and Society*, 17 (2): 227–246.

Pateman, C. (1988) *The Sexual Contract*, Cambridge: Polity Press.

Paules, G. F. (1996) 'Resisting the symbolism of service among waitresses' in C. MacDonald and C. Sirianni (eds) *Working in the Service Society*, Philadelphia: Temple University Press.

Paull, G. and Taylor, J. with Duncan, A. (2002) *Mothers' employment and childcare use in the UK*, London: Institute of Fiscal Studies.

Payne, G. (1992) 'Competing views of contemporary social mobility and social divisions', in R. Burrows and C. Marsh (eds), *Consumption and Class*, Basingstoke: Macmillan.

Payne, G. and Abbot, P. (1990) 'Beyond male mobility models' in G. Payne and A. Abbott (eds) *The Social Mobility of Women: Beyond Male Mobility Models*, Basingstoke: Falmer Press.

Perez-y-Perez, M. (2004) *Discipline, Autonomy and Ambiguity: Organization, Work and Markets in the Sex Industry in Christchurch, New Zealand*, PhD thesis, University of Canterbury, New Zealand.

Perkins, R., Prestage, G., Sharp, R. and Lovejoy, F. (eds) (1994) *Sex Work and Sex Workers in Australia*, Sydney: University of New South Wales Press.

Perrons, D. (2003) 'The new economy and the work-life balance: conceptual explorations and a case study of new media', *Gender, Work and Organization*, 10 (1): 65–93.

Pettinger, L. (2003) *Branded stores, branded workers: selling and service in fashion retail*, PhD Thesis, Essex University.

Pettinger, L. (2004) 'Brand culture and branded workers: service work and aesthetic labour in fashion retail', *Consumption, Markets and Culture*, 7 (2): 165–184.

Pettinger, L. (2005) 'Gendered work meets gendered goods: selling and service in clothing retail', *Gender, Work and Organization*, 12 (5): 460–478.

Phillips, J., Bernard, M. and Chittendon, M. (2002) *Juggling work and care: the experience of working carers of older adults*, Joseph Rowntree Foundation Family and Work Series, Bristol: The Policy Press.

Phoenix, J. (1999) *Making Sense of Prostitution*, London: Macmillan.

Pierson, P. (2000) 'Three worlds of welfare state research', *Comparative Political Studies*, 33 (6–7): 791–821.

Pillinger, J. (1998) *Working time in Europe: European working time policy in the public services*, Brussels: European Federation of Public Service Unions.

Platman, K. (2003) 'The self-designed career in later life: a study of older portfolio workers in the United Kingdom', *Ageing and Society*, 23: 281–302.

Plumridge, E., Chetwynd, J., Reed A. and Gifford, S. (1997) 'Discourses of emotionality in commercial sex; the missing client voice', *Feminism and Psychology*, 7 (2): 165–181.

Poel, S. van der (1995) 'Solidarity as boomerang: the fiasco of the prostitutes' rights movement in the Netherlands', *Crime, Law and Social Change*, 23: 41–65.

Polanyi, K., Arensberg, C. M. and Pearson, H. W. (eds) (1957) *Trade and Market in the Early Empires*, New York: The Free Press.

Pollert, A. (1981) *Girls, Wives, Factory Lives*, London: Macmillan.

Prandy, K. (1990) 'The revised Cambridge scale of occupations', *Sociology*, 24 (4): 629–655.

Prandy, K. (1998) 'Class and continuity in social reproduction: an empirical investigation', *Sociological Review*, 46 (2): 340–364.

Prandy, K. (1999) 'The social interaction approach to the measurement and analysis of social stratification', *International Journal of Sociology and Social Policy*, 19 (9/10/11): 215–224.

Prandy, K. and Bottero, W. (1998) 'The use of marriage data to measure the social order in nineteenth-century Britain', *Sociological Research Online*, 3 (1) http://www.socresonline.org.uk/socresonline/3/1/6.html.

Prandy, K. and Bottero, W. (2000a) 'Social reproduction and mobility in Britain and Ireland in the nineteenth and early twentieth centuries', *Sociology*, 34 (2): 265–281.

Prandy, K. and Bottero, W. (2000b) 'Reproduction within and between generations: the example of nineteenth-century Britain', *Historical Methods*, 33 (1): 4–15.

Prandy, K. and Jones, F. L. (2001) 'An international comparative analysis of marriage patterns and social stratification', *International Journal of Sociology and Social Policy*, 21 (4/5/6): 165–183.

Pringle, R. (1988) *Secretaries Talk: Sexuality, Power and Work*, London: Verso.

Pringle, R. (1998) *Sex and Medicine: Gender, Power and Authority in the Medical Profession*, Cambridge: Cambridge University Press.

Prochaska, F. (1980) *Women and Philanthropy in Nineteenth Century England*, New York: Oxford University Press.

Prochaska, F. (1988) *The Voluntary Impulse: Philanthropy in Modern Britain*, London: Faber and Faber.

Prügl, E. and Boris, E. (1996) 'Introduction' in E. Boris and E. Prügl (eds) *Homeworkers in Global Perspective: Invisible No More*, New York: Routledge.

Purcell, K., Hogarth, T. and Simm, C. (1999) Whose flexibility? *The costs and benefits of non-standard employment*, Joseph Rowntree Foundation Report, York: York Publishing Services, Joseph Rowntree Foundation.

Qureshi, H. (1990) 'Boundaries between formal and informal care-giving work', in C. Ungerson (ed.) *Gender and Caring: Work and Welfare in Britain and Scandinavia*, London: Harvester Wheatsheaf.

Rake, K. (2001) 'Gender and new labour's social policies', *Journal of Social Policy*, 30 (2): 209–231.

Ray, L. and Sayer, A. (eds) (1999) *Culture and Economy after the Cultural Turn*, London: Sage.

Reay, D. (1997) 'Feminist theory, habitus and social class: Disrupting notions of classlessness', *Women's Studies International Forum*, 20 (2): 225–233.

Reay, D. (1998a) 'Rethinking social class: qualitative perspectives on class and gender', *Sociology*, 32 (2): 259–275.

Reay, D. (1998b) *Class Work: Mothers' Involvement in their Children's Primary Schooling*, London: UCL Press.

Reay, D. and Lucey, H. (2003) 'The limits of choice; children and inner city schooling', *Sociology*, 37 (1): 121–142.

Rees, T. (1985) 'Regional restructuring, class change and political action: preliminary comments on the 1984–85 miners' strike in South Wales', *Environment and Planning D: Society and Space*, 3: 389–406.

Reynolds, D. and Cuttance, P. (1992) *School Effectiveness: Research, Policy and Practice*, London: Cassell.

Reynolds, T., Callender, C. and Edwards, R. (2003) *Caring and counting: The impact of mothers' employment on family relationships*, Joseph Rowntree Foundation Report, York: The Policy Press.

Rezende, C. B. (1999) 'Building affinity through friendship', in S. Bell and S. Coleman (eds) (1999) *The Anthropology of Friendship*, Oxford and New York: Berg.

Richards, N. and Milestone, K. (2000) 'What difference does it make? Women's pop cultural production and consumption in Manchester', *Sociological Research Online*, 5, 1, http://www.socresonline.org.uk/5/1/richards.html.

Roberts, K. (2001) *Class in Modern Britain*, London: Palgrave.

Robinson, D., Buchan, J. and Hayday, S. (1999) *On the agenda: changing nurses' careers in 1999* IES Report no. 360, Brighton: Institute for Employment Studies.

Robinson, J. and Godbey, G. (1997) *Time for Life: the Surprising Ways that Americans use their Time*, University of Pennsylvania State Press.

Rosenberg, S. and Lapidus, J. (1999) 'Contingent and non-standard work in the United States: towards a more poorly compensated, insecure workforce', in A. Felstead and N. Jewson (eds) *Global Trends in Flexible Labour*, Basingstoke: Macmillan Business.

Royal College of Nursing (2000) *Making up the Difference*, London: Royal College of Nursing.

Royal College of Nursing (2001) *Shifting patterns: a guide to employee friendly working*, London: Royal College of Nursing.

Rubery, J., Ward, K., Grimshaw, D. and Beynon, H. (2002) 'Time and the new employment relationship' paper presented to LSE Seminar.

Rubery, J., Smith, M. and Fagan, C. (1999) *Women's employment in Europe*, London: Routledge.
Sachdev, S. (2001) *Contracting Culture: From CCT to PPS. The Private Provision of Public Services*, London: Unison.
Sainsbury, D. (ed.) (1999) *Gender and Welfare State Regimes*, Oxford: Oxford University Press.
Sallis, J. (1991) 'Home-school contracts: a personal view', *Royal Society of Arts News*, 4: 7.
Sanchez Taylor, J. (2001) 'Dollars are a girl's best friend: female tourists' sexual behaviour in the Caribbean', *Sociology*, 35 (3): 749–764.
Sandberg, J. F. and Hofferth, S. L. (2001) 'Changes in children's time with parents: US 1981–1997', *Demography*, 38 (3): 423–436.
Savage, M. (1997) 'Social mobility and the survey method: a critical analysis', in D. Bertaux and P. Thompson (eds) *Pathways to Social Class: A Qualitative Approach to Social Mobility*, Oxford: Clarendon Press.
Savage, M. (2000) *Class Analysis and Social Transformation*, Buckingham: Open University.
Scharpf, F. and Schimdt, V. (eds) (2000) *Welfare and Work in the Open Economy. From Vulnerability to Competitiveness*, Oxford: Oxford University Press.
Schor, J. (1992) *The Overworked American: the Unexpected Decline of Leisure*, New York: Basic Books.
Scott, J. (2001) 'If class is dead, why won't it lie down?' in A. Woodward and M. Kohli (eds) *Inclusions and Exclusions in European Societies*, London: Routledge.
Scott, K. and Lockhead, C. (1997) *Are Women Catching Up in the Earnings Race?*, Ottawa: Canadian Council on Social Development.
Seddon, V. (ed.) (1996) *The Cutting Edge: Women and the Pit Strike*, London: Lawrence and Wishart.
Self, H. (2003) *Prostitution, Women and Misuse of the Law: the Fallen Daughters of Eve*, London: Frank Cass.
Sennett, R. (1998) *The Corrosion of Character: The Personal Consequences of Work in the New Capitalism*, London and New York: W. W. Norton and Company.
Sharma, U. and Black, P. (2001) 'Look good, feel better: beauty therapy as emotional labour', *Sociology*, 35 (4): 312–913.
Sheard, J. (1992) 'Volunteering and society, 1960 to 1990', in R. Hedley and J. Davis Smith (eds) *Volunteering and Society: Principles and Practices*, London: Bedford Square Press.
Sherrott, R. (1983) '50 Volunteers', in S. Hatch (ed.) *Volunteers: Patterns, Meanings and Motives*, Berkhampstead: The Volunteer Centre.
Shrage, L. (1994) *Moral Dilemmas of Feminism: Prostitution, Adultery and Abortion*, New York: Routledge.
Simmel, G. (1949) 'The Sociology of Sociability', *American Journal of Sociology*, 55 (3): 254–261.
Siranni, C. and Walsh, A. (1991) 'Through the prison of time: temporal structures in post-modern America' in A. Wolfe (ed.) *America at Century's End*, Beverley Hills, CA: Sage.
Skeggs, B. (1997) *Formations of Class and Gender: Becoming Respectable*, London: Sage.
Skilbrei, M. (2001) 'The rise and fall of the Norwegian massage parlours: changes in the Norwegian prostitution setting in the 1990s', *Feminist Review*, 67: 63–77.
Skinner, C. (2003) *Running Around in Circles. Coordinating Childcare, Education and Work*, Bristol: The Policy Press.
Slater, D. and Tonkiss, F. (2001) *Market Society. Markets and Modern Social Theory*, Cambridge: Polity.
Smelser, J. and Swedberg, R. (eds) (1994) *The Handbook of Economic Sociology*, Princeton N.J.: Princeton University Press.
Smith, D. and Griffith, A. (1990) 'Coordinating the uncoordinated: mothering, schooling and the family wage', *Perspectives on Social Problems* 2 (1): 25–43.
Smith, G. and Seccombe, I. (1998) *Changing times: a survey of registered nurses in 1998*, IES Report no. 351, Brighton: Institute for Employment Studies.
Southerton, D. and Tomlinson, M. (2003) *'Pressed for time' – the differential impacts of a 'time squeeze'*, Discussion Paper No 60, ESRC Centre for Research on Innovation and Competition, University of Manchester/UMIST.